A WOMAN IN ARABIA

GERTRUDE BELL (1868–1926), daughter of pioneers of the Industrial Revolution, turned her back on privilege and society to become a renowned traveler, mountaineer, stateswoman, Arabist, linguist, archaeologist, photographer, and writer. She was born in County Durham, England, and in her youth met such distinguished men of the day as Robert Louis Stevenson, William Morris, Charles Darwin, and Charles Dickens when they visited her grandfather and father in Yorkshire. She began her career at age twenty by becoming the first woman to gain first-class honors in Modern History at Oxford University. She survived seven independent desert expeditions, and during World War I she served as intelligence expert, army major, and adviser for the British armed forces in the Middle East, rising to become the most powerful woman in the British Empire and contributing to the defeat of the Ottoman Empire. On first-name terms with the leaders of the British Empire, she was treated as an equal by the sheikhs and mullahs of Arabia as well. In the administration of Mesopotamia after the war, she achieved her self-imposed mission of delivering self-determination to the Arabs and, along with Winston Churchill and T. E. Lawrence, succeeded in placing King Faisal on the throne of the new Iraq. Her influence spread to Southern Arabia, where her early advice on the threat of Ibn Saud led the British government to modify his territorial ambitions, and to Palestine, where she predicted that the establishment of a Zionist state would cause endless future conflict. In 1917 Bell was named a Commander of the British Empire (CBE) for her service in the war. She died in Baghdad two days before her fifty-eighth birthday.

GEORGINA HOWELL (1942–2016) wrote the acclaimed biography *Gertrude Bell: Queen of the Desert, Shaper of Nations* and was a journalist for *Vanity Fair*, *Vogue*, *The Sunday Times*, *The Observer*, and *Tatler*. She had one son and lived in London and Brittany with her husband, Christopher Bailey.

GERTRUDE BELL

A Woman in Arabia

The Writings of the Queen of the Desert

Edited by GEORGINA HOWELL

PENGUIN BOOKS

PENGUIN BOOKS
An imprint of Penguin Random House LLC
375 Hudson Street
New York, New York 10014
penguin.com

ISBN 978-0-14-310737-8

Printed in the United States of America
9 10 8

I dedicate this book to my son,
Dr. Thomas Buhler, and to Charlotte Stafford, who
have resolved so many of my dilemmas with their
knowledge of both literature and publishing

Contents

Introduction   ix
A Note on the Text and Acknowledgments   xxiii
Chronology   xxv

A WOMAN IN ARABIA

The Linguist   3
The Poet   11
The "Person"   18
The Mountaineer   26
The Archaeologist   40
The Desert Traveler   59
The Lover   105
The Prisoner   115
The War Worker   132
The Intrusives   150
The Nation Builder   176
The Kingmaker   204
The Courtier   229
Epilogue   241

Index   257

Introduction

The phenomenal Gertrude Lowthian Bell came from a family of wealthy British industrialists in the north of England in the mid-nineteenth century. From sheep farmers and blacksmiths they had become the sixth-richest family in Britain. The Bells at their most powerful employed some forty-five thousand workers at their steel and chemical works and mines. They made the steel components, weighing fifty thousand tons, for the Sydney Harbour Bridge and the track for hundreds of thousands of miles of railways all over the world. They were intellectuals, Liberal voters, and anti-aristocracy, although they had begun to marry into the nobility. In childhood, Gertrude met the scientists, writers, and statesmen of the day as they visited her grandfather and her father in Yorkshire: men such as Charles Dickens, Charles Darwin, Robert Louis Stevenson, and William Morris. Even as a child, Gertrude was intimidated by no one, telling a divinity teacher that she "didn't believe a word of it." She began her adult life at twenty, in 1888, by becoming the first woman to gain first-class honors in Modern History at Oxford University. After a life full of adventure and rule-breaking and exploration, she did something of unique importance: she founded a nation, the nation of Iraq.

Her father, Hugh Bell, was married at twenty-three to Mary Shield. A beautiful local girl, she was the daughter of a Newcastle merchant. Gertrude was their first child, born in 1868. Tragically, Mary Bell survived only three weeks after the birth of their second child, Gertrude's brother Maurice.

Hugh became for a time a poignant figure, working six days a week at the Clarence steelworks in Middlesbrough. His sister

Ada moved in to run the house and look after the children. Hugh had to share his Sundays with his sister, a wet nurse, and some half-dozen servants. Through the matchmaking of his two sisters, he met and then married Florence Eveleen Eleanore Olliffe. She had been born and brought up in Paris, where her father was physician to the British Embassy. The good-hearted Florence, who now became "Mother" to Gertrude, adored children and domestic life. She wrote plays and novels, and became heavily involved in social work into which she would co-opt Gertrude whenever she was at home for long enough. Florence wrote a groundbreaking factual book, *At the Works*, the result of thirty years of interviews with the families of steelworkers, exposing the suffering they endured.

The bond between Hugh and the eight-year-old Gertrude was extraordinary. They were everything to each other and would remain so even when living on opposite sides of the world. Florence was to write a novel concerning the second wife of a man whose bond with his daughter was so strong as almost to exclude his wife. The deep mutual affection was "to both the very foundation of existence until the day she died." Florence never tried to divide them, but she had difficulty with Gertrude, who was used to bossing the household and running rings around her unfortunate governesses. She was domineering and willful. She would climb on the greenhouse roof, she played the garden hose down the laundry chimney and flooded the fire, and she galloped about the countryside and beaches on her ponies while her small brother tried to follow her, coming home covered with cuts and bruises.

It was not long before Florence had her own children: Hugo, Elsa, and Molly. Gentle and forbearing as Florence was, she found the teenage Gertrude too much for her: scowling, noisy, argumentative, opinionated, bursting with energy, and thirsty for knowledge. And so, most unusually for a girl of her wealth and class, Gertrude was sent to school in London: to Queen's College in Harley Street, and from there to Lady Margaret Hall, Oxford. Having done that with brilliance, Gertrude came back to a Florence determined to get rid of her "Oxfordy manner" and turn her into a marriageable prospect. For a while, before becoming a debutante presented to the Queen at court, she was entrusted with housekeeping, care of her sisters and brothers, and bookkeeping. As a reward, she was given a wardrobe of wonderful clothes and sent on holiday to embassies in Bucharest, Tehran, and Berlin, where her uncle was British ambassador. She went around the world twice, once with her brother Maurice and the second time with her half-brother Hugo.

She must be one of the best-documented women of all time. There are seventy-five feet of shelving in the Bell archive, with its sixteen thousand letters, sixteen diaries, seven archaeological field books, dozens of small leather notebooks, and the three thousand items collected under the heading "Miscellaneous." Then there are her eight published books and hundreds of political position papers. There are also seven thousand glass plates of the photographs she took of archaeological sites now ransacked or crumbled away, and images of Middle Eastern life as it had been lived for thousands of years. Those are the papers and photographs in Newcastle University alone.

As a highly skilled photographer and a member of the Royal Photographic Society, she carried two cameras into the desert: one that took glass plates 6.5 inches high by 4.25 inches wide, the other designed for panoramic views. To scan an entire archaeological site she would combine carefully angled shots to give exact panoramas, which are prized by Newcastle's School of Historical Studies for their depiction of monuments and churches before they were further eroded and damaged.

Her first book in print was *Persian Pictures*, a collection of essays written about her stay in Tehran and her introduction to the desert. She thought this book to be too slight but was persuaded to publish nonetheless. *Poems from the Divan of Hafiz* was a collection of work of the fourteenth-century Sufi master who is Persia's most famous poet. Gertrude became fluent in the language to make the translations and then rendered them in lyrical English. *The Desert and the Sown* was the account of her 1905 trip across the Syrian Desert from Jericho to Antioch. *The Thousand and One Churches,* written with scholar Sir William Mitchell Ramsay, was an investigation of the Hittite and Byzantine site of Binbirkilise in Turkey in 1907; the book led to Gertrude's election as a fellow of the Royal Geographical Society. The private diaries she wrote for her lover Dick Doughty-Wylie, containing the account of her incarceration in Hayyil, were edited by Rosemary O'Brien and published in 2000 under the title *The Arabian Diaries, 1913– 1914*. *Amurath to Amurath* came from her 1909 six-month journey through Syria and along the unexplored banks of the Euphrates. *The Palace and Mosque at Ukhaidir* and *The Vaulting System at Ukhaidir* contained her meticulous drawings and measurements of the enormous ruined palace she discovered in the desert near Karbala. *The Churches and Monasteries of the Tur Abdin* took her back to Ukhaidir and north to Turkey in 1911. Gertrude's handbook *The Arab of Mesopotamia,* written by request as an introduction to the region for the military officers and civil servants who were posted there after World War I, is a collection of essays. Some of these are rigorously informative and some are eccentric and amusing. A book-length white paper for the British government, *Review of the Civil Administration of Mesopotamia,* explained the problems and solutions that confronted the High Commission when it arrived in Basra, and then in Baghdad, after the Turkish retreat.

From the time she took up her post as "Major Miss Bell" in the Intelligence Bureau in Cairo in 1915, and no longer had time to keep a diary, she told her father that her letters to the family would in future be her diary and asked him to keep them. Her work at the bureau was secret, and there was much she omitted to tell, but she continued to write home two or three times a week. The letters were so regular over so many years that their rare cessation signaled an interval of a few days during which she was doing something secret. There are three missing days and nights in November 1915, which give the clue to a mystery that has perplexed historians for a hundred years (see "The Lover"). The second time, during the period in which she was an intelligence officer in Basra, was

April 16–27, 1916. Those were exactly the days in which her friends T. E. Lawrence and Aubrey Herbert—with whom she had discussed "vast schemes for the government of the universe" the previous week—were entrusted with the attempt to break the Turkish siege of Kut, in which starving British soldiers and townspeople were reduced to eating rats and dogs. According to Gertrude's letters home, she went "up the Shatt al' Arab to check the maps." After her death, King Faisal referred to further unrecorded adventures in which she nearly lost her life, saying, "She could play a man's part in the action. . . . She ventured alone and disguised into the remotest districts . . . Death held no fear for her. Her personal safety was her last consideration." In the same interview he added the extraordinary assertion that she had on one occasion led some tribesmen in an attack on the Turks and on another been taken prisoner by the Turks but had managed to escape. Even in her midfifties, when she and Haji Naji, a gardener and great friend, were harassed by a mad dervish with an iron staff, she snatched it up and struck him with it. He left.

During her lifetime she made seven expeditions into the vast regions of the Middle East and Turkey, first as a wealthy tourist but soon as an archaeologist, explorer, and information gatherer for the British government. They were possibly the happiest times of her life. Once she was based in an office, whether engaged on war work or administration, she worked harder and longer than anyone but occasionally yearned for adventure again. "It's sometimes exasperating to be obliged to sit in an office when I long to be out in the desert, seeing the plans I hear of and finding out about them for myself . . . one can't do much more than sit and record if one is of my sex, devil take it," she wrote from Basra. And, in 1924 when she was fifty-six, "I'm planning a two days' jaunt by myself in the desert. I want to feel savage and independent again instead of being [Oriental] Secretary in a High Commissioner's office. The truth is I wonder how I bear being so civilised and respectable after the life I've led."

The wisdom of establishing a nation as conflicted as Iraq is often questioned. Gertrude soldiered on, year after year, as political officer and then Oriental secretary with her self-imposed mission to grant as complete a measure of autonomy to her beloved Arabs as was compatible with some temporary British guidance and support. Her dream was that Iraq should gain ultimate independence. She dedicated her life in Baghdad to the championing of the Arab cause, reaching the very limits of her purview as a loyal administrator employed and paid by Britain. She placed little faith in politicians: the British who betrayed the promise to give the Arabs self-determination; the French who bombed their way to control of Syria; and the Americans who proposed a benevolent world order, including a League of Nations, and then did nothing to support it.

She had to fight her corner every inch of the way, and she often had to fight her own side. There were objections to her as a woman alongside the military, objections to her rank, objections to her being in the front line. She had to fight when an interim boss tried to have her sacked, when Winston Churchill wanted to pull out of Iraq altogether, and again when political machinations brought all her achievements to the brink of disaster. Her lifelong creed was to seek out and engage with the opposition in order to understand their point of view. This was regarded with the deepest suspicion by some of her colonialist colleagues, who knew that her Baghdad house was frequented by dangerous nationalists subversive to the British administration.

In guiding the new British administration of Iraq, she was doing the most important work she had ever undertaken. To the people queuing up outside the secretariat in Baghdad, she was more than an administrator; she was someone they could trust. She spoke their language and had never lied to them. She respected them and their ways to the point of entrusting her life to them while traveling alone through their deserts. She understood Bedouin etiquette and the hereditary lines of Arab families. She also understood the priorities of the Bedouin nomads and those who had begun to farm, the traders and landowners, the Christian professionals, the clerks and teachers, and each of the explosive mixtures of races and religions in the unmapped territories the Arabs shared with the Armenians, Assyrians, Turks, Persians, and Kurds.

Once face-to-face with Gertrude, the Oriental secretary, and Sir Percy Cox, the high commissioner, the sheikhs and Mesopotamian notables lodged their interests with the brandnew British administration of the summer of 1917. They were welcomed, listened to, their situations comprehended. They were assured that the British administration would be benevolent and was prepared for the huge expenditure in effort and money that would secure their various ways of life. Each one of the representatives had to be met with proper traditional courtesies, such as the giving of small presents, and lengthy discussions had to take place. In the meeting of the two agendas, those of the administration and the population, a good part of Gertrude's day was spent in trading government favors to establish cooperation.

If the American and British invaders of 2003, after ousting Saddam Hussein, had read and taken to heart what Gertrude had to say on establishing peace in Iraq, there might have been far fewer of the bombings and burnings that have continued to this day. She wrote of the importance on the part of the administration of "a just comprehension of the conflicting claims of different classes of the population" and its ability to "command the confidence of the people so as to secure the co-operation of public opinion."

One key to stability in Iraq is contained in a sweeping pronouncement she made in 1918 that "There is nothing easier to manage than tribes if you'll take advantage of tribal organization and make it the basis of administrative organization . . . and establish familiar relations with sheikh and headman and charge them with their right share of work and responsibility."

Since civilization began, Mesopotamia had been a melting pot of races, with inevitable and frequent conflict. Of course she knew that Iraq would risk continual disruption. She was fulfilling the promise of self-determination, but it must not be forgotten that Gertrude had another urgent reason for wanting Iraq established. Had Britain evacuated Iraq after World War I, as Winston Churchill advocated, the Turks would have surged back from the north to exact revenge and reinstate the institutionalized corruption and the appropriation of taxes of their old Ottoman Empire. There was a very real threat from the Russian Bolshevik army, planning to drive the Communist revolution south to conquer the Middle East. In the south, Ibn Saud and his fearsome Wahhabis were already attacking the borders. Without western endorsement and British support, Iraq would have faced three powerful enemies without an army to defend it. The peoples of the Middle East who had failed to make their case for nationhood or political identity at the time of the Paris Peace Conference—for instance, the Kurdish people—remained at the mercy of massacres and incursions by their neighbors. The country needed to be inclusive enough and large enough to raise an army capable of repelling enemies.

Her influence spread beyond the borders of Iraq, to Palestine and southern Arabia. There had been Jewish settlements in Palestine before World War I, and some of those had been attacked by the Arabs. In November 1917, Lord Arthur James Balfour, Prime Minister Lloyd George's languid foreign secretary, issued a declaration sympathetic to the Zionist cause, stating that the British government approved "the establishment in Palestine of a national home for the Jewish people." When the first draft of the Balfour Declaration had been put to the Cabinet, the secretary of state for India, Sir Edwin Montagu, mounted a violent opposition despite being Jewish himself. In support of his argument he read to the Cabinet a strongly argued letter from Gertrude against it, forecasting future trouble without end.

This Document is the Property of
His Britannic Majesty's Government

Circulated by the Secretary of State for India

SECRET

Zionism

1. I am sorry to bother the Cabinet with another Paper on this subject, but I have obtained some more information which I would like to lay before them.

2. We have received at the India Office a series of valuable papers on Turkey in Asia from the pen of Miss Gertrude Lowthian Bell, the remarkable woman who, after years of knowledge gained by unique travel in these regions, is acting as Assistant Political Officer in Baghdad. She writes:—

Not least among the denationalising forces is the fact that a part of Syria, though like the rest mainly inhabited by Arabs, is regarded by a non-Arab people as its prescriptive inheritance. At a liberal estimate the Jews of Palestine may form a quarter of the population of the province, the Christians a fifth, while the remainder are Mohammedan Arabs. Jewish immigration has been artificially fostered by doles and subventions from millionaire co-religionists in Europe; the new colonies have now taken root and are more or less self-supporting. The pious hope that an independent Jewish state may some day be established in Palestine no doubt exists, though it may be questioned whether among local Jews there is any acute desire to see it realised, except as a means of escape from Turkish oppression; it is perhaps more lively in the breasts of those who live far from the rocky Palestinian hills and have no intention of changing their domicile. Lord Cromer took pleasure in relating a conversation which he had held on the subject with one of the best known English Jews, who observed: 'If a Jewish Kingdom were to be established at Jerusalem I should lose no time in applying for the post of Ambassador in London'. Apart from the prevalence of such sentiments two considerations rule out the conception of an independent Jewish Palestine from practical politics. The first is that the province as we know it is not Jewish, and that neither Mohammedan nor Arab would accept Jewish authority; the second that the capital, Jerusalem, is equally sacred to three faiths, Jewish, Christian and Moslem, and should never, if it can be avoided, be put under the exclusive control of any one local faction, no matter how carefully the rights of the other two may be safeguarded.

Sir Edwin went on to list some hundred prominent Jews who were anti-Zionist and to make the point that the bond that united Israel was not one of politics but of a common religion. This paper, headed by Gertrude's contribution, achieved the change of a single word in the Balfour Declaration: Palestine would become *a* home for the Jews—not *the* home. Even this minimal change probably prevented both the slaughter of those Jews already living in Palestine and sympathetic Arab uprisings elsewhere. She continued to affirm: "Palestine for the Jews has always seemed . . . an impossible proposition. I don't believe it can be carried out—personally I don't want it to be carried out, and I've said so on every possible occasion . . . to gratify Jewish sentiment you would have to override every conceivable political consideration, including the wishes of the large majority of the population." As early as 1922 the Arabs, refusing to accept the Balfour Declaration, massacred Jews in their settlements.

Gertrude warned the British government of Ibn Saud's growing power even before the war. In the east, it would have been next on his agenda to invade the Gulf states to control the flow of oil down the Persian Gulf. Britain provided the funds that persuaded him to keep his territorial ambitions in check. After the war he went on to take Mecca and the Hejaz.

Lawrence said that he thought Gertrude was "born too

gifted." The extraordinary range of her talents and abilities highlighted in this book do not tell the whole story. As Sir Ignatius Valentine Chirol wrote in her obituary, "With all the qualities which are usually described as virile, she combined in a high degree the charm of feminine refinement, and though only revealed to a few, even amongst her intimates, great depths of tender and even passionate affection." She adored clothes, bought many dresses from Paris, and from Iraq would continually ask Florence and her sisters to send her the clothes she had no other way of buying. Other books of her quotes could be collected concerning her quest for perfect clothes and her love for flowers: she was enchanted by the sheets of wildflowers she discovered in the desert after the rains, by a rare iris hidden among the ruins of an Anatolian temple, or by a knot of violets under an Alpine rock. She sent home mandrakes and cedars of Lebanon to be planted on the lawns of Rounton Grange, the huge and splendid family house built by architect Philip Webb for Hugh's father, the great ironmaster Isaac Lowthian Bell, at the height of the family fortunes. There, in a wood of beautiful old trees, Gertrude created a rockery of mountainous boulders surrounding a lake and a network of little streams. Once a showcase garden and now ruined and overgrown, it still produces unexpected plants in the spring. In Baghdad, she planted cottage garden flowers, ordering the seeds from England.

Her legacy includes the Iraq Museum, from which fifteen thousand items were looted immediately before and during the invasion of 2003, and half recovered later. She had collected items from seven thousand years of Mesopotamian history, including clay tablets recording the invention of the written word. Through her position as honorary director of antiquities for Iraq she supervised the teams of foreign archaeologists who came to dig the precious sites of Ur and Babylon—the latter eventually bulldozed for an American military base. She kept the most interesting pieces for Iraq, allowing the world's museums to take the pieces that they would better be able to reconstruct and conserve.

In all, she traveled an unbelievable twenty thousand miles

through the deserts on camel or horse, mapping terrain, photographing archaeological sites, and passing on intelligence to the government. Toward the end of her last, longest, and most dangerous journey, she questioned whether the adventure was worth it: "It is nothing, the journey to Nejd, so far as real advantage goes, or any real addition to knowledge." She had no idea that in the years to follow, this expedition would open the way into the most exciting and rewarding part of her life.

Gertrude would never know the happiness of having a husband and children, which she once said she would have preferred to all her triumphs and achievements. As her best woman friend, Janet Courtney, said of her: "She was, I think, the most brilliant creature who ever came amongst us; the most alive at every point, with her tireless energy, her splendid vitality, her unlimited capacity for work, for talk, for play. She was always an odd mixture of maturity and childishness, grown up in her judgement of men and affairs, child-like in her certainties, and most engaging in her entire belief in her father and the vivid intellectual world in which she had been brought up."

It is her own voice, so personal, visionary, and humorous, that this book has been designed to serve. The text is arranged by subject to highlight the diversity of her talents and abilities, and I have been led by her writings in deciding how to frame the chapters. In the case of some subjects, her observations over the years needed only a short headnote. In others, where history or her personal story developed in reaction to events, I have set her writings in an explanatory narration. The Chronology at the beginning of the book provides the time line necessarily missing from this approach.

The majority of her quotes come from letters to her beloved father and stepmother, to whom as a sacred duty she wrote almost daily. In letters written to her great friend and mentor Sir Valentine Chirol, she often exposed her emotional state more clearly than to her parents, whom she always tried to protect from anxiety about her well-being. In addition to letters, there are extracts from her books, diaries and official papers, reports, reviews, and bulletins. I hope this volume will stand in for the autobiography she never wrote.

Formidable as she could be as a stateswoman and figurehead, she was the most devoted family member, affectionate friend, and loyal aide. Her favorite sister, Elsa Richmond, wrote this of her:

"Eternally young, she lived every moment to the full. The years went by, but they could not chill her warm heart. To the end of her life she remained what she was at the beginning: self-willed, impatient, infinitely loving, pouring herself out in devotion to those dear to her. And now all her brilliance, her waywardness, her sympathy, her affection lie buried in the sandy cemetery of Baghdad, the memory of that vital nature remains as a possession to those who knew and loved her."

A Note on the Text
and Acknowledgments

Most of Gertrude Bell's letters, diaries, and papers are reproduced here by kind permission of the Robinson Library, University of Newcastle upon Tyne. Her appendix to "Self-Determination in Mesopotamia" and her letters to Valentine Chirol are reproduced by kind permission of Durham University Library. The majority of the letters are taken from *The Letters of Gertrude Bell,* selected by Lady Bell, DBE, first published by Ernest Benn Limited, London, in September 1927. Many letters not included in Lady Bell's collection have been taken from *Gertrude Bell: From her Personal Papers, Volume 1, 1889–1914,* and *Volume 2, 1914–1926,* edited by Elizabeth Burgoyne. Both volumes were published by Ernest Benn Limited, London, in 1961. T. E. Lawrence's letter of November 4, 1927, written to Sir Hugh Bell more than a year after Gertrude's death, is included by kind permission of the Seven Pillars of Wisdom Trust.

Other works of great importance to this volume include a summary of Gertrude's life compiled by the Robinson Library's late archivist Lesley Gordon to accompany a 1994 exhibition based on Gertrude's archaeological work, titled "Gertrude Bell 1868–1926"; *Gertrude Bell: The Arabian Diaries, 1913–1914,* edited by Rosemary O'Brien, published by Syracuse University Press in 2000; and *A Prince of Our Disorder: The Life of T. E. Lawrence* by John Mack, published by Harvard University Press in 1976.

Unless otherwise stated, all letters quoted in this volume are addressed to Gertrude's father and stepmother.

Gertrude's spelling was not her strongest point, and on

desert journeys in unmapped areas, or guided by inadequate maps, her rendition of place names was inconsistent. This book maintains her spelling throughout, whether in English or when quoting Arabic. Similarly, she sometimes found it difficult to keep track of the date. After her death, her stepmother wrote: "Gertrude hardly ever dated her letters except by the day of the week, sometimes not even that." The dates have been clarified where possible.

Whenever Gertrude mentions monetary amounts, they are given in British pounds as she wrote them, followed in brackets by a figure adjusted first to the 2014 value for British pounds by the change in the Retail Price Index (RPI), then converted into U.S. dollars at a value of £1 = $1.60 (www.measuringwealth.com, 2014).

There are many people to thank for making this book possible. I was fortunate that John Siciliano at Penguin Random House wanted to include the writings of Gertrude Bell among the eminent publications in the Penguin Classics. I want to thank him and Emily Hartley in his office for their enthusiasm, guidance, and patience throughout. Nancy Bernhaut's meticulous copyediting has brought consistency to the book, which draws on Gertrude's huge and varied output ranging from political papers to family letters. Thanks also to artist Paul X. Johnson for the cover image of Gertrude Bell; it evokes wonderfully the character of the young Gertrude. Cartography for the maps of Gertrude Bell's journeys in the Middle East was done by Raymond Turvey.

Chronology

1807	Gertrude Bell's great-grandfather Thomas Bell, the son of a blacksmith, manufactures alkali using a new chemical process at Walker near Newcastle upon Tyne
1809	Thomas Bell, with partners James Losh and George Wilson, opens an iron foundry at Walker
1816 February	Grandfather (Isaac) Lowthian Bell born on the 15th to Thomas and Katherine (née Lowthian), elder brother of John and Tom
1832 June	King William IV signs the First Reform Act to increase the franchise and address electoral corruption
1835	Lowthian joins his father's ironworks at Walker, later becoming a partner
1837 June	Queen Victoria succeeds William IV on the 20th
1842 July	Lowthian marries Margaret Pattinson on the 20th
1844 February	Gertrude's father (Thomas) Hugh Bell, born at Walker on the 10th; future elder brother of Charles, Mary (Maisie), Florence, Ada, and Sophie
	Gertrude's mother, Maria (Mary) Shield, born
	Lowthian creates a new company, Bell Brothers, with Thomas and John to operate the Wylam Ironworks, Port Clarence, Middlesbrough
1845	Lowthian takes control of Walker ironworks upon the death of his father

1850   Lowthian opens Washington Chemical Company
                with father-in-law, metallurgical chemist Hugh
                Lee Pattinson FRS, and brother-in-law

                The company pioneers steel rope and undersea cable
                manufacture with Robert S. Newall (company be-
                comes Brunner Mond, 1872)

1851 September GLB's future stepmother, Florence, born on the
                9th to Dr. Sir Joseph and Lady Olliffe (née Cubitt)
                in Paris

May–October   Great Exhibition at Crystal Palace, London, receives
                6 million visitors from May 1 to October 3

1852   Bell Brothers begins iron production at the new
                Clarence Ironworks

1854   Lowthian elected Lord Mayor of Newcastle (and
                again in 1863); begins building new home, Wash-
                ington New Hall (the old hall being the birthplace
                of George Washington)

1858 August   On the 16th, first message sent by cable across the
                Atlantic; half the cable length made by Lowthian
                Bell's Washington works

1859   Lowthian opens Britain's first factory to manufac-
                ture aluminum at Washington; tours Newcastle
                wearing a top hat of aluminum, which was more
                expensive than gold

1865   Lowthian incorporates his Cleveland Railway into
                the North Eastern Railway Company (later Lon-
                don and North Eastern Railway)

1867 April   Hugh Bell marries Maria (Mary) Shield on the 23rd

1868 July   Gertrude Margaret Lowthian Bell (GLB) born
                at grandfather's home, Washington New Hall, on
                the 14th

1869   Lowthian Bell is founding organizer of the British
                Iron and Steel Institute

1870   Hugh Bell and family move to newly built Red
                Barns, Redcar, near Middlesbrough

1870	Franco-Prussian War; Olliffe family evacuate from British embassy in Paris as Prussians approach
1871 March	GLB's brother, Maurice Hugh Lowthian Bell, born on the 29th
April	Mother dies on the 19th, aged 27; Hugh's sister Ada manages household
1872	Lowthian Bell starts building Rounton Grange on newly acquired estate near Northallerton
1874	Hugh Bell elected mayor of Middlesbrough
	Lowthian Bell elected Fellow of the Royal Society
February–June	Lowthian also elected member of Parliament for North Durham; his object was to press the government to support technical education in Britain
1875	Lowthian wins by-election as member of Parliament for Hartlepool
1876	Sir Edward Poynter paints Gertrude and Hugh
	Rounton Grange complete
August	Hugh Bell marries Florence Eveleen Eleanore Olliffe on the 10th
1877	Lowthian Bell is founding organizer of the British Institute of Chemistry (later, Royal Institute)
	Queen Victoria declared empress of India
1878	Lowthian Bell awarded Légion d'Honneur
	GLB's half-brother Hugh (Hugo) born
1879	GLB's half-sister Elsa born
1880	Lowthian Bell resigns from Parliament
1881	GLB's half-sister Mary (Molly) born
1882	Forth Bridge Railway Company formed to construct and operate the world's largest bridge; Hugh Bell appointed as a director
1884	Lowthian Bell appointed high sheriff of County Durham; rebuilds East Rounton church; his masterwork

is published, *Principles of the Manufacture of Iron and Steel: With Some Notes on the Economic Conditions of Their Production*

Hugh again elected mayor of Middlesbrough; River Tees ferry *Hugh Bell* launched

April	GLB attends Queen's College, London, living with stepgrandmother, Lady Olliffe, at 95 Sloane Street
1885	Lowthian Bell accepts baronetcy
	Maurice Bell goes to Eton College, there until 1889
1886 April	GLB attends Lady Margaret Hall, Oxford University
July–August	Lodges with a family in Weilheim, Germany
November	Grandmother Dame Margaret Bell dies on the 18th
1887	Great-uncle John Bell, Sir Lowthian's business partner, dies
1888 June	GLB leaves Oxford with first-class honors
December	Stays in Bucharest with Sir Frank and Mary Lascelles (aunt); meets Valentine Chirol and Charles Hardinge; befriended by Queen Elizabeth of Romania (aka Carmen Sylva)
1889	GLB returns with cousin Billy Lascelles via Constantinople and Paris
	GLB acts as housekeeper for her stepmother at Red Barns; does social work in Middlesbrough
	GLB "comes out" in the London season, presented to Queen Victoria
	GLB aids Florence's group studying lives of local working families; becomes treasurer of its committee
	War in South Africa resumes after Boer attack on Cape Colony
1891	Washington New Hall given away as an orphanage, named Dame Margaret's Hall
1892 April	GLB travels to Persia with cousin Florence Lascelles to stay with her parents in Tehran; studies

	Persian; begins reading the poetry of Hafiz; romance with legation secretary Henry Cadogan in Tehran; betrothal intended
July	Hugh Bell stands for Parliament as a Unionist Party candidate, unsuccessful
December	GLB's parents refuse permission for her to marry Cadogan, she returns to London with cousin Gerald Lascelles
1893	Cadogan dies
January	GLB goes to Switzerland and northern Italy with Mary Talbot
April	Travels to Algiers with father to visit great-uncle John Bell's widow, Lizzie
May	Returns to London with Mary Talbot via Switzerland and Weimar where Maurice is staying
June–December	GLB in England, learning Persian and Latin; starts Arabic studies
1894 January–February	GLB and Hugh tour Italy
March–July	GLB in England; *Safar Nameh: Persian Pictures* published
1895	Sir Lowthian awarded Albert Medal of the Royal Society of Arts (granted the right to use the term *Royal* in 1908)
September	GLB in England working on *Poems from the Divan of Hafiz*
1896 March–April	GLB visits Italy with Hugh; takes Italian lessons
September	GLB visits the Lascelles, Ambassador Sir Frank and Lady Mary, at embassy country house in Potsdam
October–December	Retums to England, continues Persian and Arabic studies
1897 January–March	With cousin Florence visits the Lascelles in Berlin; takes tea with the German emperor and empress

April	Lady Mary Lascelles dies
June	*Poems from the Divan of Hafiz* published
July–August	GLB begins climbing during family visit to La Grave, France
December	GLB and Maurice go on world tour, visiting the West Indies, Mexico, San Francisco, Honolulu, Japan, China, Singapore, Hong Kong, Burma; then return via Egypt, Greece, and Constantinople
1898	Sir Lowthian acquires the estate of Mount Grace Priory and restores the house
June	GLB and Maurice return to England
October	GLB in England, studying Arabic with Sir Denison Ross
1899 March	GLB travels to Italy, meets Hugh in Athens; studies Greek antiquities, meets archaeologist David Hogarth; returns alone via Constantinople, Prague, and Berlin
August–September	Visits Bayreuth in Germany to attend opera and returns to the French Alps to climb the Meije and Les Écrins
September–November	GLB in England
	Bell Brothers becomes a public company, 50 percent owned by Dorman Long
November	GLB goes to Jerusalem to stay with the Rosens at the German Consulate; travels via Damascus, visiting Baalbek and Beirut, Athens and Smyrna; studies Arabic and Hebrew
1900 January	Maurice Bell leaves for the Boer War, commanding Volunteer Service Company of the Yorkshire Regiment
	Hugh Bell's sister, Aunt Ada, dies
February–June	GLB's first lone desert journey begins in Jerusalem, visiting Petra, Damascus, Palmyra, Baalbek, Beirut, returning along the Mediterranean coast
June–July	GLB in England

August–September	In the Alps, climbs Mont Blanc, the Crepon, and the Dru
September–December	GLB in England
1901 January–February	In London, watches funeral procession of Queen Victoria; Edward VII succeeds to the throne
March–August	GLB in Redcar and London
	Sir Lowthian sells majority holdings in the Bell companies and merges steel interests with Dorman Long (in 1902), releasing substantial funds; Hugh takes directorships in all Bell associated companies
August	GLB in Bernese Oberland, climbs Schreckhorn and Engelhörner range; Gertrudspitze named in her honor
September–December	In England, takes up photographic developing
1902 January–May	Travels with father and Hugo to Malta, then to Sicily, to be guided by Winston Churchill; travels on alone to Greece, Turkey, Lebanon, and Palestine
	Maurice Bell returns from South Africa wounded
	Ibn Saud regains Riyadh from Rashid dynasty in night attack
May	Boer War ends
July	GLB in Switzerland; via new route almost reaches summit of Finsteraarhorn, frostbitten
September–November	GLB in England, engages lady's maid Marie Delaire
November	GLB leaves for second world tour, with Hugo
December	GLB attends Delhi durbar as guest of the Viceroy
1903	GLB and Hugo continue to Afghanistan, the Himalayas, Burma, Singapore, Hong Kong, China, Korea, Japan, Vancouver, the Rocky Mountains, Canada, Boston, and Chicago
July	Return to England

1904 January	Half-sister Molly marries Charles Trevelyan
February	Sir Lowthian gives £5,000 ($752,000 RPI adjusted) to each of his grandchildren
April	Entente Cordiale established between Britain and France
August	GLB at Zermatt, climbs the Matterhorn
September	GLB in England
November	Studies antiquities in Paris with Salomon Reinach
December	Sir Lowthian, 88, dies on the 20th at London home, Belgravia; Hugh succeeds to baronetcy and inherits £750,000 ($112,816,000 RPI adjusted)
	GLB goes on archaeological trip via Paris, Marseilles, Naples, Beirut, Haifa, and Jerusalem; then takes desert route to Druze mountains, Damascus, Homs, Baalbek, Orontes valley, and Aleppo; continues on horseback to Antioch, Osmaniye, Adana, Tarsus, and Karaman; then by train to Konya, explores Binbirkilise
1905 April	GLB recruits Fattuh, her principal servant on future desert journeys
May	Stays in Constantinople before returning to England to begin writing *The Desert and the Sown*
	Sir Hugh and family move to Rounton Grange
October	Studies ancient manuscripts in Paris with Reinach; writes essay on the geometry of the cruciform structure
November–December	Begins to transform the Rounton Grange gardens
December–February (1906)	Travels to Gibraltar, Tangier, Spain, and Paris with Sir Hugh
1906 February–December	GLB in England
	Sir Hugh appointed Lord Lieutenant of the North Riding of Yorkshire (25-year tenure)

December	GLB and Sir Hugh arrive in Cairo, joined by Hugo from Australia
1907 February	Return to England, delayed by Sir Hugh's illness
March–July	GLB in Turkey, travels on horseback across Anatolia visiting ancient sites; works with Professor Sir William Ramsay in Binbirkilise; meets Dick Doughty-Wylie
July	Half-sister Elsa marries Herbert, later Admiral Sir Herbert Richmond
August	GLB takes Fattuh to hospital in Constantinople; guest of the grand vizier
August–December	GLB in England; publication of *The Desert and the Sown*
October	GLB trains in surveying and mapmaking with the Royal Geographical Society
1908	Young Turks' Committee of Union and Progress rises against Sultan, taking six more years to achieve full power over Ottoman Empire
	GLB in England all year; becomes founding secretary of the Women's National Anti-Suffrage League; drafts *The Thousand and One Churches*; holidays in North Wales with Valentine Chirol and Frank Balfour
	Doughty-Wylie unofficially rallies Turkish troops to stop massacre of Armenians, is wounded but organizes relief for 22,000 refugees
September	Hugo Bell ordained priest; curate of Guiseley, Leeds
1909 January–July	GLB travels to Syria and Mesopotamia on horseback, follows Euphrates River to Baghdad, measures palace of Ukhaidir, then follows Tigris River to Turkey
July	GLB in England; publication of *The Thousand and One Churches*; draws palace of Ukhaidir; writes about Armenian monasteries for Josef Strzygowski; meets Sir Percy Cox, discusses with him proposed desert journeys; begins *Amurath to Amurath*; continues

developing Rounton gardens, now becoming a show-piece

Florence becomes first president of the North Riding branch of the British Red Cross (until 1930)

1910 January Hugh Bell stands as Liberal parliamentary candidate for the City of London

February GLB visits archaeological sites in Italy; pays flying visit to Munich

May George V succeeds Edward VII

1911 January–May GLB goes via Beirut and Damascus across the desert to Baghdad to check measurements of Ukhaidir; travels north along Tigris; meets T. E. Lawrence at Carchemish in Syria working for David Hogarth

June Returns to England; publication of *Amurath to Amurath*

1912 GLB in England all year; involved in worldwide fund-raising for relief of Constantinople after the great fire; creates new water garden at Rounton; meets Doughty-Wylie in London

1913 GLB in England; completes *The Palace and Mosque at Ukhaidir*

Elected to the Fellowship of the Royal Geographical Society; presented with a miniature theodolite as its Gill Memorial Award; she is the first woman to receive an RGS award

Woodrow Wilson becomes 28th president of the United States

November GLB travels to Damascus to organize journey to Hayyil, with intention of meeting Ibn Saud in Riyadh

December GLB and caravan leave for Hayyil

1914 February GLB arrives in Hayyil, put under house arrest by the ruling Rashids, then released

February–May	Continues to Baghdad; journeys through Mesopo-tamian and Syrian deserts
	Returns to England
June	Churchill persuades British parliament to approve Admiralty purchase of 51 percent of Anglo-Persian oil company to secure fuel for navy
	Archduke Franz Ferdinand of Austria shot at Sara-jevo on the 28th
July	GLB awarded Gold Medal by the Royal Geo-graphical Society
August	First World War begins; GLB gives speeches to raise troops
	Publication of *The Palace and Mosque at Ukhaidir*
	Maurice mobilized as Lieutenant Colonel com-manding 4th (territorial) Battalion, Green Howards
October	Turkey joins war as ally of Germany
November	GLB works at Lord Onslow's Hospital, Clandon Park, Surrey
	British Indian Army expeditionary force occupies Shatt al Arab and creates a base at Basra
	GLB takes charge of the Red Cross Wounded and Missing Bureau in Boulogne
1915 April	Maurice Bell on Western Front leads attack at Fortuin
	Lady Florence sets up auxiliary convalescent hos-pital for the Red Cross at Rounton Village Institute
	British begin Gallipoli campaign against the Turks on the 25th; Dick Doughty-Wylie dies there on the 26th
April–November	GLB opens new London office at 20 Arlington Street for the Red Cross Wounded and Missing Bureau
May	British Liberal prime minister Asquith invites Bo-nar Law's Conservatives to join a coalition gov-

ernment; Churchill forced to resign from the
Admiralty

September   British win decisive battle against Turkish/Arab army
                at Kut and advance to Ctesiphon near Baghdad

November   17th: GLB leaves Sloane Street, London

                20th: She embarks at Marseilles for Egypt

                26th: She dines in Port Said with Lawrence and
                Hogarth

                27th–29th: She is missing, probably took ship to
                Dardanelles, climbing beach to visit the grave of
                Doughty-Wylie

                30th: GLB back in Port Said, takes train to Cairo

                British defeated by Turkish force at Ctesiphon,
                retreat to Kut

November–   GLB works in Cairo for Gilbert Clayton, director
December   of military intelligence and also responsible for
                Egyptian civil intelligence

December   British encircled at Kut, siege begins

1916 January–   GLB in India, advises viceroy
February
                Arab Bureau established in Cairo to collect intelli-
                gence of Middle Eastern affairs and disseminate
                information to British government departments

February–   GLB in Basra as assistant political officer with rank
December   of major under Chief Political Officer Sir Percy Cox,
                reporting to General Officer Commanding-in-Chief
                (GOC) Indian Expeditionary Force in Iraq

February   Hogarth in Cairo office initiates the "Arab Bulle-
                tin" as a regular intelligence report; GLB is the
                principal contributor from Basra

March   British evacuate Gallipoli

                Maurice wounded in France

April   T. E. Lawrence arrives in Basra with authority to
                bribe the Turks to lift the siege of Kut; he and GLB

"had great talks and made vast schemes for the government of the universe"

Turks enter Kut, population massacred; many British troops die in forced march northward

May	Secret Sykes-Picot Agreement anticipates postwar division of influence in Middle East between France, Britain, and Russia
June	GLB appointed head of Iraq branch of the Arab Bureau as an officer of the Indian Expeditionary Force D (IEFD; based in Basra) while also serving Cox

Hashemite family leads inconclusive revolt of Arabs against Turkish rule in western Arabia

September	GLB in hospital with jaundice; then holidays on Euphrates
October	Cox signs treaty with Ibn Saud defining boundaries to limit his military incursions into Iraq
November	GLB arranges visit of Ibn Saud to Basra

Hashemite emir Hussein, Sharif of Mecca, proclaimed king of the Hejaz

December	Lloyd George becomes Prime Minister of Britain
1917 January– March	GLB continues in Basra as Oriental secretary to the civil administration of Cox, as well as head of the Arab Bureau (Iraq)
January	In western Arabia, Emir Faisal with Lawrence starts march of Arab army northward
March	Turkish army vacates Baghdad; British occupy
April	President Wilson asks U.S. Congress to declare war on Germany; American troops engaged in France

GLB moves to Baghdad after nine-day journey up the Tigris

May	GLB occupies her permanent home in Baghdad

Cossack troops commit atrocities in northern Mesopotamia

June	Lawrence takes Aqaba with Arab irregulars
	Maurice invalided out of active service permanently deafened
July	Cox appointed civil commissioner of Mesopotamia reporting to the secretary of state for India in London
August	British defeat Turkish army in Gaza
October	Bolsheviks take control of the Russian Revolution
	British Cabinet approves Balfour Declaration favoring Palestine as a national home for the Jews (announced November 2)
	GLB awarded Commander of the Order of the British Empire (CBE)
	Suffering from exhaustion, GLB admitted to convalescent hospital
	Appointed editor of newspaper *Al Arab* writing "The Arab of Mesopotamia" for British officials
December	British take Jerusalem
1918 January	President Wilson makes his "fourteen points" speech outlining his principles for world peace including a "general association of nations"
March	Russia makes peace with Germany; Allied troops fight Red Army in Russia; GLB awarded Founder's Medal of the Royal Geographical Society
May	GLB starts Tuesday soirees for wives of prominent Arabs
July	Holidays on horseback in Persian mountains
	Women over 30 gain the vote in Britain if they were either a member of or married to a member of the Local Government Register, were a property owner, or were a graduate voting in a university constituency
September	GLB arranges durbar of sheikhs in Iraq
	Cox posted to Tehran; provisionally replaced by Sir Arnold Wilson as acting civil commissioner; GLB's role restricted

	Lady Florence made Dame Commander of the Order of the Indian Empire (DCIE) for her work for the Red Cross; Sir Hugh awarded Companion of the Order of the Bath
October	Emir Faisal's army takes Damascus with Lawrence; Turks fight last battle at Sharqat, then withdraw; Turks sign Mudros Armistice, end of Ottoman Empire
November	Allies sign armistice with Germany; First World War ends
December	Influenza pandemic reaches Baghdad
1919 February–March	GLB prepares a paper for the Paris Peace Conference on the future of Mesopotamia, attending the conference in March
April–May	GLB tours France and visits Algiers with Sir Hugh; returns to Peace Conference until A. T. Wilson arrives
May–September	GLB in England
June	Germany signs Treaty of Versailles accepting peace conditions; Covenant of the League of Nations signed by 44 nations on the 28th
September	GLB visits Cairo, Jerusalem, Damascus, Beirut, and Aleppo
	President Wilson collapses while campaigning for the United States to join the League of Nations
October	President Wilson suffers massive stroke on the 2nd, leaving him permanently incapacitated
November	U.S. Senate fails to ratify the Treaty of Versailles on the 19th
	GLB returns to Baghdad; starts writing *Review of the Civil Administration of Mesopotamia*
	GLB's maid, Marie Delaire, joins her permanently in Baghdad
1920 January	Sir Frank Lascelles dies on the 2nd

	Arab Bureau in Cairo winds down
	GLB takes archaeological trip to the site of Babylon
February	GLB organizes funding for a women's hospital in Baghdad
March	Emir Faisal elected and crowned king of Syria
March–April	Sir Hugh visits Baghdad
April	San Remo Conference agrees to terms of British mandate over Iraq while instituting self-government
	GLB to compile annual reports on the state of Iraq required by the League of Nations
June	Cox makes official visit to Baghdad
July	French occupy Damascus; King Faisal deposed
August	Treaty of Sevres between Allies and Turkey confirms terms for end of hostilities
October	Cox returns to Baghdad as high commissioner to Iraq
	The naqib of Baghdad agrees to form a provisional Arab government and selects cabinet members
	A. T. Wilson leaves public service
	GLB prepares fortnightly reports to the Colonial Office on the progress of the administration in Iraq
November	GLB resumes duties as Oriental secretary
	First meeting of Iraqi Council of State; future meetings frequently held at GLB's house
December	Publication of *Review of the Civil Administration of Mesopotamia,* presented to British parliament
1921 February	Churchill appointed secretary of state for the colonies (including responsibility for the Middle East)
March	GLB attends Churchill's Cairo Conference
	Holidays in Egypt with Sir Hugh; returns to Baghdad

June	Faisal arrives in Basra; he greets GLB upon his arrival in Baghdad
	GLB elected president of new Baghdad Public Library
	Ibn Saud takes Hayyil; Rashid dynasty ends; Shammar tribesmen flee into Iraq
	Three-month British miners' strike hits steel industry
July	GLB announces result of Iraq referendum; naqib declares Faisal king-elect on behalf of Iraqi Council of State
August	Faisal ibn Hussein ibn Ali crowned Faisal I of Iraq
September	King invites the naqib to form a cabinet
November	GLB's half-brother Hugo marries Frances Morkill
1922 April–May	Iraq's Constituent Assembly passes electoral law
	Sir Hugh joins GLB for break in Jerusalem
July	GLB drafts antiquities law for Iraq
August	Bell finances diminish during international economic recession
October	Aiming to comply with the terms of the mandate, Cox and the naqib as prime minister sign a Treaty of Alliance between Iraq and Great Britain giving 20 years of British occupation in advisory capacity
	Faisal proclaims Treaty of Alliance on the 13th
November	Allies and Turkey sign peace treaty officially ending war with Turkey
	Macmillan Company donates books to Baghdad Public Library
	Lloyd George's wartime coalition government collapses; Bonar Law's Conservatives win election; Churchill is replaced by the Duke of Devonshire with responsibility for Middle East
	GLB's brother-in-law Charles Trevelyan elected member of Parliament for Newcastle upon Tyne

	Faisal, with Iraq Cabinet approval, appoints GLB honorary director of antiquities for Iraq
	Air Marshal Sir John Salmond takes command of British forces in Iraq; RAF tasked with controlling tribal dissension
December	Sir Henry Dobbs arrives as prospective high commissioner, in charge while Cox visits London
	GLB asked to continue as Oriental secretary
	Cox signs treaties with Ibn Saud
1923 April	Cox signs treaty reducing British advisory occupation of Iraq to four years
	Cox retires, leaves Iraq
May	Transjordan declared independent under Faisal's elder brother Emir Abdullah by treaty with Britain, later to be the Kingdom of Jordan
July	League of Nations ratifies Turkish Peace Treaty at Conference of Lausanne
	Constituent Assembly passes the draft constitution of Iraq (signed as the Organic Law by Faisal in March 1925)
July–August	GLB travels to England via Haifa, stays with Sir Herbert Samuel, high commissioner for Palestine
	John Singer Sargent draws a portrait of GLB
	GLB corresponds with Lawrence on publication of *Seven Pillars of Wisdom*
September	GLB amends her will, leaving £6,000 ($478,000 RPI adjusted) to the British Museum for a British School of Archaeology in Iraq
October	GLB founds the Iraq Museum
1924 January	Ramsay MacDonald forms first Labour government in coalition with Liberals; Charles Trevelyan in Cabinet as president of Board of Education
February	First national elections in Iraq

March	King Faisal opens Iraq National Assembly
	King Hussein of the Hejaz proclaims himself caliph of Islam following abolition of the title by Mustafa Kemal Atatürk, but without pan-Islamic acclamation
	Dorman Long wins contract to prepare final design and supply nearly 50,000 tons of steel components for the Sydney Harbour Bridge; Hugh Bell as director
September	Anglo-Iraqi Treaty of Alliance accepted by League of Nations as meeting the League's covenant
	Ibn Saud's Wahhabis raid the Hashemite summer palace of Taif in the Hejaz; townspeople massacred
October	Mecca falls to Ibn Saud; King Hussein of the Hejaz abdicates in favor of his son Ali
December	Faisal ratifies the Treaty of Alliance following its approval by George V in November
1925 January	GLB prepares briefs and translates for the League of Nations Commission of Inquiry investigating the unresolved Iraq-Turkey frontier
February	Hugh Bell visits Sydney to inspect the construction site of the bridge
July–October	GLB's last visit to England; returns to Baghdad via Beirut with Sylvia Henley
Autumn	Sir Hugh, Dame Florence, and Maurice move to Mount Grace Priory to economize; Rounton Grange closed
December	Ibn Saud ousts Faisal's brother Ali as king of the Hejaz; annexes the territory
1926 February	GLB's half-brother Hugo dies of pneumonia
March	Vita Sackville-West stays with GLB in Iraq
May	British General Strike; seven-month miners' strike cripples steel industry
June	First room of Iraq Museum opened on the 14th

July	GLB dies on the 12th; funeral with military honors; buried in British cemetery, Baghdad; Memorial service at St. Margaret's Church, Westminster
	Ministers pay tribute to GLB in British parliament
	Treaty between Britain, Iraq, and Turkey defines borders of Mosul district
1927	Dame Florence holds pageant at Mount Grace Priory in presence of Queen Mary, partly financed by sales of signed editions of Dickens's works and his letters to the family
April	Tributes paid to GLB at Royal Geographical Society, London
August	Publication of *The Letters of Gertrude Bell* by Dame Florence, who gives celebratory dinner inviting King Faisal, Iraq prime minister Jafar, the Dobbses, the Coxes, and the Richmonds
October	Turkish Petroleum Company, a consortium of international oil companies, strikes oil near Kirkuk
1928	Window dedicated to GLB in St. Lawrence's Church, East Rounton
1929	Turkish Petroleum Company changes its name to the Iraq Petroleum Company, developing what had been identified as the largest discovered oil field in the world
1930	Commemorative bronze plaque unveiled by King Faisal; bust of GLB identifies the Gertrude Bell Principal Wing of the Iraq Museum
May	Dame Florence Bell dies on the 16th
1931 June	Sir Hugh Bell dies; Maurice succeeds to baronetcy on the 29th
1932	British School of Archaeology in Iraq founded in London; £4,000 ($388,000 RPI adjusted) donation from Sir Hugh
	Iraq joins League of Nations as independent state
1933	King Faisal dies; succeeded by son, Ghazi

1939	King Ghazi dies in motoring accident, succeeded by son Faisal II
1940	Rounton Grange used as a home for Second World War evacuees and for Italian prisoners of war
1947	British Treasury grant enables formation of the British Archaeological Expedition to Iraq under auspices of the School of Archaeology; permanent base in Baghdad established
1953	Rounton Grange demolished
1958	Faisal II of Iraq assassinated in coup; Iraq declared a republic
1991 January	Iraq Museum closed during the Gulf War
2000 April	Iraq Museum reopened
2003	Immediately before and during the invasion of Iraq by Americans and British, the museum was looted of some 15,000 items, many of which have been recovered; later reopened to archaeologists and school visits
2015 February	Iraq Museum again opened to the public

A Woman in Arabia

THE LINGUIST

Florence, Gertrude's stepmother, had been brought up in Paris and spoke English with a charming French accent. Most of the family's holidays abroad were taken in Italy and Germany, and Gertrude was not the kind of traveler who would visit a country without mastering at least the basics of the language. As soon as she arrived at Weimar she arranged to have German lessons, and as soon as she arrived in Venice, she arranged to have Italian lessons. Gradually she acquired, besides her English and French, fluent Italian, German, Arabic, Persian, and Turkish. The latter she learned very quickly, but it was the only language she found difficult to remember. Her around-the-world trips gave her enough Hindustani to dispense with an interpreter, and a smattering of Japanese and Urdu. She described her progress in each language, somewhat boastfully, in her letters home to her family.

Of all the languages, Arabic proved the most difficult for her to learn. Staying in Jerusalem in 1900 with family friends Nina and Freidrich Rosen—he was the German consul—she took six lessons in Arabic a week, which did not prevent her from reading Genesis in Hebrew before dinner, for light relief.

Persia, from Gula Hek, the Summer Resort of
the British Legation, June 18, 1892,
Letter to Her Cousin Horace Marshall

. . . Is it not rather refreshing to the spirit to lie in a hammock strung between the plane trees of a Persian garden and read the poems of Hafiz—in the original mark you!—out of a book curiously bound in stamped leather which you have bought in the bazaars. That is how I spend my mornings here; a stream murmurs past me which Zoroastrian gardeners guide with long handled spades into tiny sluices leading into the flower beds all around. The dictionary which is also in my hammock is not perhaps so poetic as the other attributes—let us hide it under our muslin petticoats!

I learn Persian, not with great energy, one does nothing with energy here. My teacher is a delightful old person with bright eyes and a white turban who knows so little French (French is our medium) that he can neither translate the poets to me nor explain any grammatical difficulties. But we get on admirably nevertheless and spend much of our time in long philosophic discussions carried on by me in French and him in Persian. His point of view is very much that of an oriental Gibbon. . . .

London, February 14, 1896

My Pundit was extremely pleased with me, he kept congratulating me on my proficiency in the Arabic tongue! I think his other pupils must be awful duffers. It is quite extraordinarily interesting to read the Koran with him—and it *is* such a magnificent book!

London, February 24, 1896

My Pundit brought back my poems yesterday—he is really pleased with them. . . . Arabic flies along—I shall soon be able to read the Arabian Nights for fun.

Jerusalem, December 1899

I'd rather do this than be in London, it's more worthwhile on the whole. I'm very sorry but one can't do everything and I would rather well get hold of Arabic than anything in the world.

. . . I don't think I shall ever talk Arabic, but I go on struggling with it in the hope of mortifying Providence by my persistence . . .

My teacher's name is Khalil Dughan and . . . I learnt more about pronunciation this morning than I have ever known. . . . I either have a lesson or work alone every morning for 4 hours—the lesson only lasts 1 ½ hours. I have 3 morning and 3 afternoon lessons a week. I am just beginning to understand a little of what I hear and to say simple things to the servants, but I find it awfully difficult. The pronunciation is past words, no western throat being constructed to form these extraordinary gutturals. . . .

Comes my housemaid, "The hot water is ready for the Presence" says he. "Enter and light the candle" say I. "On my head" he has replied. . . . That means it's dressing time.

Jerusalem, January 11, 1900

. . . Language is very difficult [and] there are at least three sounds almost impossible to the European throat. The worst I think is a very much aspirated H. I can only say it by holding down my tongue with one finger, but then you can't carry on a conversation with your finger down your throat, can you? . . .

I took Ferideh* for a drive . . . and talked Arabic extremely badly and felt desponding about it. However there is nothing to be done but struggle on with it. I should like to mention that there are five words for a wall and 36 ways of forming the plural.

Jerusalem, February 18, 1900

Do you know these wet afternoons I have been reading the story of Aladdin to myself for pleasure, without a dictionary! . . . I really think that these months here [in Jerusalem] will permanently add to the pleasure and interest of the rest of my days! Honest Injun. Still there is a lot and a lot more to be done first—so to work!

*Ferideh Yamseh, a schoolteacher who helped Gertrude with her Arabic.

Ain Tulma, Palestine, February 28, 1900

I hurried on . . . with 5 little beggar boys in my train. They were great fun. We had long conversations all the way home. It's such an amusement to be able to understand. The differences of pronunciation are a little puzzling at first to the foreigner. There are two k's in Arabic—the town people drop the hard k altogether and replace it by a guttural for which we have no equivalent; the country people pronounce the hard k soft and the soft k ch, but they say their gutturals beautifully and use a lot of words which belong to the more classical Arabic. The Bedouins speak the best; they pronounce all their letters and get all the subtlest shades of meaning out of the words.

From Her Tent Pitched at Ayan Musa, March 20, 1900

We were soon surrounded by Arabs who sold us a hen and some excellent sour milk, "laban" it is called. While we bargained the women and children wandered round and ate grass, just like goats. The women are unveiled. They wear a blue cotton gown 6 yards long which is gathered up and bound round their heads and their waists and falls to their feet. Their faces, from the mouth downwards, are tattooed with indigo and their hair hangs down in two long plaits on either side. . . . Our horses and mules were hobbled and groomed. Hanna brought me an excellent cup of tea and at 6 a good dinner consisting of soup made of rice and olive oil (very good!) an Irish stew and raisins from Salt, an offering from Tarif. My camp lies just under Pisgah. Isn't it a joke being able to talk Arabic!

March 25, 1900

I . . . came back to my tent where I was presently fetched by a little Turkish girl, the daughter of an Effendi, who told me her mother was sitting down in the shadow of the wall a little below my camp and invited me to come and drink coffee. We went down hand in hand and I found a lot of Turkish women sitting on the ground under a fig tree, so I sat down too and was given coffee and as they all but one talked Arabic, we had a cheerful conversation.

Of Her Druze Muleteers, April 2, 1900

They both talk with the pretty, soft, sing-song accent of the Lebanon. I have a good variety of accents with me, for Tarif has the Bedouin and Hanna the real cockney of Jerusalem. They appeal to me sometimes to know which is right.

Gertrude traveled to Malta and Italy with her family, then went on alone to several countries farther east.

Haifa, Palestine, April 7, 1902

This is my day: I get up at 7, at 8 Abu Nimrud comes and teaches me Arabic till 10. I go on working till 12, when I lunch. Then I write for my Persian till 1.30, or so, when I ride or walk out. Come in at 5, and work till 7, when I dine. At 7.30 my Persian comes and stays until 10, and at 10.30 I go to bed. You see I have not much leisure time! And the whole day long I talk Arabic.

Haifa, April 2, 1902

It's perfectly delightful getting hold of Persian again, the delicious language! But as for Arabic I am soaked and saddened by it and how anyone can wish to have anything to do with a tongue so difficult when they might be living at ease, I can't imagine. . . . The birds fly into my room and nest in the chandelier!

"My First Night in the Desert," May 16, 1900

My soldiers are delighted that I can talk Arabic; they say it's so
dull when they can't talk to the "gentry." They talk Kurdish
together, being of Kurdish parentage, but born in Damascus.
Their Arabic is very good. Mine is really getting quite presentable. I think I talk Arabic as well as I talk German (which isn't
saying much perhaps!), but I don't understand so well. It's so
confoundedly—in the Bible sense!—rich in words.

On Gertrude's second around-the-world journey, she was
accompanied by her half-brother, Hugo.

India, in the Train from Alwar to Delhi, January 18, 1903

My thrice blessed Hindustani, though it doesn't reach to any
flowers of speech, carries us through our travels admirably and
here we were able to stop where no one has a word of English,
without any inconvenience.

Burma, on the Irrawaddy River, March 2, 1903

We came to a very small steam boat. . . . A steep and slippery
plank led out to the boat. I took my courage in both hands,
crept along it, lifted the awning, and received a broadside of the
hottest, oiliest, most machinery laden air, resonant with the
snores of sleepers. I lit a match and found that I was on a tiny
deck covered with the sheeted dead, who, however, presently sat
up on their elbows and blinked at me. I announced firmly in
Urdu that I would not move until I was shown somewhere to
sleep. After much grumbling . . . one arose, and lit a lantern;
together we sidled down the plank and he took us back to one of
the mysterious hulks by the river bank. It was inhabited by an
old Hindu and a bicycle and many cockroaches.

Tokyo, May 24, 1903

In one of the temples, a wonderful place all gold lacquer and carving set in a little peaceful garden, a priest came up to me and asked if I were an American. I said no, I was English. . . . I replied in Japanese, in which tongue the conversation was being conducted. . . .

During the years in Mesopotamia she came to speak many Arabic dialects so well that she once disguised herself and was able to tease King Faisal by convincing him that she was a talkative camel driver.

Baghdad, November 29, 1920

I love walking with the beaters (at a shoot) and hearing what they say to each other in the broadest Iraq dialect, which I'm proud to understand.

Baghdad, June 23, 1921

. . . I have been elected President of the Bagdad Public Library. . .*

Notice Distributed by Gertrude to English Publishers, Asking if They Would Care to Donate Books to the Salam Library, 1921

*Ultimately called the Salam Library.

NOTICE
TO
ALL AUTHORS, PUBLISHERS
AND BOOKSELLERS

The Salam Library, Bagdad, intends to issue a periodical publication—in Arabic and English—the object of which is to review books published in Oriental languages, Arabic, Persian, Turkish, Hebrew, Syriac, Hindustani, etc.; and also books published in European languages, English, French and German, etc.

This publication will deal only with books presented to the library with a request from the publisher or author asking for a review or notice of the book.

It will also give an account of such manuscripts as may be found in the library or are to be found in local bookshops. Thus the Salam Library's periodical publication will be the best means for introducing European books to Orientals and Oriental books to Europeans and will serve as a means to facilitate the sale of books.

The Committee of the Salam Library is composed of Arab and British members who will undertake the publication of the periodical.

(Signed) GERTRUDE BELL

President, Salam Library

BAGDAD

THE POET

In 1892, when Gertrude was twenty-four, she was invited to stay with her aunt Mary and uncle Sir Frank Lascelles, ambassador to Persia (now Iran) in Tehran. For six months in advance, she learned Persian, then continued to study the language in Tehran. She was much encouraged in this by an agreeable and scholarly legation secretary, Henry Cadogan, a grandson of the 3rd Earl Cadogan, who found her a teacher and gave her books of Persian poetry to read. Exploring and riding out together on picnics and expeditions, Henry would produce a book from his pocket and read Sufi poetry aloud to her, describing the yearning for the Beloved that filled the vacuum between the profane and the divine. It was not long before she fell in love for the first time and wrote to her father to ask if she and Henry might become engaged. After a short delay, Hugh Bell's reply arrived, and it was unequivocal: no engagement was possible, and she must leave and come home at once. Gertrude, of course, was an heiress, and her father had heard that not only was Henry penniless, but he was also a gambler. Not a year after a brokenhearted Gertrude left Persia, Henry fell into an icy river while fishing and died of pneumonia. Partly as a tribute to his memory, and a lingering suspicion that it might have been suicide, Gertrude wrote and, in 1897, published *Poems from the Divan of Hafiz,* an English rendering of forty-three poems of the fourteenth-century Sufi mystic Shemsuddin Mahommad, better known by his pen name Hafiz. These Persian *ghazals,* or odes, range in length from ten to sixteen couplets, all on one rhyme and each containing a new idea, and always introducing the poet's name in the last couplet.

In London, she continued her Persian lessons with Sir Edward Denison Ross, director of the School of Oriental and African Studies. The foremost linguist of his day, he could read forty-nine languages and speak thirty but had the modesty to write of Gertrude at the end of the 1890s that he had had "the healthy experience of realising in the presence of such a brilliant scholar my own limitations." Gertrude's *Poems of the Divan of Hafiz* was published together with her biography of the poet set in the context of his contemporary history—a tour de force in its own right, there being no written history of Islamic Persia at the time. It received as large an acclaim as a book of poetry can elicit. The greatest authority on Persian literature of her day, Edward G. Browne, said that with the single exception of Edward FitzGerald's paraphrase of the quatrains of Omar Khayyam, her translations were "probably the finest and most truly poetical renderings of any Persian poet ever produced in the English language."

She beautifully and rather freely rendered the verses into English poetry imbuing them with great sadness, coloring Hafiz' work with the melancholy of her own poignant loss, and occasionally departing rather noticeably from the original. In the second poem below—"the nightingale with drops of his heart's blood . . . "—Hafiz was writing of the death of his son; but Gertrude was undoubtedly thinking of Henry.

Denison Ross in his preface demonstrated the exact material she had to work on by giving a literal translation of the original of one of Gertrude's renderings.

> *Dast az talab nadaram ta kam-i dil bar ayad*
> *Ya tan rasad bijanan, ya jan zi tan bar ayad*

literally means,

> I will not hold back from seeking till my desire is
> realised,

Either my soul will reach the beloved, or my soul will
    leave its body.

Gertrude wrote,

I cease not from desire till my desire
Is satisfied; or let my mouth attain
My love's red mouth, or let my soul expire,
Sighed from those lips that sought her lips in vain.

Piecing together the scattered facts of Hafiz' life, she
sketched the elusive history of Sufism and referred to the
"interminable, the hopeless mysticism, the playing with words
that say one thing and mean something totally different, the
vagueness of a philosophy that dare not speak out, which
repels the European just as much as it attracts the Oriental
mind." For such a pragmatic personality to illuminate the
highest aim of the Sufi—the annihilation of the actual—was a
considerable feat, although in the translator's preface she could
not resist writing, "I have a shrewd suspicion that the Cup-
bearer [teacher] brought him a wine other than that of divine
knowledge, and that his mistress is considerably more than an
allegorical figure." In the same vein, she fearlessly guides the
average European reader: "The tavern . . . is the place of instruction or worship, of which the tavern-keeper is the teacher
or priest, and the wine the spirit of divine knowledge . . . the
idol is God; beauty is the divine perfection; shining locks the
expansion of his glory; down on the cheek denotes the cloud of
spirits that encircles his throne; and a black mole is the point
of indivisible unity." As if aware that leading Sufis would disdain
these mundane translations, she concluded, "I am very conscious
that my appreciation of the poet is that of the Western . . . what
his compatriots make of his teaching it is perhaps impossible
to understand."

In 1903, Denison Ross was amused to receive a telegram
from Gertrude in Rangoon, on the second of her around-the-
world tours, which asked: "Please send first hemistich of verse
ending *Wa khayru jalisin fi zaman kitabu.*" He was able to

telegraph immediately in reply: "*zahru sabihin A'azz makanin fiddunya*" [sic]:

> The finest place in the world is the back of a swift horse,
> And the best of good companions is a book.

FROM A VERSE OF THE POET AL-MUTANABBI

Gertrude remained a lover of poetry all her life but never wrote another poem. As Florence wrote, this passion for reading poetry was "a strangely interesting ingredient in a character capable on occasion of very definite hardness, and of a deliberate disregard of sentiment."

On all her desert expeditions, Gertrude always carried a pocket set of Shakespeare in her saddlebag. On one occasion on her final expedition, when it was raining too heavily to go on, she wrote in her diary, "I sat in my tent and read Hamlet from beginning to end and as I read, the world swung back into focus. Princes and powers of Arabia stepped down into their true place and there rose up above them the human soul conscious and answerable to itself."

Four Poems by Hafiz, Rendered in English by Gertrude Bell

> I cease not from desire till my desire
> Is satisfied; or let my mouth attain
> My love's red mouth, or let my soul expire,
> Sighed from those lips that sought her lips in vain.
>
> Others may find another love as fair;
> Upon her threshold I have laid my head,
> The dust shall cover me, still lying there,
> When from my body life and love have fled.
>
> My soul is on my lips ready to fly,
> But grief beats in my heart and will not cease,
> Because not once, not once before I die,
> Will her sweet lips give all my longing peace.
> My breath is narrowed down to one long sigh

For a red mouth that burns my thoughts like fire;
When will that mouth draw near and make reply
To one whose life is straitened with desire?

When I am dead, open my grave and see
The cloud of smoke that rises round thy feet:
In my dead heart the fire still burns for thee;
Yes, the smoke rises from my winding-sheet!
Ah, come, Beloved! for the meadows wait
Thy coming, and the thorn bears flowers instead
Of thorns, the cypress fruit, and desolate
Bare winter from before thy steps has fled.

Hoping within some garden ground to find
A red rose soft and sweet as thy soft cheek,
Through every meadow blows the western wind,
Through every garden he is fain to seek.
Reveal thy face! that the whole world may be
Bewildered by thy radiant loveliness;
The cry of man and woman comes to thee,
Open thy lips and comfort their distress!

Each curling lock of thy luxuriant hair
Breaks into barbed hooks to catch my heart,
My broken heart is wounded everywhere
With countless wounds from which the red drops start.
Yet when sad lovers meet and tell their sighs,
Not without praise shall Hafiz' name be said,
Not without tears, in those pale companies
Where joy has been forgot and hope has fled.

———

The nightingale with drops of his heart's blood
Had nourished the red rose, then came a wind,
And catching at the boughs in envious mood,
A hundred thorns about his heart entwined.
Like to the parrot crunching sugar, good

Seemed the world to me who could not stay
The wind of Death that swept my hopes away.

Light of mine eyes and harvest of my heart,
And mine at least in changeless memory!
Ah, when he found it easy to depart,
He left the harder pilgrimage to me!
Oh Camel-driver, though the cordage start,
For God's sake help me lift my fallen load,
And Pity be my comrade of the road!

My face is seamed with dust, mine eyes are wet.
Of dust and tears the turquoise firmament
Kneadeth the bricks for joy's abode; and yet . . .
Alas, and weeping yet I make lament!
Because the moon her jealous glances set
Upon the bow-bent eyebrows of my moon,
He sought a lodging in the grave—too soon!

I had not castled, and the time is gone.
What shall I play? Upon the chequered floor
Of Night and Day, Death won the game—forlorn
And careless now, Hafiz can lose no more.

————

Thus said the Poet: "When Death comes to you,
All ye whose life-sand through the hour-glass slips,
He lays two fingers on your ears, and two
Upon your eyes he lays, one on your lips,
Whispering: Silence." Although deaf thine ear,
Thine eye, my Hafiz, suffer Time's eclipse,
The songs thou sangest still all men may hear.

Songs of dead laughter, songs of love once hot,
Songs of a cup once flushed rose-red with wine,
Songs of a rose whose beauty is forgot,
A nightingale that piped hushed lays divine:

And still a graver music runs beneath
The tender love notes of those songs of thine,
Oh, Seeker of the keys of Life and Death!

———

Return! that to a heart wounded full sore
Valiance and strength may enter in; return!
And Life shall pause at the deserted door,
The cold dead body breathe again and burn.
Oh come! and touch mine eyes, of thy sweet grace,
For I am blind to all but to thy face.
Open the gates and bid me see once more!

Like to a cruel Ethiopian band,
Sorrow despoiled the kingdom of my heart—
Return! glad Lord of Rome, and free the land;
Before thine arms the foe shall break and part.
See now, I hold a mirror to mine eyes,
And nought but thy reflection therein lies;
The glass speaks truth to them that understand.

Night is with child, hast thou not heard men say?
"Night is with child! what will she bring to birth?"
I sit and ask the stars when thou'rt away.
Oh come! and when the nightingale of mirth
Pipes in the Spring-awakened garden ground,
In Hafiz' heart shall ring a sweeter sound,
Diviner nightingales attune their lay.

THE "PERSON"

The moral and intellectual debate of the age was female suffrage, and from the moment of being allowed to join the adults for meals, Gertrude heard the issue being discussed passionately from all points of view. Hugh and Florence were opposed to it for cogent reasons, but some of their friends were adamant in its support. All the Bells agreed with John Stuart Mill, the greatest proponent of women's emancipation of his time, that it was vital for a woman to be a "Person": it became a family joke that the women seldom felt themselves to be quite enough of a Person.

It has gone down in history that Gertrude was an antifeminist. In 2004, London's National Portrait Gallery mounted an exhibition of pioneering women travelers called "Off the Beaten Track." Gertrude's corner was accompanied by a four-line caption—all that was devoted to her—stating "Despite her own achievements she actively opposed British women being given the right to vote." Technically correct, the statement is a crude assessment of her ultimate intentions and one that takes no account of the complex politics of the times, or her position as a daughter of the Industrial Revolution. This oversimplification is often leveled against her and has been partially responsible for the way in which her achievements have been undervalued.

While the Reform Bill of 1832 and its successors had increased voters from 500,000 to 5 million by 1884, the vote was still limited to men of property. Only one quarter of the men in Britain had the vote. While the franchise was denied to so many men, Parliament could not have contemplated giving the vote

to women. In discussions about giving the vote only to women
of property, Parliament came up against an insuperable difficulty: the property laws. The possessions of wives automati-
cally became their husbands' property on marriage. This was
the law that led Gertrude's father to refuse her marriage to
Henry Cadogan, known to be a gambler. So married women
would be denied the vote, while much of the franchise would
have been granted to widows, prostitutes, and spinsters. As
independent and rational women such as Gertrude and Florence Nightingale felt, women's suffrage could not be addressed
until the property laws were transformed.

Matters such as health, schooling, men's leisure activities,
social services, the Poor Laws, subsistence benefit, and the
workhouses and almshouses were dealt with by local government. In these issues Florence Bell and most of the women she
knew were involved up to the hilt. Unfortunately, when they
and other women across Britain achieved the local vote, men
rioted in the streets of several towns. These women dreaded a
reaction to the demands of the suffragists—who kept within
the law—and the suffragettes—who broke it—that would
bring retribution and destroy the advances that women had
already made.

Whenever Gertrude stayed at home too long, she would be
drawn into Florence's social work, summed up by Florence in
her book *At the Works*. Factually exhaustive, exposing the
suffering endured by the poorer working families and especially when they struck hard times, it poses no remedies. Capi-
talists and employers as the Bells were, Hugh saw no conflict
between masters and men—he saw them as mutually dependent. He paid his men fairly according to the dictates of the
day, he was active in Liberal politics, and he believed in the
role of the new trade unions. As civic leaders and local bene-
factors, the Bells built assembly rooms, libraries, schools, and
offices. They also opened a Middlesbrough center where
exhausted workers could go and where Florence would play
the piano and lead the songs.

At the time the vote, considered today to be a universal
human right, was judged to be a serious business requiring

education and political acumen. The government of the day
was concerned with such issues as defense, Irish Home Rule,
free trade, penal reform, the Reform Bill, and political corruption. What could a wife with a houseful of children know of
these issues, asked Florence, and how could she find the time
to learn to read if she was illiterate?

If anything tipped Gertrude into action, other than family
pressure, it was the militancy of Christabel Pankhurst, who by
1904 was leading women against what she called "the noxious
character of male sexuality." The suffragettes were engaged in a
war against men, employing methods tantamount to terrorism.
They denounced marriage as legalized prostitution, and they
attacked property, smashing windows and train carriages and
slashing paintings of nude women in galleries. They assaulted
random men who happened to resemble Prime Minister Herbert Asquith. They sent packages of sulfuric acid to his succes-
sor, Lloyd George, later attempting to burn down his house.

Gertrude joined the movement against women's suffrage in
1908 and became a member of the Anti-Suffrage League. Being
the person she was, she initially entered the fray with zest, and
it was probably Gertrude who collected 250,000 signatures for
the anti-suffrage petition of 1909; but soon her letters betrayed
a lack of mission, which suggests she had taken on the work
mostly to please Florence.

In Iraq, from 1915, she made few female friends. There were
exceptions, but she made cutting remarks about the British
wives of her colleagues in Baghdad. "A little woman" was one
of her deadliest assessments. She conceded that her great friend
Haji Naji, who regularly sent her fruit and vegetables from his
garden, was "an odd substitute for a female friend but the best
I can find."

Later in life, her work for Muslim women would be considerable. In her earliest encounters with women of the harem, and
particularly in Hayyil, Gertrude had heard their tragic stories
and remained deeply impressed by their subjection. She heartily
disliked the restrictions placed on Muslim women in the Islamic
societies of the East and did what she could to help. She orga-

nized a series of health lectures by a woman doctor, which were well attended by the Muslim wives. She helped found the first girls' school in Baghdad, and she led the fund-raising for a women's hospital. Her regular Tuesday tea parties for women put her on a friendly footing with the chief families of Baghdad.

Gertrude was to become a supremely civilized and able woman. With no husband or children to preoccupy her, her abilities spanned the spectrum from poetry to administration, from pioneering adventure and sportsmanship to archaeology. She possessed a rare grasp of world history and contemporary political debate alongside a love of gardening and pretty clothes. She was proficient in six languages. And all of this was well grounded in the gentler human qualities: a deep sense of family, of landscape and architecture, and a love of life itself. Few have rivaled her in the sheer range of her capabilities. As a Person she came to fulfill the highest aspirations that John Stuart Mill had imagined possible for women.

Mount Carmel, Haifa, March 30, 1902

I am much entertained to find that I am a Person in this country—they all think I am a Person! . . . Renown is not very difficult to acquire here.

Damascus, February 27, 1905

I find the Government here has been in an agony of nervousness all the time I was in the Jebel Druze! They had three telegrams a day from Salkhad about me. . . . The governor here has sent me a message to say would I honour him by coming to see him, so I've answered graciously. . . . An official lives in this hotel. He spent the evening talking to me and offering to place the whole of the organisation of Syria at my disposal. He also tried to find out all my views on Druze and Bedouin affairs, but he did not get much forrader there. I have become a Person in Syria!

95 Sloane Street, London, March 28, 1913

Last night I went to a delightful party at the Glenconners' and
just before I arrived 4 suffragettes set on Asquith and seized
hold of him. Whereupon Alec Laurence in fury seized 2 of them
and twisted their arms till they shrieked. Then one of them bit
him in the hand till he bled. When he told me the tale he was
steeped in his own gore.

In 1917, Gertrude's friend Sheikh Fahd Beg ibn Hadhdhal
came to Baghdad on a visit early in the British administration
of Iraq and described the powerful effect on him produced by
one of her letters. She wrote home of what he said to her colleagues in the secretariat.

June 1, 1917

"I summoned my sheikhs" he wound up (I feeling more and
more of a Person as he proceeded). "I read them your letter and
I said to them, Oh Sheikhs"—we hung upon his words—"This
is a woman—what must the men be like!" This delicious perora-
tion restored me to my true place in the twinkling of an eye.

Of Religious Leaders and the Veiling of Women

. . . Their tenets forbid them to look upon an unveiled woman
and my tenets don't permit me to veil—I think I'm right there,
for it would be a tacit admission of inferiority which would put
our intercourse from the first out of focus. Nor is it any good
trying to make friends through the women—if the women were
allowed to see me they would veil before me as if I were a man.
So you see I appear to be too female for one sex and too male for
the other. [March 14, 1920]

Of British Women Abroad

As for the wife, why she comes abroad I can't imagine for she has the meanest opinion of foreigners and their ways and their cooking. She dismisses the whole French cuisine at one blow:—they give you no potatoes. [April 23, 1893]

. . . The devil take all inane women. [September 6, 1917]

. . . A collection of more tiresome women I never encountered. [September 27, 1920]

I'm left without any female I can trouble to be intimate with and it's a very great drawback. [October 13, 1921]

Of Some of the Wives of Her Colleagues

These idle women . . . take no sort of interest in what's going on, know no Arabic and see no Arabs. They create an exclusive (it's also a very second-rate) English society quite cut off from the life of the town. I now begin to understand why British Government has come to grief in India, where our women do just the same thing. [Baghdad, June 19, 1921]

But she made good friends with Aurelia Tod, and much regretted her absence when the Tods left Baghdad.

I miss her dreadfully. She is the only intimate friend I have here; there isn't one of the other women whom I care about or can talk to with complete frankness. It's such a comfort to have someone to whom you can say everything! And besides she adds very greatly to the pleasure of life by making a centre for us where we can meet cheerfully and agreeably. [Baghdad, May 8, 1921]

Of Muslim Wives

They [the ladies of Baghdad] never see anything or go anywhere, think of it! Some of them remain quite human and cheerful but a great many are hysterical and nerve-ridden. They look like plants reared in a cellar. [Baghdad, May 4, 1918]

The poor thing never leaves the house or sees anyone. There are many families where the women are entirely secluded. I'm bound to say they hate it, and my heart aches with boredom when I think of them. [Baghdad, December 27, 1918]

Last night I dined with Sir Aylmer* to meet Ja'far† and Nuri‡ and their wives! I doubted whether they would be bold enough to bring them, the wives I mean, but they were—it certainly is a great step forward. . . . They behaved perfectly, their complete absence of self-consciousness giving them a natural distinction which many great ladies might envy. [December 8, 1921]

Of the First Women's Club Established in Baghdad

I'm wholly in favour of it—it's the first step in female emancipation here—and yet wholly against it because it's going to give me such a lot of trouble.

Aren't we advancing Moslem women? There's a quite considerable women's movement going on.

Of Reactions to a Lecture She Gave to an Audience of Muslim Women

I discoursed to them on the ancient history of Iraq and modern excavation. Some of them listened and some didn't—they haven't got the habit of attention. But they'll have to learn it. [January 30, 1924]

---

*General Sir Aylmer Haldane, chief of the British army.

†Ja'far Pasha al-Askari, Iraq minister of defense, ambassador to Great Britain (later became prime minister of Iraq).

‡Nuri Pasha al-Said, brother-in-law of Ja'far (later became prime minister of Iraq).

Of Her First Meeting with King Faisal's Wife and Daughters

Just think of the life they've all led, imprisoned in the Mecca
palace with a pack of women and slaves! Just to sit on their balcony and see the Tigris flowing must be wonderful to them.
[December 23, 1924]

Gertrude much admired a Muslim woman who refused to
submit herself to the usual Islamic rules.

She is an intrepid woman, holds her own against her men folk
and goes about in Najaf scarcely veiled. . . . [December 5, 1920]
   She is really a very remarkable woman, speaks English as well
as I do and French better, and is quite free of the veil though a
good Moslem. [October 12, 1922]

She wondered if the veiling of women might become a thing of
the past, at least as a universal institution.

May 15, 1921

The women who have come back from Syria or Constantinople
find the Baghdad social observances very trying. They have
been accustomed to much greater freedom. As soon as we get
our local institutions firmly established they will be bolder.
They and their husbands are afraid that any steps taken now
would set all the prejudiced old tongues wagging and jeopardize
their future. Nevertheless these new men bring their wives to see
me which is an unexpected departure from Baghdad customs,
according to which a man would never go about with his wife. I
welcome everything that tends in this direction but again one
can do little but give sympathetic welcome to the woman. They
must work out their own salvation and it wouldn't help them to
be actively backed by an infidel, even if the infidel were I who
am permitted many things here.

THE MOUNTAINEER

During the 1899–1904 climbing seasons, Gertrude Bell became one of the most prominent women climbers in the Alps. While her traverse of the Schreckhorn was officially her most important ascent, she will always be remembered for the glorious failure of her attempt on the Finsteraarhorn. Her safe retreat under such conditions was a tremendous performance. "There can be in the whole Alps few places so steep and so high," wrote Ulrich Fuhrer to her father, years later. "The climb has only been done three times, including your daughter's attempt, and is still considered one of the greatest expeditions in the whole Alps. The honour belongs to Miss Bell. Had she not been full of courage and determination, we must have perished."

Her achievements are all the more extraordinary because mountaineering was just one of her interests. Seen in the context of her whole life, her climbing was little more than a hobby she took up for a while, less important to her than traveling, learning languages, archaeology, or photography but more important, perhaps, than her rock gardening, hunting, or fencing.

From childhood, Gertrude had possessed an extraordinary vitality of mind and body. Small but strong and athletic, she needed considerable quantities of exercise, the harder the better. She hunted, danced, bicycled, played golf, shot, fished, fenced, gardened, and skated. She discovered climbing as a result of a family holiday in the French Alps. The first mountain she climbed was the snow-covered ridge of the Meije, which towered over the village of La Grave and the inn where the Bells were staying in August 1897. There Florence and her sisters sat on the balcony and drank hot chocolate, while Hugh and Gertrude got up early and bicycled or walked. They scrambled up a local peak together, the Bec de l'Homme, but Gertrude was soon going off by herself with the local mountain guides, Mathon and Marius, and beginning to climb minor peaks. Before she left, she went over the Brèche by the easy route and spent one night in the mountain refuge. It was enough to convince her of the thrill and danger of climbing, and as she ran down the last slope into the village, she resolved to come back and climb to the peak of the 13,068 foot Meije another year.

She fulfilled her promise a couple of seasons later, having been around the world in the meantime. She came on alone from Bayreuth, as much of a novice as she had been two years previously. It was not unusual at the time for male climbers, often British students on holiday, to tackle the Alps without any experience, as long as they could find good guides. Crampons would not be in use for nearly a decade, carabiners had not been invented, and without the benefit of nylon the ropes were thick and heavy, and even heavier when saturated. Women mountaineers were so rare that there were no "right clothes" for them. At first, Gertrude would take off her skirt and climb in her combinations. Later, she would wear a pair of men's trousers tightly belted under her skirt. Eventually, she achieved a blue climbing suit with trousers into which she would change at the base hut. From a written request to her sister for "two gold pins for my necktie, and thick black garters," it is clear that her trim and masculine appearance on the mountains set the fashion for the women skiers of the next few decades.

She met up with Mathon and Marius, and they started up the Meije. She was soon supporting her own weight and managing so well that she didn't realize she had completed one of the trickiest maneuvers of the climb, the Pas du Chat. They reached the Grand Pic, fifteen feet of almost perpendicular rock, followed by a twenty-foot overhang and the summit. The way down was longer than the way up, and just as difficult.

Arriving back at the inn, she went straight to bed and slept for eleven hours.

Now she set her heart on climbing the highest summit of the southern French Alps, the Barre des Écrins. They started at 1:10 a.m. in intense cold only three days later. Accidents happened that day. She fell onto her back on the ice but was caught on the rope by Mathon. Both cut their hands, he badly. She took photographs, her numb fingers fumbling with the camera. Bitter winds drove clouds of snow around them at midday, delaying the descent from the peak. On the way down, she twisted her foot painfully.

For the climbing season of 1900, Gertrude chose the Swiss Alps and met her new guides at Chamonix. Ulrich Fuhrer and his brother Heinrich would take her on all her major climbs thereafter. She had decided to tackle Mont Blanc. At 15,771 feet, it is physically demanding and the highest summit in the Alps. Only a year after her first mountain, she succeeded in climbing Mont Blanc and two other major peaks in the range, the Grepon and the Dru. Her fame as a mountaineer began to spread, and she became overconfident. She was riding for a fall, but she was so natural and agile a climber, combining such strength and courage, that it would be some time before the reckoning.

In 1901, she met Ulrich and Heinrich again, this time in the Bernese Oberland. Her first ambition was to climb the Schreckhorn, dominated only by the immense razor of the Finsteraarhorn. From her letter home she appears to have found the Schreckhorn easy, including even the two-thousand-foot rock tower at its crest. At the summit she announced to the Fuhrers her latest ambition: to climb the Finsteraarhorn by the unconquered northeast face.

Ulrich, whatever his private doubts, now put her through an intensive period of difficult climbing in preparation for this daunting challenge. Systematically, she climbed all the perpendicular peaks of the Engelhörner range. During the course of two weeks she climbed seven virgin peaks, one of which was named after her and remains in all the literature to this day as

Gertrudspitze (Gertrude's Peak). At her personal best she undertook the most difficult ascent of the year, the unclimbed first-
class traverse of the Urbachthaler Engelhorn. In a long letter to
her family, she describes the key moments of what proved to be
a horrific day's climbing in bad weather, which involved Ulrich
standing on Gertrude's shoulders and then her upstretched
hand in order to reach a small handhold. The ascent could have
been fatal for all three and would have deterred almost any
other climber, but in 1902 Gertrude returned to hold Ulrich to
his promise to take her up the Finsteraarhorn.

She discovered that she had become famous when the train
guard came to ask her if she were the same Miss Bell who had
climbed the Engelhorn the previous year. However, she had
rivals, and rather comically she ran into one of them, Fräulein
Kuntze, in the same inn at Rosenlaui, and again when both were
attempting the first ascent of the Lauteraarhorn-Schreckhorn
traverse. There was, apparently, an acrimonious exchange between the two ladies, with Gertrude coming off best. Amused
and on her mettle, she achieved the first ascent without much
trouble, although, according to the *Alpine Journal,* the climb
remains technically her most important climb.

Now she had truly earned her attempt on the Finsteraarhorn, the highest mountain in the Oberland, approaching the
summit by the new and difficult route that she and Ulrich had
been working up to for a couple of years. Sharp as a blade, this
remote and bad-tempered mountain rises perpendicular to a
razor ridge at 14,022 feet, its steeple point visible for a hundred
miles. It is notorious for bad weather and frequent avalanches,
and many an experienced climber had turned away from the
challenge that this thirty-five-year-old woman and her guide
now set themselves. This was to be Gertrude's most dangerous
mountain exploit, and at her death it would still be regarded as
one of the greatest expeditions in the history of Alpine climbing. It is clear from her vivid letter home afterward that she
could have lost her life several times in the attempt, as the three
climbers gave up the ascent in despair and struggled to descend
the precipice at night in a raging storm.

After their fifty-seven hours on the mountain, the village inn and its occupants had given them up for dead. A hot bath, supper in bed, and twenty-four hours of sleep followed, but Gertrude woke up with frostbitten hands and feet. She had to delay her return to England until she could wear shoes again.

Her last climb of note was the Matterhorn, in August 1904, once more with Ulrich and Heinrich. Until she had climbed this final giant, she felt that she had unfinished business in the Alps. It was her last great mountain, and her interests were now to focus on the desert and archaeology. In 1926, Colonel E. L. Strutt, then editor of the *Alpine Journal*, wrote that there had been no more prominent female mountaineer than Gertrude Bell:

> Everything that she undertook, physical or mental, was accomplished so superlatively well, that it would indeed have been strange if she had not shone on a mountain as she did in the hunting-field or in the desert. Her strength, incredible in that slim frame, her endurance, above all her courage, were so great that even to this day her guide and companion Ulrich Fuhrer— and there could be few more competent judges—speaks with an admiration of her that amounts to veneration. He told the writer, some years ago, that of all the amateurs, men or women, that he had travelled with, he had seen but very few to surpass her in technical skill and none to equal her in coolness, bravery and judgment.

La Grave, August 28, 1899
The Meije

Well, I'll tell you—it's awful! I think if I had known exactly what was before me I should not have faced it, but fortunately I did not, and I look back on it with unmixed satisfaction—and forward to other things with no further apprehension. . . .

Gertrude and her two guides, Mathon and Marius, left La Grave on Friday afternoon and walked to the inn. The next evening, accompanied by two Germans, they arrived at the hut, where they were joined by a young Englishman called Turner and his guide, Rodier. All seven crammed in for the night.

We were packed as tight as herrings, Mr. Turner next to me, then the two Germans and Rodier. Mathon and the porters lay on the ground beneath us. Our night lasted from 8 to 12, but I didn't sleep at all!

At the Snow Line

I gave my skirt to Marius, Mathon having said I couldn't possibly wear it. He was quite right, but I felt very indecent . . . We had about two hours and a half of awfully difficult rock, very solid fortunately, but perfectly fearful. There were two places which Mathon and Marius literally pulled me up like a parcel. I didn't a bit mind where it was steep up, but round corners where the rope couldn't help me! . . . And it was absolutely sheer down. The first half-hour I gave myself up for lost. It didn't seem possible that I could get up all that wall without ever making a slip. You see, I had practically never been on a rock before. However I didn't let on and presently it began to seem quite natural to be hanging by my eyelids over an abyss. . . . There were two little lumps to hold on to on an overhanging rock and there [was] La Grave beneath and there was me in mid-air and Mathon round the corner holding the rope tight, but the rope was sideways of course—that's my general impression of those ten minutes. Added to which I thought at the time how very well I was climbing and how odd it was that I should not be afraid.

The Barre des Écrins, September 4, 1899

The wind blew merrily, and the snow swept round in clouds. However, at last it ended in a great big enormous *schrund,* and I thought I never should let myself down round the corner of it, but I did after all. I was now in rags, so I put on my skirt for

decency—at least Mathon did, for I couldn't feel at all with my
fingers. . . . We felt we had a real good day's mountaineering
behind us; but it was too long—nineteen hours. . . .

Starting with the 1900 season, her guides were Ulrich and
Heinrich Fuhrer. They met up at Chamonix and discussed her
ambitious plan to climb Mont Blanc. Her success in managing
this and the Grepon and Dru went to her head.

I am a Person! And one of the first questions everyone seems to
ask everyone else is "Have you ever met Miss Gertrude Bell?"
    Ulrich is as pleased as Punch and says I'm as good as any
man, and from what I see of the capacities of the ordinary
mountaineer, I think I am. . . . I rather hanker after the Matterhorn and must try to fit it in. . . .
    [I feel] keener and keener the more I do, the fact being that I now
feel a considerable amount more confidence in my power of doing
things. Guess I can manage any mountain you like to mention.

In just two weeks in late August and early September 1901,
Gertrude climbed seven virgin peaks, one of them first-class
and two "old" peaks, all of them new routes or first ascents.
She began with the thirteen-thousand-foot Schreckhorn, continued with the peaks of the Engelhörner range, and finished
with the most challenging climb of the year, the first-class traverse of the Urbachthaler Engelhorn itself.

September 8, 1901
The Urbachthaler Engelhorn

We . . . halted at the bottom of a smooth bit of overhanging
rock. The great difficulty of it all was that it was so exposed,
you couldn't ever get yourself comfortably wedged into a chimney, there was nothing but the face of the rock and up you had
to go. . . . Here we were on an awfully steep place under the
overhanging place. Ulrich tried it on Heinrich's shoulder and
could not reach any hold. I then clambered up on to Heinrich,

Ulrich stood on me and fingered up the rock as high as he could. It wasn't high enough. I lifted myself still a little higher—always with Ulrich on me, mind!—and he began to raise himself by his hands. As his foot left my shoulder I put up a hand, straightened out my arm and made a ledge for him. He called out, "I don't feel at all safe—if you move we are all killed." I said, "All right, I can stand here for a week," and up he went by my shoulder and my hand. It was just high enough. Once up he got into a fine safe place and it was now my turn. I was on Heinrich's shoulder still with one foot and with one on the rock. Ulrich could not help me because he hadn't got my rope—I had been the last on the rope, you see, and I was going up second, so that all I had was the rope between the two guides to hold on to. It was pretty hard work, but I got up. Now we had to get Heinrich up. He had a rope round his waist and my rope to hold, but no shoulder, but he could not manage it. The fact was, I think, that he lost his nerve, anyhow, he declared that he could not get up, not with 50 ropes, and there was nothing to do but to leave him. He unroped himself from the big rope and we let down the thin rope to him, with which he tied himself, while we fastened our end firmly on to a rock. There we left him like a second Prometheus—fortunately there were no vultures about!

Lady Bell writes that Gertrude told her later that Ulrich had said to her after their successful climb of the Engelhorn, "If, when I was standing on your shoulders and asked you if you felt safe, you had said you did not, I should have fallen and we should all have gone over." And Gertrude had replied, "I thought I was falling when I spoke."

It was 7 o'clock before we reached the foot of the rocks. It was too late and too dark to think of getting down into the valley so we decided that we would sleep at the Engen Alp at a shepherd's hut. . . . At 9.30 we hove up against a chalet nestled in to the mountain side and looking exactly like a big rock. We went in and found a tiny light burning; in a minute 3 tall shepherds, with pipes in their mouths, joined us and slowly questioned us as to where we had come from. . . . We said we . . . would like to

eat and sleep. One of the shepherds lighted a blazing wood fire
and cooked a quantity of milk in a 3-legged cauldron and we fell
to on bowls of the most delicious bread and milk I ever tasted.
The chalet was divided into two parts by a wooden partition.
The first part was occupied by some enormous pigs, there was
also a ladder in it leading up to a bit of wooden floor just under
the roof, where the fresh hay was kept. Here I slept. . . . It was so
enchanting waking up in that funny little place high up on the
mountain side with noisy torrents all round it. The goats came
flocking home before we left . . . they bleated loud complaints as
they crowded round the hut, licking the shepherd's hand.

In 1902, Ulrich put Gertrude through her paces, climbing several "impossibles" by way of preparation for the unclimbed
northeast face of the highest mountain in the Oberland, the
Finsteraarhorn.

Meiringen, August 3, 1902
The Attempt on the Finsteraarhorn

On Tuesday we set out at 1 a.m. and made for a crack high up
on the Wetterhorn rocks which we had observed through
glasses. We got up to it after about 3 hours' climbing only to
find to our sorrow that . . . it would have been madness to
attempt it for we could see from the broken ice on the rocks that
the great blocks were thrown from side to side as they fell and
swept the whole passage . . . ; we turned sadly back. I record
this piece of prudence with pleasure.

The Second Attempt

The arête . . . rises from the glacier in a great series of gen-
darmes and towers, set at such an angle on the steep face of the
mountain that you wonder how they can stand at all and indeed
they can scarcely be said to stand, for the great points of them

are continually overbalancing and tumbling down into the couloirs . . . and they are all capped with loosely poised stones, jutting out and hanging over and ready to fall. . . .

Crossed the séracs just at dawn. . . . We breakfasted then followed a difficult and dangerous climb. It was difficult because the rocks were exceedingly steep . . . it was dangerous because the whole rock was so treacherous. I found this out very early in the morning by putting my hand into the crack of a rock which looked as if it went into the very foundations of things. About 2 feet square of rock tumbled out upon me and knocked me a little way . . . till I managed to part company with it on a tiny ledge. . . .

About 2 o'clock I looked round and saw great black clouds rolling up from the west. . . . We . . . pushed on steadily for another hour while the weather signs got worse and worse. . . . The first snow flakes began to fall. . . . We were then 1000 feet below the summit. . . . We sat down to eat a few mouthfuls, the snow falling fast, driven by a strong wind, and a thick mist marching up the valley below, . . . then we crept along the knife edge of a col, fastened a rope firmly round a rock and let Ulrich down on to a ledge below the overhang of the tower. He tried it for a few moments and then gave it up. The ledge was very narrow, sloped outwards and was quite rotten. Anything was better than that. So we tried the left side of the tower: there was a very steep iced couloir running up. . . . Again we let ourselves down on the extra rope to the foot of the tower, again to find that this way also was impossible.

But even with the alternative before us of the descent down the terrible arête, we decided to turn back; already the snow was blowing down the couloir in a small avalanche, small but blinding, and the wind rushed down upon us carrying the mists with it. . . . By the time we had been going down for half-an-hour we could see nothing of the mountain side to the right or to the left except an occasional glimpse as one cloud rolled off and another rolled over. The snow fell fast and covered the rocks with incredible speed. Difficult as they had been to go up, you may imagine what they were like going down when we could no longer so much as see them. . . .

We . . . got on to a sloping out rock ledge with an inch of new snow on it; there was a crack in which you could stand and with one hand hold in the rock face, from whence you had to drop down about 8 feet on to deep snow. We fixed the extra rope and tumbled down one after the other on to the snow; . . . I shall remember every inch of that rock face for the rest of my life. . . . We toiled on till 8, by which time a furious thunderstorm was raging. We were standing by a great upright on the top of a tower when suddenly it gave a crack and a blue flame sat on it for a second. . . . My ice axe jumped in my hand and I thought the steel felt hot through my woollen glove—was that possible? I didn't take my glove off to see! Before we knew where we were the rock flashed again . . . we . . . tumbled down a chimney as hard as ever we could, one on top of the other, buried our ice axe heads in some shale at the bottom of it and hurriedly retreated from them. It's not nice to carry a private lightning conductor in your hand in the thick of a thunderstorm. It was clear we could go no further that night, the question was to find the best lodging while there was still light enough to see. We hit upon a tiny crack sheltered from the wind. . . . There was just room for me to sit in the extreme back of it on a very pointed bit of rock. . . . Ulrich sat on my feet to keep them warm and Heinrich just below him. They each of them put their feet into a knapsack which is the golden rule of bivouac. The other golden rule is to take no brandy because you feel the reaction more after. I knew this and insisted on it. It was really not so bad. . . . I went to sleep quite often and was wakened up every hour or so by the intolerable discomfort of my position. . . . We tied ourselves firmly on to the rock above lest as Ulrich philosophically said one of us should be struck and fall out. The rocks were all crackling round us and fizzing like damp wood which is just beginning to burn . . . And as there was no further precaution possible I enjoyed the extraordinary magnificence of the storm with a free mind: it was worth seeing. Gradually the night cleared and became beautifully starry.

The day came wrapped in a blinding mist and heralded by a cutting, snow-laden wind. . . . When we stepped out of our crack in the first grey light about 4 (too stiff to bear it a moment longer) everything was deep in it. I can scarcely describe to you

what that day was like. We were from 4 a.m. to 8 p.m. on the
arête; during that time we ate for a minute or two 3 times and
my fare was 5 ginger bread biscuits, 2 sticks of chocolate, a slice
of bread, a scrap of cheese and a handful of raisins. . . . Both the
ropes were thoroughly iced and terribly difficult to manage, and
the weather was appalling. It snowed all day sometimes softly as
decent snow should fall, sometimes driven by a furious bitter
wind which enveloped us not only in the falling snow, but lifted
all the light powdery snow from the rocks and sent it whirling
down the precipices and into the couloirs. . . . The couloirs were
all running with snow rivers. . . . As soon as you cut a step it
was filled up before you could put your foot into it. But I think
that when things are as bad as ever they can be you cease to
mind them much. You set your teeth and battle with the fates. . . .
I know I never thought of the danger except once and then quite
calmly. . . . We had to fix our rope in [the chimney] twice, the
second time round a very unsafe nail. I stood in this place holding Heinrich, there was an overhang. He climbed a bit of the
way and then fell on to soft snow and spun down the couloir till
my rope brought him up with a jerk. Then he got up on to a bit
of rock. . . . Ulrich came down to me and I repeated Heinrich's
process exactly, the iced extra rope slipping through my hands
like butter. Then came Ulrich. He climbed down to the place we
had both fallen . . . , then he called out "Heinrich, Heinrich, ich
bin verloren" and tumbled off just as we had done and we held
him up in the couloir, more dead than alive with anxiety. We
gave him some of our precious brandy on a piece of sugar. . . .
We thought the worst was over but there was a more dangerous
place to come . . . a steep but short slope of iced rock . . . now
covered with about 4 inches of avalanche snow and the rocks
were quite hidden. It was on the edge of a big couloirs down
which raced a snow river. We managed badly; . . . Ulrich and I
found ourselves on a place where there was not room for us both
to stand. . . . He was very insecure and could not hold me, Heinrich was below on the edge of the couloir, also very insecure.
And here I had to refix the extra rope on a rock a little below me
so that it was practically no good to me. But it was the only possible plan. The rock was too difficult for me, the stretches too

big, I couldn't reach them: I handed my axe down to Heinrich
and told him I could do nothing but fall, but he couldn't, or at
any rate, didn't secure himself and in a second we were both
tumbling head over heels down the couloir. . . . How Ulrich held
us I don't know. . . . I got on to my feet in the snow directly I
came to the end of my leash of rope and held Heinrich and
caught his ice axe and mine and we slowly cut ourselves back up
the couloir to the foot of the rock. But it was a near thing and I
felt rather ashamed of my part in it. This was the time when I
thought it on the cards we should not get down alive. . . .

And so we went on for 6 hours more of which only the last
hour was easy and at 8 found ourselves at the top of the Finster-
aar glacier. . . . It was now quite dark, the snow had turned into
pouring rain, and we sank 6 inches into the soft glacier with
every step. . . . Not a single match would light. Then we tried to
go on and after a few steps Heinrich fell in . . . almost up to his
neck and Ulrich and I had to pull him out with the greatest difficulty and the mists swept up over the glacier and hid everything; that was the only moment of despair. . . . Here we were
with another night out before us. And a much worse one than
the first, for we were on the shelterless glacier and in driving
drenching rain. We laid our three axes together and sat on them
side by side. . . . My shoulders ached and ached. . . . Before we
expected it a sort of grey light came over the snow. . . . We could
hardly stand but after a few steps we began to walk quite credit-
ably. About 6 we got to where we could unrope—having been 48
hours on the rope—and we reached here at 10 on Saturday. . . .

Now that I am comfortably indoors, I do rather wonder that
we ever got down the Finsteraarhorn and that we were not frozen at the bottom of it. What do you think?

In 1904, Gertrude made her last climb, the Matterhorn.

Zermatt, August 31, 1904

It is very imposing, the Matterhorn . . . the great faces of rock
are so enormous, so perpendicular. . . . It was beautiful climbing,

never seriously difficult, but never easy, and most of the time on a
great steep face which was splendid to go upon. . . . The most difficult place on the mountain is an overhanging bit above the Tyn-
dall Grat and quite near the summit. There is usually a rope
ladder there, but this year it is broken and in consequence scarcely
any one has gone up the Italian side. There is a fixed rope which
is good and makes descent on this side quite easy, but it is a different matter getting up. We took over 2 hours over this 30 or 40
ft. . . . At the overhanging bit you had to throw yourself out on
the rope and so hanging catch with your right knee a shelving
scrap of rock from which you can just reach the top rung which is
all that is left of the ladder. That is how it is done. I speak from
experience, and I also remember wondering how it was possible
to do it. And I had a rope round my waist which Ulrich, who went
first, had not. Heinrich found it uncommonly difficult.

Gertrude's mountaineering career ended after the 1904 season, when she was becoming increasingly drawn to desert
adventures.

THE ARCHAEOLOGIST

Gertrude had been fascinated by archaeology since a holiday in Greece in 1899, when she was thirty-one. With her father and her uncle, a classical scholar, she made an excursion to Melos, a six-thousand-year-old city, and was shown the excavation by Dr. David Hogarth, brother of her Oxford friend Janet. She was so interested that she stayed several days to watch and join the dig.

Two years later, she extended a holiday to join archaeological digs at Pergamos, Magnesia, and Sardis. She evidently enjoyed the excavation work more than the rather dull cruise that preceded it, chiefly memorable for a day's sightseeing in Santa Flavia with Winston Churchill, who was staying in a villa there to paint.

By 1904, Gertrude was immersed in plans for an imminent journey through western Syria and Asia Minor, her first expedition after Jerusalem. To give substance to her archaeological credentials, she had written an essay on the geometry of the cruciform structure, which she wanted to place in an eminent magazine, the *Revue Archéologique*, whose offices were in Paris. She wanted to make herself known to the editor, Professor Salomon Reinach, the scholar who had proselytized for the East as the origin of civilization. He was also the director of the Saint-Germain Museum of National Antiquities.

When she called on Reinach, he welcomed her warmly, taking to her immediately and opening up his address book for her. Armed with his letters of introduction, she was gladly received in every library and museum that she had time to visit. Reinach also gave her what amounted to a crash course in archaeological history. Under his aegis she examined Greek manuscripts and early ivories, buried herself in the Bibliothèque nationale de France, spent a day in the Musée de Cluny, toured a new Byzantine museum not yet open to the public, and spent evenings poring over books in his library. She spoke to Reinach of her forthcoming journey, and he encouraged her to study Roman and Byzantine ruins and learn about the impact of these civilizations upon the region. From this point on, Byzantine culture would become Gertrude's special field of study.

She was well aware that she lacked the qualifications of an archaeologist—for instance, a knowledge of epigraphy. Between her carefully planned expeditions, therefore, she set out to learn new practical skills, so that she would be able to pinpoint the sites, make maps, and finally recognize what she found and fit it into the historical and archaeological context as she recorded it. She attended courses that taught her how to measure and draw up her finds, she learned to make casts, and she became a skilled photographer and a member of the Royal Photographic Society—as such, she was able to have her film professionally printed.

Even without qualifications, she had great advantages: her energy and enthusiasm, her willingness to go into dangerous territories, and, not least, the financial freedom to follow her ends. No mountain was too high for her, no cave too full of snakes and spiders, no journey too far.

Mapping the Euphrates in 1909, Gertrude examined 450 miles of sites before arriving south of Baghdad. Not far from Karbala, at Ukhaidir, she found an immense and beautiful desert palace in a remarkable state of repair. For a time, when it was found that her plan of the palace was the first to be made, she believed that she had discovered an unknown citadel. The following year she published a preliminary paper on Ukhaidir. But returning to the site in 1911, she found to her bitter disappointment that the monograph she intended to publish, with its 168 pages of plans and 166 photographs, would not be the first. She discovered that German archaeologists had been to the site during the two years of her absence

and were close to publishing their own book. Exhibiting much
grace under pressure, she wrote in the preface to her monograph of her respect for the "masterly" German volume and
even apologized for offering a second version:

> ... My work, which was almost completed when the German
> volume came out, covers not only the ground traversed by my
> learned friends in Babylon, but also ground which they had nei-
> ther leisure nor opportunity to explore ... with this I must take
> leave of a field of study which formed for four years my princi-
> pal occupation, as well as my chief delight.

Gertrude's entry in the *Prolegomena*, the Who's Who of
archaeology, names her as "the remarkable pioneer woman of
Byzantine architecture." After publishing *The Thousand and
One Churches* about Binbirkilise in 1909, together with Professor William Ramsay, she concentrated on the high Anatolian plateau of Turkey, publishing the material she gathered
there as her seventh book, *The Churches and Monasteries of
the Tur Abdin,* in 1913.

Toward the end of her life, in Baghdad, she became increasingly worried about the wholesale looting of Iraq's national
treasures. She discussed with King Faisal the need for a law of
excavations, to protect the many important sites in Iraq and
also to prevent all the country's treasures being exported to
foreign museums. He made her the honorary director of
archaeology and helped her to frame the writing of a law giving due weight to the rights of the nation and the excavators:
these had proliferated after the war with scientific expeditions
from many countries attempting to construct the history of
the region. Once Gertrude had begun to think in terms of
exacting the country's rights to its own past, she was determined to establish a museum of Iraq. Zealous in claiming the
prize objects from each dig, she soon acquired the richest collection in the world of objects representing the early history of
Iraq. In cloche hat and 1920s short skirt, she became a dreaded
figure at British, American, and German excavations, walking
briskly from her office car to the table of finds to claim or

bargain for the most precious objects. When discussions reached an impasse, she reverted to her favorite expedient: she tossed a coin.

In 1926, the year of her death, she turned her full attention to archaeology. Her object was to create a proper museum where her antiquities could be displayed. Her Babylonian Stone Room was opened by the king in June. As always, once she was committed to a project, she took on even the most uncongenial of tasks. Alone or with a clerk, sometimes with a Royal Air Force (RAF) officer who was a keen amateur, she laboriously cataloged the finds from Ur and Kish, sometimes getting up at 5 a.m. to do the work before the midday heat became overwhelming.

The descriptions and accounts below are taken from her letters home to her stepmother and father.

Athens, Spring 1899

Mr. Hogarth . . . showed us his recent finds—pots of 4000 B.C. from Melos. Doesn't that make one's brain reel?

On a Lecture by Professor Dorpfield About the Acropolis

. . . He took us from stone to stone, and built up a wonderful chain of evidence with extraordinary ingenuity, until we saw the Athens of 600 B.C. rise before us.

Pergamos, Turkey, March 1902

You should see me shopping in Smyrna—quite like a native, only I ought to have more flashing eyes. At Pergamos, I went all over the Acropolis and examined temples and palaces and theatres and the great altar of which the friezes are at Berlin.

Sardis, March 3, 1902

I've just succeeded in getting a second hand Herodotus* in French to my enormous delight. . . .

Sardis, March 7, 1902

I was delighted that I had Herodotus so fresh in my mind. . . . It's a madly interesting place. . . .

Sardis, March 9, 1902

Some day I shall come and travel here with tents, but then I will speak Turkish, which will not be difficult. . . .

Paris, November 7, 1904

After lunch I drove out, left some cards and went to see Salomon Reinach, whom I found enthusiastically delighted to see me. There were 2 other men there. . . . We sat for an hour or more while Salomon and Ricci piled books round me and poured information into my ears. It was delightful to hear the good jargon of the learned. . . . But bewildering. This morning I read till 11 about Byzantine MSS, which I'm going to see at the Bibliothéque Nationale; then I went shopping with the Stanleys and bought a charming little fur jacket to ride in in Syria—yes, I did! Then I came in and read till 2 when Salomon fetched me and we went together to the Louvre. We stayed till 4.30—it was enchanting. . . . There is nothing more wonderful than to go to a museum with my dear Salomon. We passed from Egypt through Pompeii and back to Alexandria. We traced the drawing of horns from Greece to Byzantium. We followed the lines of

*Herodotus, Greek historian of the fifth century, known as the "Father of History."

Byzantine art into early Europe ... while Salomon developed
an entirely new theory about eyelids ... and illustrated it with a
Pheidean bust and a Scopas head. It *was* nice.

November 11, 1904

I've seen all the ivories that concern me, and I find to my joy that
I am beginning to be able to place them. .... This happy result is
a good deal caused by having looked through such masses of
picture books with Reinach. Last night he set me guessing what
things were—even Greek beads—it was a sort of examination—
I really think I passed. Reinach was much pleased but then he
loves me so dearly that perhaps he is not a good judge. He has
simply set all his boundless knowledge at my disposal. ....

On Her 1905 Expedition Through the Syrian Desert
to Asia Minor Qallat Semaan, March 31, 1905

I have had the most delightful day today, playing at being an
archaeologist.

April 3, 1905

I shall not forget the misery of copying a Syrian inscription in
the drenching rain, holding my cloak round my book to keep
the paper dry. The devil take all Syrian inscriptions, they are so
horribly difficult to copy.

Anavarza, April 21, 1905

I got up at dawn and at 6 o'clock started out to grapple with my
churches. .... I took my soldier with me and taught him to hold
the measuring tape. He soon understood what I wanted and
measured away at doors and windows like one to the manner

born. . . . One of the biggest of the churches is razed to the ground. . . . I looked round about for any scraps of carving that might give an indication of the style of decoration and found, after much search, one and one only—and it was dated! It was a big stone which from the shape and the mouldings I knew to have been at the spring of two arches of the windows of the apse, and the date was carved in beautiful raised Greek letters between the two arch mouldings—"The year 511."

Two things I dislike in Anavarza. The mosquitoes and the snakes; the mosquitoes have been the most hostile of the two: the snakes always bustle away in a great hurry and I have made no experiments as to what their bite would be like. There are quantities of them among the ruins. They are about 3 ft long— I wonder if they are poisonous. . . . We dislodged the vultures who were sitting in rows on the castle top—they left a horrid smell behind them.

Karaman, May 7, 1905

I daresay it does not often occur to you to think what a wonderful invention is the railway, but it is very forcibly borne in upon me at this moment for I am going to Konia in 3 hours instead of having a weary two days' march across a plain of mud. Yesterday I rode in here some 35 miles.

Binbirkilise, May 13, 1905

We . . . set off across the plain to Binbirklisse. The name means *The Thousand and one Churches*. . . . It lies at the foot of the Kara Dagh, a great isolated mountain arising abruptly out of the plain. . . . I fell in love with it at once, a mass of beautiful ruins gathered together in a little rocky cup high up in the hills—with Asia Minor at its feet. . . . It has made a delightful end to my travels. . . .

May 16, 1905

I . . . took the train and came back to Konia. The Consul and
his wife met me at the station and dined with me at the hotel
and I found there besides Professor Ramsay, who knows more
about this country than any other man, and we fell into each
other's arms and made great friends.

This was Gertrude's first meeting with the archaeologist Sir
William Mitchell Ramsay, and it led to their collaboration on
a book about the ruins of Binbirkilise. On this occasion, she
showed him an inscription she had copied on her brief visit
there. Professor Ramsay wrote in the preface to their book,
"Miss Gertrude Bell was impelled by [Strzygowski's] book to
visit Bin Bir Kilisse; and, when I met her at Konia on her
return, she asked me to copy an inscription on one of the
churches, in letters so worn that she could not decipher it,
which she believed to contain a date for the building. Her
belief proved well founded and the chronology of the Thousand and One Churches centres round this text."

They met again at Binbirkilise at the end of May 1907 for a
month of excavations, worked together on the results at Rounton, and published the book, *The Thousand and One Churches*,
in 1909.

Lake of Egerdir, on the Journey to Binbirkilise, May 1, 1907

There was a place which Ramsay had begged me to try and visit
on the eastern shore of the lake . . . a holy site long before the
Christian era, sacred to Artemis of the Lake who was herself a
Psidian deity re-baptised by the Greeks. . . . The rocks drop here
straight into the lake and at their foot there is a great natural
arch some 15 feet wide through which glistens the blue water of
the lake. In the rock above is a small rock-cut chamber into
which I scrambled with some difficulty and found a slab like a
loculus in it . . . probably the slab was sacrificial. . . . So we rode
back. . . . Almost joined to the shore by beds of immensely tall

reeds there is a little island which no one had yet succeeded in visiting. I, however, found . . . a very old and smelly boat, so I hired the three fishermen for an infinitesimal sum and rowed out to the island. . . . It was completely surrounded by ruined Byzantine walls dropping into the water in great blocks of masonry; here and there there was a bit of an older column built into them and they were densely populated by snakes. There was only one thing of real interest, a very curious stele with a female figure carved on it, bearing what looked like water skins, and two lines of inscription above . . . unfortunately the whole stone was covered by 18 inches or more of shimmering water. It had fallen into the lake and there it lay. I did all I knew to get the inscription. I waded into the water and tried to scrub the slime off the stone, but the water glittered and the slime floated back and finally I gave it up and came out very wet and more than a little annoyed.

Maden Sheher (The Lower Town of Binbirkilise), May 21, 1907

The habit of building everything on the extreme top of hills is to be deprecated. It entails so much labour for subsequent generations. . . . I had found . . . a ruined site with a very perfect church on the top of a hill near my camp, and in the church was a half-buried stone which I thought was probably the altar. So I took up some of my men with picks and crowbars and had it out and it was the altar. . . . My Cast! oh my Cast! it's more professional than words can say.

Maden Sheher, May 25, 1907

The Ramsays arrived yesterday. I was in the middle of digging up a church when suddenly 2 carts hove into sight and there they were. . . . They instantly got out, . . . Lady R. made tea (for they were starving) in the open and R. oblivious of all other considerations was at once lost in the problems the church presented. . . .

Now I must tell you something very very striking. The church on the extreme point of the Kara D., at which I worked for 2 days before R. came, has near it some great rocks and on the rocks I found a very queer inscription. The more I looked at it the queerer it became and the less I thought it could be Christian . . . I took it down with great care, curious rabbit-headed things and winged sort of crosses and arms and circles, and with some trembling I showed it to R. The moment he looked at it he said, "It's a Hittite inscription. This is the very thing I hoped most to find here." I think I've never been so elated. We now think of nothing but Hittites all the time. . . .

I haven't told you half enough what gorgeous fun it's being! You should see me directing the labours of 20 Turks and 4 Kurds!

May 29, 1907

I get up at 5 and breakfast before the Ramsay family have appeared and go off before 6 to wherever we are digging, and stay there till 12 superintending and measuring as we uncover. . . . After lunch I go back to the diggings and stay there till 5 or later. R. generally appears on the scene about 7 or 8 in the morning and about 3 in the afternoon . . . he can't physically do more. I shall have all the measuring and planning to do and I'm at it some 12 hours a day on and off. Nor can it be otherwise for that's the part that I have undertaken.

Daile, June 14, 1907

You would be surprised to see the scene in the middle of which I am writing. Thirty-one Turks are busy with picks and spades clearing out a church and monastery. At intervals they call out to me "Effendim, effendim! is this enough?"

July 5, 1907

We spent the whole morning going from village to village along the side of the Karajadagh looking for ruins and inscriptions. The

manner of proceeding is this: you arrive in a village and ask for
inscriptions. They reply that there are absolutely none. You say very
firmly that there are certainly inscriptions and then you stand
about in the hot sun for 10 minutes or so while the villagers gather
round. At last someone says there is a written stone in his house.
You go off, find it, copy it, and give the owner two piastres, the
result of which is that everybody has a written stone somewhere. . . .

Early in 1909, Gertrude made one of her most important desert expeditions, discovering the immense castle of Ukhaidir,
crossing the desert between hostile tribes to get there.

Ukhaidir, March 23, 1909

We are through! without mishap and without adventure and I
am exceedingly glad I took the desert road since all has turned
out so well. . . . It's extraordinarily peaceful and beautiful and
all of us have a sense of relief as of people who have come safely
out of perilous ways.

March 26, 1909

It is an enormous castle, fortress, palace—what you will—155
metres by 170 metres, the immense outer walls set all along
with round towers, and about a third of the inside filled with
court after court of beautiful rooms, vaulted and domed, covered
with exquisite plaster decorations—underground chambers—
overhead chambers—some built with columns, some set round
with niches, in short the most undreamt-of example of the finest
Sassanian art that ever was. It is not seen on the map, it has
never been published, I never heard its name before. I hear from
the Arabs that a foreigner* came here last year and worked at it
for a few days. As soon as I saw it I decided that this was the
opportunity of a lifetime. It doesn't matter in the least if

*M. Massignon, with whom Gertrude corresponded later in the year.

someone else publishes it before I do; I myself shall learn more of Eastern art of the sixth century by working at it than I should learn from all the books that ever were. I place it at the time of Ctesiphon, but I expect that it was built not for the Sassanians but for the Lakhmid princes. . . .

I set out with a measuring tape and a foot rule to plan the whole palace. . . . I've brought up my whole camp from Kerbela. . . . I confess I felt some misgivings about the enterprise, but Fattuh* is so capable and plucky, that if he did meet with robbers they would probably come off the worst. He was armed with Maurice's rifle, which has been invaluable. . . .

March 29, 1909

Last night my castle gave me a different entertainment. I had gone to bed early, but I was too tired to sleep, and I lay and turned over in my mind all the work I had been doing. . . . Suddenly a rifle shot rang out, and a bullet whizzed over us. All my men jumped up, and I could hear Fattuh putting the muleteers as outposts round the camp. I got up too, and came out to see the fun. Meanwhile three or four more shots had been fired. Presently 'Ali and several others hurried past us, all armed in some fashion, and Fattuh, all eagerness, ran off with them into the desert. I climbed on to a heap of ruins to watch them, but they soon disappeared into the glimmering moonlight. A few minutes later we saw shots flash out red in the distance; and after about a quarter of an hour 'Ali and his men returned, singing a wild song as they came, their rifles over their shoulders. . . . They declared that the enemy had been raiders of the Dafi'ah, a hostile tribe.

She published her own quarto volume on Ukhaidir in 1914, paying graceful deference to "my learned friends in Babylon" who had published their book two years previously, and regretfully turned her back on the subject.

*Her beloved servant whom she had taken on in Adana in 1905, and who was to accompany her throughout most of her desert journeys.

A subject so enchanting and so suggestive . . . is not likely to present itself more than once in a lifetime, and as I bring this page to a close I call to mind the amazement with which I first gazed upon its formidable walls; the romance of my first sojourn within its precincts; the pleasure, undiminished by familiarity, of my return; and the regret with which I sent back across the sun drenched plain a last greeting to its distant presence.

Her final desert journey in 1913 to 1914 was followed by the First World War, after which she was in full employment in Cairo, Basra, and Baghdad. A decade passed before she had the time to take up archaeology once more. By then, in Iraq, she was becoming worried about protecting the archaeological sites and treasures of the country.

July 20, 1922

Today the King ordered me to tea and we had two hours most excellent talk. First of all I got his assistance for my Law of Excavations* which I've compiled with the utmost care in consultation with the legal authorities. He has undertaken to push it through Council—he's perfectly sound about archaeology—having been trained by T.E. Lawrence—and has agreed to my suggestion that he should appoint me . . . provisional Director of Archaeology to his Govt, in addition to my other duties.

Baghdad, October 13, 1923

I've been spending most of the morning at the Ministry of Works where we are starting—what do you think? the Iraq Museum! It will be a modest beginning, but it is a beginning.

*One of its provisions was that there should be a fifty-fifty division of all finds between Iraq and the excavators. Gertrude represented Iraq.

Baghdad, January 9, 1924

I'm planning a two days' jaunt by myself in the desert. I want to feel savage and independent again instead of being [Oriental] Secretary in a High Commissioner's Office.

Mr. Woolley* at Ur has been making wonderful finds and has written urgently to me to go down. . . . I've a great scheme for visiting some mounds this side of Nasiriyah which I hope will come off.

Baghdad, January 22, 1924

We spent 3 hours walking over the site [of Kish] and examining the excavations. When we got back to the tents . . . there was no car, so I climbed to the top of the zigurrat, hailed in 4 horsemen and requisitioned their horses, on two of which J.M.† and I mounted and prepared to ride into Hillah.

After an early breakfast, I went down to the river, crossed in a ferry to Khidhr village and presented myself at the house of the Mudir, who provided me (via the report) with a horse and escort to ride to Warka, which is Erech, the great Babylonian capital of the south. We rode hard for two hours on the mound; I was riding on a policeman's saddle. I've got a peculiar sort of skin that comes off if you look at it; it did. When we reached the mound we found quantities of people digging and rounded them up. They all screamed and cried when they saw me, but I gave them the salute and they were comforted. I said "Have you any anticas?" "No," they answered, "by God, no." I observed "What are those spades and picks for? I'll give you backsheesh for anything you have." At that a change came over the scene

*Later Sir Leonard Woolley, he had worked at Carchemish with T. E. Lawrence and was now heading a joint expedition organized by the British Museum and the University of Pennsylvania to dig Ur of the Chaldaes.

†J. M. Wilson was the architectural adviser to the Ministry of Public Works.

and one after another fumbled in his breast and produced a cyl-inder or a seal which I bought for the museum for a few annas.

February 13, 1924

I pursued my explorations round Kadhimain. . . . I espied half an elephant planted on the top of the courtyard wall—so I rode into the court and asked who lived there. . . . I asked [the propri-etor] if there were an idol in the house. "Oh, yes," he said, and taking me into the inner court, lifted up a mat, and there was the Assyrian statue. It's very roughly blocked out but so like a statue of Semiramis that was found at Assur that . . . it may be no other than she. It is said to have been brought from Babylon. Only the upper part remains, down to about the waist. It seems to have bobbed hair. . . . But I must have it for my museum. . . . I shall leave the elephant.

Baghdad, March 6, 1924

On Friday after lunch J.M. Wilson and I took the so called express and went to Ur to do the division. We arrived at 5.10 a.m. on Sat. . . . I had a bare half hour to get up and pack my bed and things. So I jumped up, put on my clothes, neither washed nor did my hair and J.M. and I, with old 'Abdul Qadir, my curator walked out to Ur in the still dawn. . . . We . . . went off to the zigurrat to see the uncovered stair. It's amazing and unexpected, a triple stair. . . . laid against the zigurrat with blocks of masonry between the stairways. It's latest Babylo-nian . . . and must cover an Ur 3rd dynasty stair of which as yet we know nothing. . . . By this time the workmen began to arrive, . . . and next Mr. Woolley, so we marvelled at the stair and all the rest and I went back to the house to wash, summar-ily, and do my hair. . . . Before 9 we started the division (it began by my winning the gold scarab on the toss of a rupee). . . . The really agonizing part was after lunch when I had to tell them that I must take the milking scene. I can't do otherwise. It's

unique and it depicts the life of the country at an immensely
early date. In my capacity as Director of Antiquities I'm an Iraqi
official and bound by the terms on which we gave the permit for
excavation. J.M. backed me but it broke Mr. Woolley's heart. . . .

Baghdad, March 18, 1924

I fell into one of the worst passions I've ever been in. I found old
'Abdul Qadir mending the flowers from Ur with huge blobs of
plaster of Paris so that the stone petals quite disappeared in
them. I . . . told him he was never to mend anything again and
sent for a friend of mine, an antiquity dealer to repair the dam-
age, which he has done.

Kish, March 24, 1924

I . . . explained that my object was to leave, as far as possible,
the tablets to them for they should be at the disposition of students. On the other hand, they would have to make up by part-
ing with some other fine objects. "Who decides," said the
Professor [S. H. Langdon], "if we disagree?" I replied that I
did. . . . There was one unique object, a stone tablet inscribed
with what is probably the oldest known human script. . . . So I
took it. Then we went to a little room where all the other objects
were and began on the beads and jewels. There was a lovely
pomegranate bud earring, found in the grave of a girl, time of
Nebuchadnezzar, and he set against it a wonderful copper stag,
early Babylonian and falling into dust. It was obvious that we
here could not preserve the latter. . . . I took the pomegranate
bud . . . turned to the necklaces and we picked, turn and turn
about. . . . Isn't it fantastic to be selecting pots and things four
to six thousand years old! I got a marvellous stone inlay of a
Sumerian king leading captives and not being at all nice to
them . . . .

Baghdad, May 4, 1924

I burst with pride when I show people over the Museum. It is becoming such a wonderful place. It was a great morning because there were 6 boxes from Kish to be unpacked. . . . Such copper instruments as have never before been handed down from antiquity; the shelves shout with them.

Baghdad, April 22, 1925

J.M. and I had got permission from the A.V.M. [air vice-marshal] to go up to Kirkuk by air mail in order to see a little excavation. . . . We went yesterday morning and came back this morning—2 ½ hours up and 2 hours down, with a following wind. I like flying. The only contretemps was that they forgot to put my little valise into the plane and I arrived with nothing. . . . However . . . once you have made up your mind that you have no luggage, it is rather an exhilarating feeling.

Baghdad, March 16, 1926

We got to Ur. . . . I had to take the best thing they have got. . . . I'm getting much more knowing with practice. I now can place cylinder and other seals at more or less their comparative date and value, so that I don't choose wildly according to prettiness. . . .

Baghdad, March 23, 1926

I have been . . . trying to learn a little about arranging a museum. Oh dear! there's such a lot to do. . . . I shall concentrate on exhibiting the best objects properly and get the others done little by little. Meantime the new museum building has to be re-roofed, for the present mud and beams could be cut through almost by a penknife.

Baghdad, May 12, 1926

You ask about my plans for the summer. . . . My duty to the museum is of the first importance. I can't go away and leave all those valuable things half transferred. . . . It will take months and months. . . .

Baghdad, May 26, 1926

. . . Already I know that I ought to have all my time for the Museum. As it is I now go there from 7 to 8.30 or so every morning and get to the office about 9. That has meant a pretty strenuous 4½ hours but I find that I can just get through the work. . . . One big room downstairs, the Babylonian Stone Room, is now finished and I am only waiting for the catalogue, which I have written, to be translated and printed, to ask the King to open it—just to show them that we are doing something. But this is the easiest of all the rooms. . . . The serial number of the Baghdad Museum has to be put onto everything and until each object is in the catalogue we can't number it. . . . I have moved about half the things from the old room into the new Museum and they are lying about, some on tables, some on the floor, a desolating spectacle. . . . I don't think I could possibly leave it like this.

Baghdad, June 9, 1926

I am enclosing the catalogue of the Babylonian Stone Room of the Museum and two picture postcards of the exhibits. . . . No. 7 is the thing I am proudest of—there is nothing like it in any museum in the world. . . . The King is going to open this room on Monday. . . .

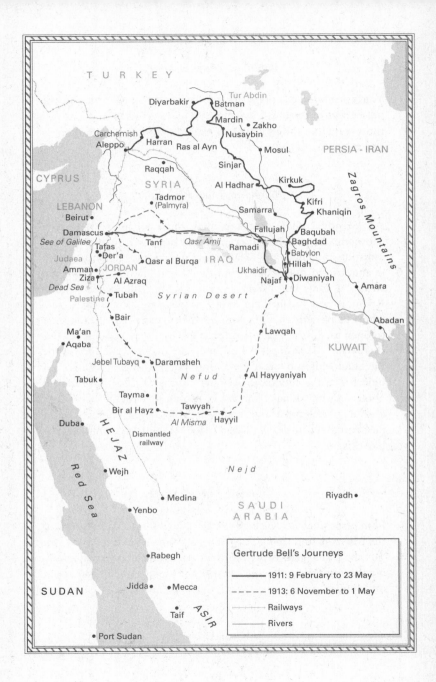

Gertrude Bell's Journeys

— 1911: 9 February to 23 May
--- 1913: 6 November to 1 May
······· Railways
—— Rivers

THE DESERT TRAVELER

In March 1905, Gertrude came to Qallat Semaan, a two and a half days' march from Homs, Syria, and stopped to reflect.

> This is the place where St. Simon lived upon a pillar. While the servants pitched my tents I went out and sat upon St. Simon's column—there is still a little bit of it left—and considered how very different he must have been from me. And there came a big star and twinkled at me through the soft warm night, and we agreed together that it was pleasanter to wander across the heavens and the earth than to sit on top of a pillar all one's days.

Gertrude's first desert journeys were undertaken at the age of thirty-one, in 1900, comparatively late in her life. Her first glimpse of the desert had been on holiday with her aunt and uncle eight years previously, when she had written ecstatically of the desert around Tehran.

Persia, June 18, 1892, Letter to Horace Marshall

> Oh the desert round Teheran! miles and miles of it with nothing, *nothing* growing; ringed in with bleak bare mountains snow crowned and furrowed with the deep courses of torrents. I never knew what desert was till I came here; it is a very wonderful thing to see. . . .

It remained something to see, rather than experience, until she visited family friends, the Rosens, in Jerusalem where Fried-

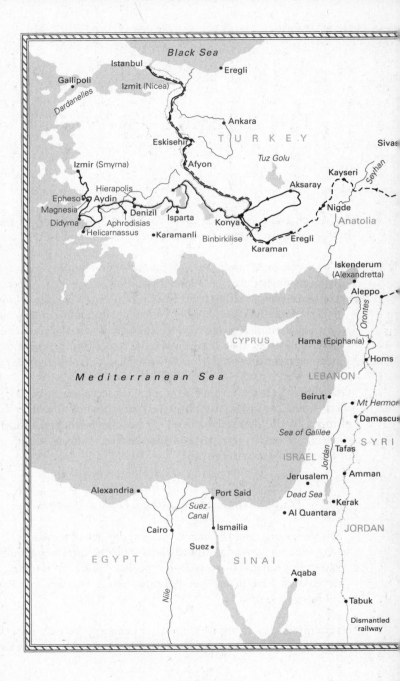

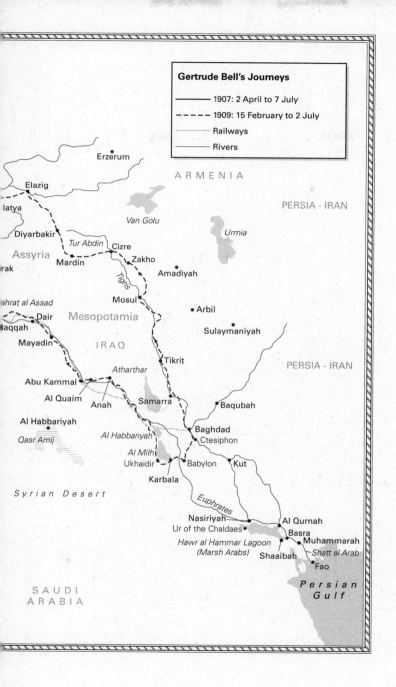

Gertrude Bell's Journeys

——————— 1907: 2 April to 7 July
– – – – – 1909: 15 February to 2 July
·············· Railways
——————— Rivers

Erzerum

ARMENIA

PERSIA - IRAN

Elazig

latya

Van Golu

Urmia

Diyarbakir

Assyria   Tur Abdin   Cizre

rak   Mardin   Zakho

Tigris

Amadiyah

Mosul

ahrat al Assad   Dair

Mesopotamia

Arbil

Raqqah

Sulaymaniyah

Mayadin

IRAQ

PERSIA - IRAN

Atharthar   Tikrit

Abu Kammal

Al Quaim   Anah   Samarra

Baqubah

Al Habbariyah

Al Habbanyah   Baghdad

Qasr Amij

Ctesiphon

Al Milh

Ukhaidir   Babylon   Kut

Karbala

Syrian Desert

Euphrates

Nasiriyah   Al Qurnah
Ur of the Chaldaes   Basra
                                         Muhammarah
Hawr al Hammar Lagoon   Shatt al Arab
(Marsh Arabs)   Shaaibah
                                    Fao

SAUDI
ARABIA

Persian
Gulf

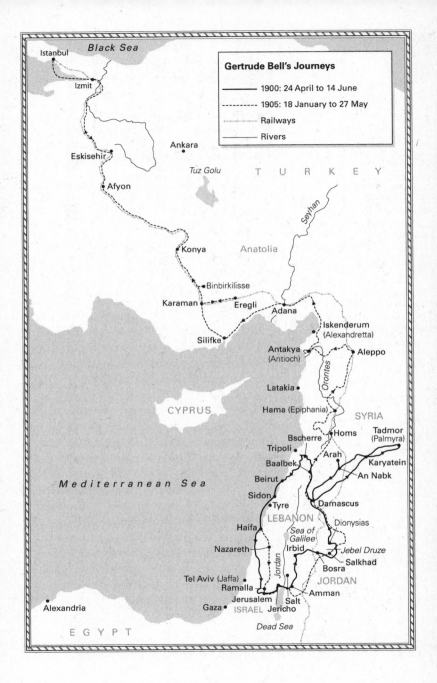

Gertrude Bell's Journeys

——— 1900: 24 April to 14 June
- - - 1905: 18 January to 27 May
······· Railways
——— Rivers

Black Sea

Istanbul

Izmit

Eskisehir

Afyon

Ankara

Tuz Golu

TURKEY

Seyhan

Konya

Anatolia

Binbirkilisse

Karaman

Eregli

Adana

Silifke

Iskenderum
(Alexandretta)

Antakya
(Antioch)

Aleppo

Orontes

Latakia

Hama (Epiphania)

SYRIA

CYPRUS

Bscherre

Homs

Tadmor
(Palmyra)

Tripoli

Arah

Karyatein

Baalbek

An Nabk

Beirut

Mediterranean Sea

Sidon

Tyre

Damascus

LEBANON

Haifa

Sea of
Galilee

Dionysias

Nazareth

Irbid

Jebel Druze

Jordan

Salkhad

Bosra

Tel Aviv (Jaffa)

JORDAN

Ramalla

Amman

Alexandria

Jerusalem

Salt

Gaza

Jericho

ISRAEL

Dead Sea

EGYPT

rich was the German consul. She took lessons in Arabic and embarked on horseback expeditions to Palmyra, Damascus, Baalbek, and Beirut. But her long, groundbreaking expeditions did not begin for five more years, until she undertook the journey through the Syrian Desert to Asia Minor that she described in her book *The Desert and the Sown:* the title arising from her explanation written on a journey from Jerusalem.

> ... We came to spreading cornfields. The plan is this—the "Arabs" sow one place this year and go and live somewhere else lest their animals should eat the growing corn. Next year this lies fallow and the fallow of the year before is sown.

Meanwhile, her privileged life was full of traveling, mountaineering, hunting, society, gardening, and learning archaeology. Yet, as the prospect of marriage and children receded, she felt an increasing need for self-fulfillment. As an independent woman of great ability she was driven by the need to test herself, veering toward challenges tinged with danger and excitement. When she conquered Arabic and discovered desert travel, the challenges proliferated into an all-embracing personal experiment of which she would never reach the end. There was the risky business of staying alive and reaching her goal and the intoxication of asserting her own identity far from the world that regarded her as a spinster, an heiress, and a Bell. There were languages to perfect, customs to learn, history and archaeology to explore, techniques of surveying and navigation to master, photography and cartography skills to acquire, Middle Eastern politics to plumb, and, finally, information to gather and pass on. Up to the First World War, affairs of state were conducted as comprehensively at dinner parties, soirees, and embassy receptions as in government offices. She accessed this world and would become recognized in it as an expert.

Settling on arrival into a Middle Eastern hotel would become a happy ritual, an almost sacred preliminary to the increasingly complicated organization of Gertrude's five desert expeditions. She would book two rooms with a veranda or view, and use one as an office. She would banish all furniture except for two armchairs and two tables, and trail cigarette ash behind her as she tacked up her maps and photographs of the family.

On her first visit to Jerusalem she bought only a lively Arab stallion on which she soon departed from the tourist tracks, riding astride for the first time instead of side-saddle, leaping stone walls and whooping for joy, one hand hanging on to her gray felt hat with its black velvet ribbon.

Deraa, April 30, 1900

. . . The chief comfort of this journey is my masculine saddle, both to me and my horse. Never, never again will I travel on anything else; I haven't known real ease in riding till now. Till I speak the people always think I'm a man and address me as Effendim! You mustn't think I haven't got a most elegant and decent divided skirt, however, but as all men wear skirts of sorts too, that doesn't serve to distinguish me.

Her first expedition was the seventy-mile ride down the east bank of the Dead Sea, with a cook and a couple of muleteers. On the Jordan plain she found herself waist-deep in flowers. The flora and fauna of the desert would never fail to enchant and surprise her.

Ayan Musa, March 20, 1900

. . . The wilderness had blossomed like the rose. It was the most unforgettable sight—sheets and sheets of varied and exquisite colour—purple, white, yellow, and the brightest blue (this was a bristly sort of plant which I don't know) and fields of scarlet ranunculus. Nine-tenths of them I didn't know, but there was the yellow daisy, the sweet-scented mauve wild stock, a great splendid sort of dark purple onion, the white garlic and purple marrow, and higher up a tiny blue iris and red anemones and a dawning pink thing like a linum.

April 2, 1900

My camp is pitched half way up the hill, with . . . deep corn
fields . . . the storks walking solemnly up to their necks in
green. . . . There has been an immense flock of them flying and
settling on the hillside, and when I took a stroll I soon found
what was engaging [their] attention . . . The ground was hop-
ping with locusts. . . .

Sometimes the fauna was less enchanting.

Jericho, April 6, 1900

Madeba, in proportion to its size, must have the largest number
of mosquitoes and fleas of any inhabited spot on the globe.

She returned northward, crossing the pilgrim road leading to
Mecca.

March 22, 1900

Road of course it is not; it is about one-eighth of a mile wide and
consists of hundreds of parallel tracks trodden out by the
immense caravan which passes over it twice a year.

On the last day of the journey, instead of returning to Jerusalem,
she had decided to go on to the Nabataean ruins of Petra and
stopped for the night near an encampment of the Beni Sakhr, the
fierce tribe that had been the last to submit to Turkish rule.
    She made many mistakes and omissions that turned this
first desert journey into a steep learning curve. She learned
that she must hire a *rafiq* from each of the Bedouin tribes in
whose territories she traveled, to pass in peace. Not yet cogni-
zant of the etiquette of the desert, she did not know that when
she found herself near a desert encampment, she should immediately pay a courtesy visit to the sheikh in his tent. As a result,

her expedition soon ran into trouble and was threatened by
Beni Sakhr tribesmen, armed to the teeth. That night, nevertheless, she wrote home, "Don't think I have ever spent such a
wonderful day." She learned to distrust the maps, which were
full of errors—"one of the great difficulties of this journey is
that no one knows the distances even approximately and there
is no map worth a farthing. Another is that the population is
so scant we can't get food! This is starvation camp tonight. . . ."
Arriving at Petra, she was distracted from the fabulous ruins
by hunger.

March 29, 1900

The Bab es Sik is a passage about half a mile long. . . . Suddenly
between the narrow opening of the rocks, we saw the most
beautiful sight I have ever seen. Imagine a temple cut out of the
solid rock, the charming facade supported on great Corinthian
columns standing clear, soaring upwards to the top of the cliff
with the most exquisite proportions and carved with groups of
figures almost as fresh as when the chisel left them—all this in
the rose red rock, with the sun just touching it and making it
look almost transparent . . . .We camped under a row of the
most elaborate tombs, three stories of pillars and cornices and
the whole topped by a great funeral urn. They are extremely
rococo, just like the kind of thing you see in a Venetian
church. . . . "A rose red city half as old as Time."—I wish the
lamb had come!

As she became more experienced, she learned more. She made
herself a muslin sleeping bag to protect herself from biting
insects at night. She learned to toughen up and drink water
from wells swarming with "little red animals swimming cheerfully about." She learned how to mend a leaking water-skin,
covering the hole with a stone and tying the skin tightly around
the neck with string. She learnt to wrap up against the sun,
finding that the sun could burn her ankles and feet even
through her thick leather boots. On farther journeys she would

wear the traditional white cloth, the keffiyeh,* tied over her hat
and wound over her lower face, and over her head a fine blue veil
cut through with eyeholes. Her new divided skirt would be partly
covered by a large masculine coat in khaki cotton. Effectively,
though unintentionally, she would disguise herself as a man.

We know every detail of her life on her expeditions because
of her wonderful consistency as a writer of letters to her father
and stepmother, kept today in the Robinson Library at Newcastle on Tyne University. It was a matter of enormous importance to her to keep them in touch and unworried, and her
detailed and humorous accounts of her travels were sent in
almost daily installments; however, her dating of letters was a
little erratic. When she was pressed for time she occasionally
wrote a diary for them instead, which she sent off in batches.

From 1909 her mode of traveling was little short of majestic.
It was not only that she liked to travel in style, but she found
that the tribes would judge her status by her possessions and
her gifts, and treat her accordingly. She did not forget the
Druze chief, Yahya Beg, questioning the local villagers, "Have
you seen a queen traveling?" She packed couture evening dresses,
lawn blouses, linen riding skirts, cotton shirts, a fur coat that
would double as a blanket, sweaters, scarves, and canvas and
leather boots. Beneath layers of lacy petticoats she hid guns,
her two cameras and film, and many pairs of binoculars and
pistols as gifts for the most important sheikhs. She carried Egyp-
tian cigarettes, insect powder, a Wedgwood dinner service, silver
candlesticks and hairbrushes, crystal glasses, linen and blankets,
folding tables, and a comfortable chair. Growing tired of sleeping on the ground, she brought with her a camp bed and two
tents, one for writing as soon as they struck camp, the other for
her bed. She also brought her traveling canvas bath for when
there was enough water.

When she stopped for the night at a small distance from the
black Arab tents, she made herself known to the sheikh. As
soon as she had struck camp and had washed and changed, she
presented herself at his tent, bringing gifts suitable to his power

*Arab headdress.

and importance. With her long red hair swept up, wearing an evening dress of muslin or lace, she combined a regal appearance with assertive self-confidence. In what was now fluent Arabic, she brought news of interest to the sheikh—information about tribal movements, who had sold horses, who owned camels, who had been killed in a raid, and how much the blood money would be. He would invite her to dine, they would eat with their fingers and then wash their hands in bowls brought by slaves. After dinner and coffee when she might smoke or take her turn with the *nargile*, the water pipe in which tobacco, marijuana, or opium was smoked, she would quote from her photographic memory whole odes, or *qasidas*, of Arabic poetry, of which she probably knew more than the sheikh himself.

Camping near Tneib, after Dining in the Tent of Sheikh Fellah Isa of the Daja Tribe, February 12, 1905

I hope you realise what an Arab tent is like. It's made of black goats' hair, long and wide, with a division in the middle to separate the women from the men. The lee side of it is always open and this is most necessary, for light and warmth all come from a fire of desert scrub burning in a shallow square hole in the ground and smoking abominably. . . .

The hours riding a horse or a camel were long, and she spent days trying, in ferocious heat, to take photographs and measure ruins lying deep in snake-infested grass. At other times she had to march on through freezing weather or storm conditions. To add to these tribulations, her 1905 expedition crew were rebellious.

North of Hama, April 17, 1905

What it's like to travel in a roadless and bridgeless country after and during heavy, not to say torrential, rains you can't imagine. . . .
I was tired and wet and hungry and bad weather travelling is

exhausting to the mind and to the body. . . . We pitched camp in a downpour amid the mutual recriminations of all the servants who had had a hard time too and vented their displeasure on each other. There was nothing for it but to hold one's tongue, do the work oneself, and having seen that the horses were fed, I went to bed supperless because no one would own that it was his duty to light the fire! It was miserable I must say and this morning was just as bad. All the ropes were like iron after the rain and the tents weighed tons and as I splashed about in the deep grass . . . I thought I was a real idiot to go travelling in tents. . . . What my servants needed last night was a good beating and that's what they would have got if I had been a man—I seldom remember being in such a state of suppressed rage! . . .

North of Hama, April 22, 1905

I shall not soon forget the Cilician plain. . . . At the hands of Turkish muleteers I suffer tortures. They get into camp and when they have unloaded the mules they sit down on one of the packs and light a cigarette with an air of impartial and wholly unconcerned benevolence. I've gone to the length of dislodging them with the lash of my crop, freely applied. It makes no difference; they stroll on to the next pack and take up a position there smiling cheerfully. . . .

When she reached Adana, her luck changed. She was recommended a new servant: Fattuh, an Armenian Catholic with a wife in Aleppo. Fattuh was destined to become Jeeves to Gertrude's Wooster. She was soon writing home that he "would have been a prime minister or a commander in chief if he hadn't happened to be an ignorant Syrian peasant."

April 24, 1905

I have taken on from Mr. Lloyd one of his servants whom he does not want any longer. His name is Fattuh and he is to be

general director of the transport and spare hand all round . . . .
He seems very capable and has an excellent character from Mr.
Lloyd, and my transport arrangements have not been going well
for the last fortnight.

As the days passed, the problems melted away.

Konia, May 12, 1907, Letter to Chirol

There's one most eminently satisfactory peg on which to hang
travel and that is the man [Fattuh] I now have with me. His allegiance is divided between George Lloyd and me—I cannot
decide which of us he adores the most, but I fear it is George
Lloyd. However, I am content to have him for a rival. Once in a
life-time one gets hold of such a man, and not always so often.
He is engaged in making all my arrangements for two months in
the Kara Dagh, not an easy matter, I can assure you, in this
country where the very first essentials of existence cannot be
found. I would rather organise 50 commissariats in the desert
than one in Asia Minor. The people seem themselves to live on
bread alone . . . a lamb is quite out of the question. . . . I'm going
to take a flock of sheep up with me to the Kara Dagh, and Fattuh is to be shepherd as well as butler, head stableman, excava-
tor and friend. . . .

Binbirkilise, May 13, 1905

. . . My clothes arrived from Smyrna! If you had roughed it for 4
months with 2 tiny mule trunks you would realize what that
meant. All things are by comparison and one evening when I put
on a skirt that originally came from Paris, I felt almost too
smart to move. . . . My servants are so charming. And then Fattuh, bless him! the best servant I ever had, ready to cook my
dinner or pack a mule or dig out an inscription with equal
alacrity—the dinner is what he does least well. . . .

Dedicated to Gertrude's well-being, Fattuh was to accompany her on most of her travels thereafter. She would take good care of him when he fell ill at Binbirkilise two years later, and in 1919, when Aleppo was suffering badly from Turkish oppression, she sought him out to check on his circumstances. They were every bit as hard as she had feared. "Fattuh . . . has been through an awful time. He has lost everything he had . . . and now he has only a horse and a small cart with which he brings in wood to sell in Aleppo. . . . We have had such happy times together. . . . My poor Fattuh." She did what she could: gave him money and helped him rent a garden to grow his vegetables.

As Gertrude traveled, she investigated people and archaeological sites, took note of any Turkish barracks, and traveled far beyond help, accompanied only by male guides and camel drivers. She would spend up to ten or twelve hours in the saddle, then write her letter home and her abbreviated diaries. Having become a famous person, as soon as she arrived at a town or city and announced her presence, she would be pressed to take up residence in consulates and embassies. There, over dinner, she would add to their knowledge of the most recent tribal affiliations and enmities. A writer of innumerable letters, she would take the opportunity to send information by diplomatic bag to the Foreign Office.

As early as 1905, Gertrude's name was recognized throughout Britain as the country's best-known traveler. By 1915, she became the interpreter of all reports received from Central Arabia. Lord Cromer, a former British consul general in Egypt, later wrote that "Miss Gertrude Bell knows more about the Arabs and Arabia than almost any other living Englishman or woman."

By the outbreak of war, her encyclopaedic knowledge had benefitted from her pioneer journey into unknown territory culminating in the interval in Hayyil. She had put on the map a line of wells and a mass of new information accumulated about the tribal elements from the Hejaz railway to Sirhan and Nefud. She brought the latest news about the state of the

House of Rashid, and its relations with the Sauds. Her friend Dr. David Hogarth, later the president of the Royal Geographical Society, wrote of Gertrude: "The jaded traveller, writing in April 1914 her diary and letters at Bagdad, had no suspicion that, in little more than a year, the knowledge and experience acquired during the past four months would become of national value."

In 1900, on one of her first expeditions from Jerusalem, Gertrude was already "deep in intrigues." She had decided to go to some ruined towns north of Salkhad. She would need to travel over the Jebel Druze mountains, where she wanted to meet the Druze, a supposedly dangerous tribe feared by the Turks, whose protection she would need to go farther. Meanwhile, she needed a permit from the Turks, and in order to conceal her real intentions she told them she wanted to go to Salkhad.

Bosrah, May 2, 1900

I went first to see the Mudir,* whom I found sitting in his arched and shaded courtyard. He gave me coffee and negotiations began.

"Where was I going?"

"To Damascus."

"God has made it! there is a fine road to the west with such and such places in it, very beautiful ruins."

"Please God I shall see them! but I wish first to look upon Salkhad." (This is in the heart of the Druze country, where they [the Turkish authorities] don't want me to go.)

"Salkhad! there is nothing there at all, and the road is very dangerous. It cannot happen."

"It must happen."

"There has come a telegram from Damascus to bid me to say the Mutussarif fears for the safety of your Presence." (This isn't true.)

---

*Governor of the town, in this case Arab, but working for the Turkish authorities.

"English women are never afraid." (This also isn't true!)

"I wish to look upon the ruins." And so on and so off, till finally I told him I was going nowhere to-day and he said he would come and see me later.

We parted, he saying "You have honoured me!" and I "God forbid!"

Jebel Druze, May 3, 1900

I've slipped through their fingers, and as yet I can scarcely believe in my good fortune. . . . Last night . . . as I was sitting reading in my tent, I heard the voice of the Mudir. I blew out my light and when Hanna came to tell me of his coming, I sent him a message that I was very tired and had gone to bed. I heard this conversation: *Hanna.* "The lady has been awake since the rising of the sun; all day she has walked and ridden, now she sleeps." *Mudir.* "Does she march to-morrow?" *Hanna.* "I couldn't possibly say, Effendim." *Mudir.* "Tell her she must let me know before she goes anywhere." *Hanna.* "At your pleasure, Effendim.". . . I hastily re-arranged my plans. He knew I was going to Salkhad and when he found that I had flown, he would send after me along that road as far as he dared; I decided, therefore, to strike for a place further north, Areh, where . . . a powerful Druze sheikh lived. . . . At two Hanna called me and I got up into the shivering night. By three I was ready, and the packing up began under the stars. . . . At 4 we were off. It was a ticklish business finding our way in the dark round the walls to the east. . . . At last . . . I hit on the Jemurrin road. . . . Oh! it seemed long to the first Druze village.

The Druze made her welcome and became her firm favorites among the tribes.

Areh, May 3, 1900

I told them my tale and how I escaped from the government and came to them, interrupted by many interjections of welcome and assurance that there was no government here (Turks, that means), and that I was safe with them. . . . The sense of comfort and safety and confidence and of being with straight speaking people, was more delightful than I can tell you. . . . I asked if I could see the Sheikh. "Sheikh!" said they, "Yahya Beg is the head of all the Druzes in the land, of course you must visit him." So we went off . . . Hammad and I finger in finger, and as we went he told me that the Beg had been five years in prison in Damascus and had just been let out, three weeks ago, and warned me that I must treat him with great respect. . . . And indeed I would defy any one not to treat Yahya Beg with respect. He is the most perfect type of the Grand Seigneur, a great big man (40 to 50, I suppose) very handsome and with the most exquisite manners. . . . He piled up his cushions for me on the floor and I waited till he sat down, very politely, for he's a king, you understand, and a very good king too, though his kingdom doesn't happen to be a large one.

Gertrude traveled on north, deciding to make a considerable diversion from the route in order to visit Palmyra.

Palmyra, May 20, 1900

. . . It began to be very cold. . . . I put on gaiters, a second pair of knickerbockers and a covert coat under my thick winter coat, rolled myself up in a blacket and a cape and went to sleep. . . . As we drew near Palmyra, the hills were covered with the strangest buildings, great stone towers, four stories high. . . . They are the famous Palmyrene tower tombs. At length we stood on the edge of the col and looked over Palmyra. I wonder if the wide world presents a more singular landscape. It is a mass of columns. . . . Beyond them is the immense Temple of Baal; the modern town is built inside it and its rows of columns rise out of a mass of mud roofs. And beyond all is the desert, sand and white stretches of salt and sand again, with dust clouds whirling over it. . . . It looks like the white skeleton of a town, standing knee deep in the blown sand.

The extra journey brought a couple of comical incidents.

Karyatein, May 17, 1900

Yesterday I fell off. I was sitting sideways in my saddle with a map in one hand and a parasol in the other when suddenly my horse began to trot. I hadn't even got the reins in my hands, so I jumped off, much to the amusement of my soldiers.

Caravans crossing the desert tend to accumulate hangers-on in the form of travelers seeking protection along the way. On the return journey from Palmyra, now in the company of Sheikh Muhammad of the 'Agail Arabs and his raggle-taggle caravan—"the wildest, unkemptest camel drivers . . . carrying a club or an enormous lance 12 feet long"—she encountered a couple of pleasant tourists she knew. Miss Blount and Miss Grieve looked aghast at Gertrude's company but invited her into their horse-drawn carriage for tea and gingerbread biscuits.

May 23, 1900

. . . A carriage, driving across the desert and containing 2 Englishwomen whom I had met in Jerusalem! There they were very neat and tidy, with their dragoman on the box and their mules following behind with crowds of tents. I was glad to see them, for I liked them and it's pleasant to meet someone in the desert, but I felt rather disreputable with a troop of 'Agail on their dromedaries round me and no dragoman and no nothing! . . . I wouldn't really have changed places with them and I prefer a Sheikh from Nejd to a dragoman from Jerusalem as travelling companion. . . . I wish I could manage to travel on the approved lines, but the fates are against me. I had laid all my plans for coming back from Palmyra like a lady, but no! it was not to be.

Gertrude completed her expedition a much more experienced desert traveler.

May 24, 1900

We were only seven hours from Karyatein. . . . I came in the last hour or two on Ahmad's camel—it's the greatest relief after you have been riding a horse for 8 or 9 hours to feel the long comfy swing and the wide soft saddle of a camel beneath you.

June 10, 1900

. . . You know, dearest Father, I shall be back here before long! One doesn't keep away from the East when one has got into it this far.

———

Gertrude returned to the East briefly in 1902 and again in 1905, when she undertook the journey through the Syrian Desert to Asia Minor without requesting Turkish permission: "I laugh to think that I am marching along the Turkish frontier, so to speak, some ten miles beyond it, and they can't catch me or stop me." She took part in a *ghazu*, beat a rival to arrive first with her friends the Druze, experienced the desert in bad weather, and found that she was famous in Syria.

A Week's March from Jericho, February 13, 1905

Yesterday a great ghazu, a raid, swept over this very country and carried off 2,000 head of cattle and all the tents of one of the small outlying groups. . . . Five hundred horsemen, they say there were. . . . I must tell you what will happen to the destitute of the Beni Hassan. They will go round to the rest of the tribe and one will give a camel, and one will give a few sheep and one some pieces of goat's hair for the tent, until each man has enough to support existence—they don't need much. So they will bide their time until a suitable moment when they will gather together all the horsemen of their allies, and ride out against the Sakhr and the Howeitat who were the authors of their ills; and then if they are lucky they will take back the 2,000 head of beasts and more besides. It seems a most unreasonable industry this of the ghazu—about as profitable as stealing each other's washing, but that's how they live.

. . . To-morrow is the great feast of the Mohammmedan year. . . . After sunset there was a mighty firing off of guns. I too contributed—by request—in a modest way, with my revolver, the first, and I expect the only, time I shall use it.

February 16, 1905

Salkhad is a little black lava town hanging on to the southern slope of a volcano, and in the crater of the volcano there is a great ruined castle, most grim and splendid. This evening as I dined, . . . I heard a great sound of wild song, together with the letting off of guns, and going out I saw a fire burning on the top-most top of the castle walls. You who live in peace, what do you think this meant? It was a call to arms. I told you the Beni Sakhr and the Druzes were bitter foes. A month ago the Sakhr carried off 5,000 sheep from the Druze folds in the plain. To-morrow the Druzes are going forth, 2,000 horsemen, to recapture their flocks, and to kill every man, woman and child of the Sakhr that they may come across. The bonfire was a signal to the country side. To-morrow they will assemble here and Nasib rides at their head. There was a soldier sitting at my camp fire. He wears the Turkish uniform, but he is a Druze from Salkhad, and he hates the Turk as a Druze knows how to hate. I said: "Is there refusal to my going up?" He replied: "There is no refusal, honour us." And together under the moon we scrambled up the sandy side of the mountain. There at the top, on the edge of the castle moat we found a group of Druzes, men and boys, standing in a circle and singing a terrible song. They were all armed and most of them carried bare swords. "Oh Lord our God! Upon them! Upon them!"—I too joined the circle with my guide. "Let the child leave his mother's side, let the young man mount and be gone." Over and over again they repeated a single phrase. Then half a dozen or so stepped into the circle, each shaking his club or his drawn sword in the face of those standing round. "Are you a good man? are you a true man? Are you valiant?" they shouted. "Ha! ha!" came the answer and the swords glistened and quivered in the moonlight. Then several came up to me and saluted me: "Upon thee be peace!" they said, "the English and the Druze are one." I said "Praise be to God! we too are a fighting race." And if you had listened to that song you would know that the finest thing in the world is to go out and kill your enemy. When it was over we ran down the hill together, the Druzes took up a commanding position on the roof of a house—we happened to be on it at the time, for one always walks for choice on the roofs and not in the streets to avoid the mud—and reformed their devilish circle. I listened for a little and then took my leave and departed, many blessings following me down the hill. . . .

February 18, 1905

I hear that Mark Sykes* has come into the Jebel Druze with an official escort. . . . I am very glad I came up through the desert . . . a most amusing journey and a very valuable experience for a future expedition. You see I have laid the foundations of

---

*Sir Mark Sykes was a bombastic Catholic landowner and close neighbor of the Bells in Yorkshire. Gertrude had quarreled violently with him at a dinner in Haifa in 1905, when he called the Arabs "animals" who were "cowardly," "diseased," and "idle." Later, he accused her of tricking him in order to get to the Jebel Druze first, which she had. She had let slip to a governor in Damascus that Sykes was highly connected, ensuring he would not be allowed permission to travel without Turkish soldiers. He wrote to his wife, "Confound the silly chattering windbag of conceited, gushing, flat-chested, man-woman, globetrotting, rump-wagging, blethering ass!" Sykes became principal adviser to the British government on its wartime relations with the Arabs. In 1916, he made an agreement with François Georges-Picot that divided up Arabia between the French, British, and Russians: it nearly stopped the Arab Revolt in its tracks. The Sykes-Picot Agreement—or disagreement, as Gertrude called it—would form the basis of the San Remo Pact of 1920, which settled Arabia under British and French mandates.

friendship with several important people—of desert importance that is.

The weather worsened as she traveled north.

Saleh, the Safah Desert, February 20, 1905

All went well for the first three hours or so, except that it was so cold that I rode in a sweater . . . a Norfolk jacket and a fur coat; then we began to get into snow and it was more abominable than words can say. The mules fell down in snow drifts, the horses reared and bucked, and if I had been on a side-saddle we should have been down half a dozen times, but on this beloved saddle one can sit straight, and close. So we plunged on, the wind increasing and sleet beginning to fall till at last we came out on to a world entirely white. The last hour I walked and led my horse for he broke through the deep snow at every step. . . . Some interest surrounds me, for I am the first foreign woman who has ever been in these parts.

February 23, 1905

I left my tents behind. . . . We rode down the Druze mountains. . . . We rode on and on over all the stones in the world and at last, half an hour before sunset, just as we were deciding that we should have to sleep out, waterless, one of the Druzes caught sight of the smoke of some Arab tents. . . . Very miserable the little encampment looked. They have nothing but a few camels, the black tents and the coffee pots. They eat nothing but bread. . . . My servants and I went to the house of the Sheikh, whose name was Understanding. His two sons lighted a fire of desert thorns and we all sat round watching the coffee making. And the talk began to the accompaniment of the coffee pounding, a great accomplishment among them. They pound in a delightful sort of tune, or rather a sort of tattoo. We dined on flaps of fresh bread and bowls of dibbis and then I curled myself up in a blanket and went to sleep in a corner of the tent. The smoke of the fire was abominable, but it blew out after a bit. . . . The fleas didn't blow out.

. . . The second night in Arab tents was rather wearing, I must admit, and I felt quite extraordinarily dirty this morning. We started early and I got back to my tents at 4—the bath that followed was one of the most delightful I have ever had.

Damascus, February 27, 1905

I . . . alighted at a most fascinating hotel, with a courtyard. . . . The governor here has sent me a message to say would I honour him by coming to see him. . . . An official [Turkish] lives in this hotel. He spent the evening talking to me and offering to place the whole of the organisation of Syria at my disposal. . . . I have become a Person in Syria!

March 3, 1905

I made my way at last to the great mosque . . . left my shoes at the door with a friendly beggar and went in. It was the hour of the afternoon prayer. In the courtyard, men of all sorts and kinds, from the learned Doctor of Damascus down to the raggedest camel driver—Islam is the great republic of the world, there is neither class nor race inside the creed—were washing at the fountain and making the first prostrations before they entered the mosque. I followed them in and stood behind the lines of praying people some two or three hundred of them, listening to the chanting of the Imam. "Allah!" he cried, and the Faithful fell with a single movement upon their faces and remained for a full moment in silent adoration, till the high chant of the Imam began again: "The Creator of this World and the next, of the Heavens and the Earth, He who leads the righteous in the true path, and the evil to destruction. Allah!" And as the name of God echoed through the great colonnades, where it had sounded for near 2,000 years in different tongues, the listeners prostrated themselves again, and for a moment all the church was silence. . . .

I begin to see dimly what the civilisation of a great Eastern city means—how they live, what they think; and I have got on to terms with them.

Homs, March 9, 1905

I took a walk through the bazaars, but that was not as pleasant as it might have been on account of the interest my appearance excited. It was an interest purely benevolent but none the less tiresome, for I was never without the company of fifty or sixty people.

Kalaat el Husn, March 12, 1905

It is one of the most difficult things I know to keep one's temper when one is constantly surrounded and mobbed. . . . Only a fixed determination not to afford more amusement than I could help to the inhabitants of Homs kept me outwardly calm.

Hamah, March 16, 1905

I have just had a struggle with the authorities who insisted on giving me eight watchmen for the night. I refused to have more than two. . . . It's a perfect pest having so many, for in the first place they talk all night and in the second one has to tip them all.

———

In April 1907, Gertrude went to Asia Minor. The work she did there at the Hittite and Byzantine site of Binbirkilise with Sir William Ramsay is detailed in their 580-page book, *The Thousand and One Churches*. They worked on it for much of 1908, and it was published a year later. They met, as arranged, in

Binbirkilise, but she traveled there alone except for Fattuh and her crew, buying a couple of horses but mostly traveling by cart. On the way she stopped here and there to take notes on ancient stones that Ramsay had asked her to look at.

Back in England, she took tutorials in surveying and astronomical observations for determining positions in preparation for her next important desert expedition.

London, October 1907

I have had a wild 24 hours. I worked at the Geog. Soc. all yesterday and in the evening I went to Red Hill, getting there at 8. A young man (one of my fellow students . . .) met me at the station and we walked up on to the Common where we met Mr. Reeves. Then we took observations on stars for two hours. It was wonderfully calm and warm but the moon was so bright that even the big stars were a little difficult to see. However, I took a number of observations and shall work them out on Monday. I got back after midnight, very hungry, and this morning I was back at Red Hill before 10 and spent three hours taking bearings for a map with Mr. Reeves. That has to be plotted out too on Monday at the Geog. Soc.

———

Gertrude was back in Syria in 1909. She started from Aleppo in the middle of February for her longest journey so far. Taking the northern desert route, she crossed the Euphrates in order to explore its unmapped east bank. It was in mid-March that she left her caravan and rode with Fattuh and a small party north of Najaf. There, in a dangerous section of the desert, she discovered the ruined palace of Ukhaidir (see "The Archaeologist"). She returned via Babylon and Ctesiphon, Samarra and Ashur.

Leaving Aleppo, February 1909

There is a moment ... when one is newly arrived in the East,
when one is conscious of the world shrinking at one end and
growing at the other till all the perspective of life is changed—
after a few days it becomes a common place and one notices it
no more. . . . Some day I hope the East will be strong again and
develop its own civilisation, not imitate ours, and then perhaps
it will teach us a few of the things we once learnt from it and
have now forgotten, to our great loss. . . .

This bank of the Euphrates is in many parts untravelled and I
am therefore obliged to take a great deal of trouble about it. . . .
I forgot to tell you ... that at Der I saw the Arabs swimming
across the Euphrates on inflated skins just exactly like the Assyrian soldiers on the bas reliefs in the British Museum.

On a hill in Ashur, in northern Mesopotamia some sixty miles
south of Mosul, she sat for an hour looking down on what
would become Iraq, the country of which she would one day
become the uncrowned queen.

April 27, 1909

The whole world shone like a jewel, green crops, and blue waters and far away the gleaming snows of the mountains that
bound Mesopotamia to the north—we saw them today for the
first time. I sat on a hill top for an hour and considered the history of Asia that was spread out before me. Here Mithridates
murdered the Greek generals, here Xenophen began to have
his command, and just beyond Zab the Greeks turned and
defeated the archers of Mithridates, marching then on to Lar-
issa, the mound of Nimrud, where Xenophon saw the great
Assyrian city of Calah standing in ruins. Nimrud stood out
among the cornfields at my feet. A little further east I could
see the plain of Arbela where Alexander conquered Asia. We
people of the west can always conquer, but we can never hold

Asia—that seemed to me to be the legend written across the
landscape. . . .

––––––––

In 1911, Gertrude traveled back east from Damascus to complete
her measurements of the ruined palace of Ukhaidir, first seen by
her two years previously. From Baghdad she took a long route
northwest, exploring the Tur Abdin in southeast Turkey before
returning via Aleppo. She would write about this journey in her
next book, *The Churches and Monasteries of the Tur Abdin*.

Two Days out from Damascus, February 11 and 12, 1911

When I went to bed a hurricane was blowing. . . . About an hour
before dawn Fattuh called to me and asked whether I was cold. I
woke in surprise and putting my hand out felt the waterproof valise
that covered me wet with snow. "It is like the sea," cried Fattuh.
Therefore I lighted a candle and saw that it had drifted into my tent
a foot deep. I dug down, found my boots and hat . . . and put all
my extra clothing under the valise for warmth. . . . At dawn Fattuh
dragged out the waterproof sheet that covers the ground and with
it most of the snow. The snow was lying in great drifts. . . .

Everything in my tent was frozen stiff—yesterday's damp
skirt was like a board, my gloves like iron, my sponges—well,
I'll draw a veil over my sponges—I did not use them much. Nor
was my toilette very complicated as I had gone to bed in my
clothes. The temperature after sunrise was 30° [-1°C] and there
was a biting wind blowing sharply from the west. . . . The frozen tents took a world of time to pack—with frozen fingers
too. . . . The wet desert was like a sheet of glass and the camels
slipped about and fell down with much groaning and moaning.
They are singularly unfitted to cope with emergencies. . . .

Suddenly we got out of the snow zone and all was well. I got
on to my camel and rode her for the rest of the day. She is the
most charming of animals. You ride a camel with only a halter
which you mostly tie loosely round the peak of your saddle. A

tap with your camel switch on one side of her neck or the other tells her the direction you want her to go, a touch with your heels sends her on, but when you wish her to sit down you have to hit her lightly and often on the neck saying at the same time: "Kh kh kh kh." . . . The big soft saddle, the "shedad," is so easy and comfortable that you never tire. You loll about and eat your lunch and observe the landscape through your glasses. . . .

No sooner had the snow ceased to be a problem than they began to suffer for lack of water.

February 20, 1911

We marched yesterday thirteen and a half hours without getting anywhere. . . . And the whole supply of water which we had was about a cupful in my flask. . . . My poor little mare had not drunk for two days, and she whinnied to everyone she saw. . . . We rode to-day for six and a half hours before we got to rain pools in the Wady Hauran. . . .

Ramadi, February 25, 1911

I was sitting reading in my tent when suddenly I heard unusual sounds and stepping out saw my muleteers in the grip of about fifteen rascally young men who had picked a quarrel with them . . . I rushed into the fray . . . and soon put an end to the business, for the roughs were alarmed when they saw a European. But after they had gone Mahmud discovered that his watch was missing and Fattuh, presently returning with Government in the shape of a couple of officials, found that a revolver had been taken from one of the saddle bags.

———

Gertrude's final and most extraordinary desert journey took place during winter 1913–14. She set out in late December to escape an emotional bond with Dick Doughty-Wylie, which was causing her great misery. On this single journey she would cover sixteen hundred miles.

Leaving Damascus, December 19–21, 1913

Already I have dropped back into the desert as if it were my own place; silence and solitude fall around you like an impenetrable veil; there is no reality but the long hours of riding, shivering in the morning and drowsy in the afternoon, the bustle of getting into camp, the talk round Muhammad's coffee fire after dinner, profounder sleep than civilization ever knows—and then the road again. And as usual one feels as secure and confident in this lawless country as one does in one's own village.

The lawless element of the country soon made itself felt.

December 22, 1913

A preposterous and provoking episode has delayed us to-day. We had marched about 2 hours when we sighted camels and the smoke of tents. We took them to be (as indeed they were) Arabs of the Mountain, the Jebel Druze. . . . We tried in Dumeir to get one of the Jebel Druze Arabs as a companion and failed—and we suffered for it. Presently a horseman came galloping over the plain, shooting as he came. . . . He wheeled round us, shouting that we were foes, that we should not approach with weapons and then while he aimed his rifle at me or other of us Muhammad and Ali tried to pacify him, but in vain. He demanded of Ali his rifle and fur cloak, which were thrown to him, and by this time a dozen or more men had come galloping or running up, some shooting, all shouting, half dressed—one of them had neglected to put on any clothes at all—with matted black locks falling about their faces. They shrieked and leapt at us like men insane. One of them seized Muhammad's camel and drew the sword which hangs behind his

saddle with which he danced round us, slashing the air and hit-
ting my camel on the neck to make her kneel. Next they pro-
ceeded to strip my men of their revolvers, cartridge belts and
cloaks. My camel got up again and as there was nothing to be
done but to sit quiet and watch events that's what I did. Things
looked rather black, but they took a turn for the better when my
camel herd, a negro, was recognised by our assailants, and in a
minute or two some sheikhs came up, knew Ali and Muhammad,
and greeted us with friendship. Our possessions were returned. . . .

The account she sent her parents of being detained at Ziza,
and then obliged to absolve the Turkish authorities of responsibility for her, differs from that which she sent to Dick
Doughty-Wylie (see "The Lover"). The British ambassador to
Constantinople, Sir Louis Mallet, had already warned her not
to go to Hayyil, telling her that if she went ahead, His Majesty's Government (HMG) would disclaim all responsibility for
her. She was more anxious than she appears here, and the
Turks were more reluctant to let her go.

January 9, 1914

As I said before, paf! I'm caught. I was an idiot to come in so
close to the railway, but I was like an ostrich with its head in the
sand. . . . Besides I wanted my letters and Fattuh [arriving by
train]. . . .

  I rode off to Mshetta, which is only an hour from my camp. As
we came back Ali, the camel driver, looked up and said "Are those
horsemen or camel riders going to our tents?" I looked, and they
were horsemen and, what is more, they were soldiers, and when we
rode in they were sitting round our camp fire. More and more
came, to the number of 10, and last of all a very angry, rude (and
rather drunken) little Jack-in-Office of a Chaowish [staff sergeant],
who said they had been looking for me ever since I left Damascus.

  I sent off at once telegrams to Beyrout and Damascus to the
two Consuls, but I had to send a man with them to Madeba and

the Chaowish intercepted them and put the man, one of my camel drivers, into the Ziza castle, practically a prisoner. Thither he presently sent Fattuh also, on some imaginary insult (F. had said nothing) and then he ransacked our baggage, took possession of our arms, and posted men all round my tent. All this which he had not the slightest right to do I met with an icy calmness for which God give me the reward. . . . I am busy forging new plans for I am not beaten yet. . . . Fattuh [released that morning] observes cheerfully "I spent the first night of the journey in the railway station, and the second in prison, and now where?"

January 14, 1914

The Kaimmakam* not having arrived this morning, I came down to Amman and here I found him on his way to me, a charming, educated man, a Christian, willing and ready to let me go any-where I like. . . . I have telegraphed to Damascus for permission to visit the ruins round Ziza and if I get that . . . , I shall have relieved my friend [the Kaimmakam] of all responsibility and shall be free. . . . I shall be glad when the permission comes.

Amman, January 14, 1914

I have to-day permission from the Vali to go when I like. The permission comes just in time for all my plans were laid and I was going to run away to-morrow night.

January 19, 1914

We left Amman on the 15th, I have given the authorities at Amman an assurance that the Ott. Government was not respon-sible for me.

---

*The nearest Turkish authority authorized to issue permissions for travel.

At the end of February, after a daunting journey, Gertrude reached the desert city of Hayyil, where they refused to honor her promissory note. Without money or resources, she was held against her will (see "The Prisoner"). Finally reaching Baghdad at the end of March, she found that modern life had caught up with the ancient city.

Baghdad, March 29, 1914

The slow Tigris and the native boats loaded with steel rails, the steam cranes working under the palm trees, the great locomotives of the latest pattern standing in all stages of completion in the middle of a devastated palm garden, the blue clad, ragged Arabs working and singing as they worked and hauled, and among them the decisive military Germans, sharp of word, straight of carriage—it was the old East meeting the newest West and going down before it.

Gertrude still had to cross some 450 miles of the Syrian Desert by camel back to Damascus. Tired when she started, she was totally exhausted by the time they reached the city. There she was taken in by friends and stayed some time convalescing.

Fallujah, April 13, 1914, Diary

. . . we are travelling very light. . . . I have a very small and light native tent, with my bed in a Wolseley valise and one chair—that's all I have except a bagful of clothes. . . . My one luxury is my canvas bath! It's hot now, you know, and it will serve to water the camels in if necessary. . . . This is not desert; my bed lies on grass. . . . But it is out under the open sky again and at once my heart leaps to it. . . . Here comes the great procession of the stars—Sirius sparkled out long ago—here is the Great Bear with his eternal interrogations, and the sicle of Leo—all my friends. The Twins, and there is Capella's lovely face half veiled in heat haze; Aldebaran, and above me Procyon—a thousand welcomes!

April 23–26, 1914

... So far I have run my own show quite satisfactorily and it amuses me to be tongue and voice for myself, as I have been these days. But I am tired, and being anxious to get through and be done with travel, we are making long marches, 9 and 10 hours. Oh, but they are long hours, day after day in the open wilderness! I have come in sometimes more dead than alive, too tired to eat and with just enough energy to write my diary. . . .

On the 24th we began the day by sighting something lying in the desert with an ominous flutter of great wings over it. Assaf [her road companion] observed that it was 3 dead camels and 2 dead men, killed ten nights ago—ghazu met ghazu, said he. . . .

On the 26th . . . In the middle of the morning we met a man walking solitary in the desert. We rode up to him and addressed him in Arabic, but he made no answer. Assaf, my rafiq, said he thought he must be a Persian dervish. I spoke to him in Turkish and in what words of Persian I could muster, but he made no reply. Fattuh gave him some bread which he accepted and turned away from us into the rainy wilderness, going whither? . . . We are terribly bothered by wind, both marching and in camp, when it sheets us in dust. We march very long hours, and oh, I'm tired!

EXCERPTS FROM GERTRUDE'S TRAVEL BOOKS

Gertrude's first travel book, *Persian Pictures*, is a collection of essays detailing her initial excursion into the East in 1892. She herself called it "extraordinarily feeble" and wished it to remain unpublished, but her family was disappointed and she conceded. This extract, about a horseback excursion with an early boyfriend, stands out for the freshness and excitement of her first visit to a Zoroastrian "Tower of the Dead."

The Tower of Silence

Hundreds of years ago, when the Persian race first issued from unknown Bactria and the grim Hyrcanian forests, passing through the Caspian Gates, they came upon a fertile land lying to the north-east of the country, which was subsequently named Media. There on the edge of the province known to-day as Khorasan they founded a city, which with the rolling centuries gathered greatness and riches and power; the Greeks (for her fame had penetrated to the limits of the civilized world) called her Rages. Key to Hyrcania and Parthia, the geographical position of the Median city lent her considerable importance. The Jews knew her well: in Rages dwelt that Gabelus to whom the pious Tobit entrusted his ten talents of silver in the days of the Captivity; there Tobias was journeying when the angel Raphael met him and instructed him in the healing properties of fishes; there, relates the author of the Book of Judith, reigned Phraortes whom Nebuchadnezzar smote through with his darts and utterly destroyed.

Rages, the Ancient of Days, passed through many vicissitudes of fortune in the course of her long-drawn life. Under her walls fled the last Darius when Alexander's army chased him, vanquished at Arbela, over the wide plains of Khorasan—fled to the mountains of the Caspian to seek a luckless fate at the hands of the cruel Bactrian satrap. At Rages, perhaps, the generous Alexander mourned the untimely death of his rival, from her palaces hurled his vengeance against Bessus, and saw the satrap dragged a captive to execution. Twice the city was destroyed, by earthquake and by Parthian invaders, twice to rise up afresh under new names. At length, in the twelfth century, an enemy more devastating than the Parthian hordes, more vindictive than the earthquake, swept over pleasant Khorasan and turned the fertile province into the wilderness it is to this day. Tartars from the uttermost ends of the earth left no stone of Rages standing, and the great Median city vanished from the history of men. A few miles to the north-east Tehran has sprung up to be the capital of modern Persia—a Persia to whom the glorious traditions of the past are as forgotten as the strength of Phraortes' walls. "The Lion and the Lizard keep the courts where Jemshyd gloried and drank deep," but the foundations of Rages, the mother of Persian cities, can be traced only by conjecture.

Through waste and solitary places we rode one morning to the city and the citadel of the dead. It was still so early that the sun had not over-topped the range of eastern mountains. We rode out of sleeping Tehran, and took our way along the deserted track that skirts its walls; to our left lay the wilderness, wrapped in transparent shadow, and sloping gradually upwards to the barren foot-hills over which winds the road to Meshed. Before we had gone far, with a flash and a sudden glitter, the sun leapt up above the snow-peaks, and day rushed across the plain—day, crude and garish, revealing not the bounteous plenty of the cornfields and pastures which encircled Rages, but dust and stones and desert scrub, and the naked, forbidding mountains, wrinkled by many winters.

To us, with the headlong flight of Darius and the triumph of the conqueror surging before our eyes, the broken ground round the site of the ancient stronghold piled itself into ruined turret and rampart, sank into half-obliterated fosse and ditch. Where we imagined the walls to have been, we discovered a solid piece of masonry, and our minds reeled at the thought that it was wildly possible Alexander's eyes might have rested on this even brickwork. Time has made gates in the battlements, but the desert has not even yet established unquestioned rule within them. At the foot of the wall we came upon a living pool lying under the shadow of a plane-tree. Round such a pool the sick men of Bethsaida gathered and waited for the stirring of the waters, but in Rages all was solitude, "and the desired angel came no more."

Towards the east two parallel lines of hills rear themselves out of the desert, dividing it from the wider stretch of desert that reaches southward to Isfahan. Between the hills lies a stony valley, up which we turned our steps, and which led us to the heart of desolation and the end of all things. Half-way up the hillside stands a tower, whose whitewashed wall is a landmark to all the country round. Even from the far distant peaks of the opposite mountains the Tower of Silence is visible, a mocking gleam reminding the living of the vanity of their eager days. For the tower is the first stage in the weary journey of the dead; here they come to throw off the mantle of the flesh before their bones may rest in the earth without fear of defiling the holy element, before their souls, passing through the seven gates of the planets, may reach the sacred fire of the sun.

The tower is roofless; within, ten or twelve feet below the upper surface of its wall, is a chalky platform on which the dead bodies lie till sun and vultures have devoured them. This grim turret-room was untenanted. Zoroaster's religion has faded from that Media where once it reigned, and few and humble now are the worshippers who raise prayers to Ormuzd under the open heaven, and whose bodies are borne up the stony valley and cast into the Tower of Silence.

We dismounted from our horses and sat down on the hillside. The plain stretched below us like a monotonous ocean which had billowed up against the mountain flanks and had been fixed there forever; we could see the feet of the mountains themselves planted firmly in the waves of dust, and their glistening peaks towering into the cloudless sky; the very bones of the naked earth were exposed before us, and the fashion of its making was revealed.

With the silence of an extinct world still heavy upon us, we made our way to the upper end of the valley, but at the gates of the plain Life came surging to meet us. A wild hollyhock stood sentinel among the stones; it had spread some of its yellow petals for banner and on its uplifted spears the buds were fat and creamy with coming bloom. Rain had fallen in the night, and had called the wilderness itself to life, clothing its thorns with a purple garment of tiny flowers; the delicious sun struck upon our shoulders; a joyful little wind blew the damp, sweet smell of the reviving earth in gusts towards us; our horses sniffed the air and, catching the infection of the moment, tugged at the bit and set off at racing speed across the rain-softened ground. And we, too, passed out of the silence and remembered that we lived. Life seized us and inspired us with a mad sense of revelry. The

humming wind and the teeming earth shouted "Life! life!" as
we rode. Life! life! the bountiful, the magnificent! Age was far
from us—death far; we had left him enthroned in his barren
mountains, with ghostly cities and out-worn faiths to bear him
company. For us the wide plain and the limitless world, for us
the beauty and the freshness of the morning, for us youth and
the joy of living!

In the preface to *The Desert and the Sown*,* Gertrude's 1907
book about her experiences in Syria, she chose to write from
an unusual perspective. As noted by Rosemary O'Brien in her
introduction to the book, other European travelers regarded
and described the foreign world with the inborn conviction
that their own civilization was superior, and the interviews
they reported in their books were with the locally eminent and
powerful. Gertrude relates "the actual political conditions of
unimportant persons" and analyzes the roots and causes of
disaffection. The book cemented her early fame as a traveler
and a writer.

Those who venture to add a new volume to the vast literature of
travel, unless they be men of learning or politicians, must be
prepared with an excuse. My excuse is ready, as specious and I
hope as plausible as such things should be. I desired to write not
so much a book of travel as an account of the people whom I
met or who accompanied me on my way, and to show what the
world is like in which they live and how it appears to them. And
since it was better that they should, as far as possible, tell their
own tale, I have strung their words upon the thread of the road,
relating as I heard them the stories with which shepherd and
man-at-arms beguiled the hours of the march, the talk that
passed from lip to lip round the camp-fire, in the black tent of
the Arab and the guest-chamber of the Druze, as well as the
more cautious utterances of Turkish and Syrian officials. Their
statecraft consists of guesses, often shrewd enough, at the results

---

The Desert and the Sown, originally published in New York by E. P.
Dutton, was republished in 2001 by Cooper Square Press.

that may spring from the clash of unknown forces, of which the strength and the aim are but dimly apprehended; their wisdom is that of men whose channels of information and standards for comparison are different from ours, and who bring a different set of preconceptions to bear upon the problems laid before them. The Oriental is like a very old child. He is unacquainted with many branches of knowledge which we have come to regard as of elementary necessity; frequently, but not always, his mind is little preoccupied with the need of acquiring them, and he concerns himself scarcely at all with what we call practical utility. He is not practical in our acceptation of the word, any more than a child is practical, and his utility is not ours. On the other hand, his action is guided by traditions of conduct and morality that go back to the beginnings of civilisation, traditions unmodified as yet by any important change in the manner of life to which they apply and out of which they arose. These things apart, he is as we are; human nature does not undergo a complete change east of Suez, nor is it impossible to be on terms of friendship and sympathy with the dwellers in those regions. In some respects it is even easier than in Europe. You will find in the East habits of intercourse less fettered by artificial chains, and a wider tolerance born of greater diversity. Society is divided by caste and sect and tribe into an infinite number of groups, each one of which is following a law of its own, and however fantastic, to our thinking, that law may be, to the Oriental it is an ample and a satisfactory explanation of all peculiarities. A man may go about in public veiled up to the eyes, or clad if he please only in a girdle: he will excite no remark. Why should he? Like every one else he is merely obeying his own law. So too the European may pass up and down the wildest places, encountering little curiosity and of criticism even less. The news he brings will be heard with interest, his opinions will be listened to with attention, but he will not be thought odd or mad, nor even mistaken, because his practices and the ways of his thought are at variance with those of the people among whom he finds himself. "'Adat-hu:" it is his custom. And for this reason he will be the wiser if he does not seek to ingratiate himself with Orientals by trying to ape their habits, unless he is so skilful that he can pass as one of themselves. Let him treat the law of others respectfully, but he himself will meet with a far greater respect if he adheres strictly to his own. For a woman this rule is of the first importance, since a woman can never disguise herself effectually. That she should be known to come of a great and honoured stock, whose customs are inviolable, is her best claim to consideration.

None of the country through which I went is ground virgin to the traveller, though parts of it have been visited but seldom, and described only in works that are costly and often difficult to obtain. Of such places I have given a brief account, and as many photographs as seemed to be of value. I have also noted in the northern cities of Syria those vestiges of antiquity that catch the eye of a casual observer. There is still much exploration to be done in Syria and on the edge of the desert, and there are many difficult problems yet to be solved. The work has been well begun by de Vogüé, Wetzstein, Brünnow, Sachau, Dussaud, Puchstein and his colleagues, the members of the Princeton Expedition and others. To their books I refer those who would learn how immeasurably rich is the land in architectural monuments and in the epigraphic records of a far-reaching history.

My journey did not end at Alexandretta as this account ends. In Asia Minor I was, however, concerned mainly with archaeology; the results of what work I did there have been published in a series of papers in the "Revue Archéologique," where, through the kindness of the editor, Monsieur Salomon Reinach, they have found a more suitable place than the pages of such a book as this could have offered them.

I do not know either the people or the language of Asia Minor well enough to come into anything like a close touch with the country, but I am prepared, even on a meagre acquaintance, to lay tokens of esteem at the feet of the Turkish peasant. He is gifted with many virtues, with the virtue of hospitality beyond all others.

I have been at some pains to relate the actual political conditions of unimportant persons. They do not appear so unimportant to one who is in their midst, and for my part I have always been grateful to those who have provided me with a clue to their relations with one another. But I am not concerned to justify or condemn the government of the Turk. I have lived long enough in Syria to realise that his rule is far from being the ideal of administration, and seen enough of the turbulent elements which he keeps more or less in order to know that his post is a difficult one. I do not believe that any government would give universal satisfaction; indeed, there are few which attain that desired end even in more united countries. Being English, I am persuaded that we are the people who could best have taken Syria in hand with the prospect of a success greater than that which might be attained by a moderately reasonable Sultan. We have long recognised that the task will not fall to us. We have unfortunately done more than this. Throughout the dominions of Turkey we have allowed a very great reputation to weaken and decline; reluctant to accept the responsibility of official interference, we have yet permitted the irresponsible protests, vehemently expressed, of a sentimentality that I make bold to qualify as ignorant, and our dealings with the Turk have thus presented an air of vacillation which he may be pardoned for considering perfidious and for regarding with animosity. These feelings, combined with the deep-seated dread of a great Asiatic Empire which is also mistress of Egypt and of the sea, have, I think, led the Porte to seize the first opportunity for open resistance to British demands, whether out of simple miscalculation of the spirit that would be aroused, or with the hope of foreign backing, it is immaterial to decide. The result is equally deplorable, and if I have gauged the matter at all correctly, the root of it lies in the disappearance of English influence at Constantinople. The position of authority that we occupied has been taken by another, yet it is and must be of far deeper importance to us than to any other that we should be able to guide when necessary the tortuous politics of Yildiz Kiosk. The greatest of all Mohammedan powers cannot afford to let her relations with the Khalif of Islām be regulated with so little consistency or firmness, and if the Sultan's obstinacy in the Tabah quarrel can prove to us how far the reins have slipped from our hands, it will have served its turn. Seated as we are upon the Mediterranean and having at our command, as I believe, a considerable

amount of goodwill within the Turkish empire and the memo-
ries of an ancient friendship, it should not be impossible to
recapture the place we have lost.

But these are matters outside the scope of the present book,
and my *apologia* had best end where every Oriental writer
would have begun: "In the name of God, the Merciful, the
Compassionate!"

Early in *The Desert and the Sown*, Gertrude describes to her
parents the advantages of an Arab tent, where she would so
often go at night to eat mutton and curds, drink coffee, and
exchange information with the sheikhs.

We did not go straight back to my tents. I had been invited out
to dine that evening by Sheikh Nahār of the Beni Ṣakhr, he who
had spent the previous night in Namrüd's cave; and after consultation it had been decided that the invitation was one which a
person of my exalted dignity would not be compromised by
accepting.

"But in general," added Namrüd, "you should go nowhere
but to a great sheikh's tent, or you will fall into the hands of
those who invite you only for the sake of the present you will
give. Nahār—well, he is an honest man, though he be Meskīn,"
a word that covers all forms of mild contempt, from that which
is extended to honest poverty, through imbecility to the first
stages of feeble vice.

The Meskīn received me with the dignity of a prince, and
motioned me to the place of honour on the ragged carpet
between the square hole in the ground that serves as hearth and
the partition that separates the women's quarters from the
men's. We had tethered our horses to the long tent ropes that
give such wonderful solidity to the frail dwelling, and our eyes
wandered out from where we sat over the eastward sweep of the
landscape—swell and fall, fall and swell, as though the desert
breathed quietly under the gathering night.

The lee side of an Arab tent is always open to the air; if the
wind shifts the women take down the tent wall and set it up
against another quarter, and in a moment your house has changed

its outlook and faces gaily to the most favourable prospect. It is so small and so light and yet so strongly anchored that the storms can do little to it; the coarse meshes of the goat's hair cloth swell and close together in the wet so that it needs continuous rain carried on a high wind before a cold stream leaks into the dwelling-place.

Amurath to Amurath* is the account of Gertrude's extensive journey along the banks of the Euphrates, surveying and photographing innumerable archaeological sites along the way. She wrote in 1910, "The five months of journeying which are recounted in this book were months of suspense and even of terror. . . . The banks of the Euphrates echo with ghostly alarums." Here she tells of two near escapes in this dangerous territory and of one comical encounter with unpleasant insects.

On the leg of the journey from Hit to Karbala, Gertrude and her crew set out for Shetateh.

We were jogging along between hummocks of thorn and scrub, Muḥammad as usual singing, when suddenly he broke off at the end of a couplet and said: "I see a horseman riding in haste."

I looked up and saw a man galloping towards us along the top of a ridge; he was followed closely by another and yet another, and all three disappeared as they dipped down from the high ground. In the desert every newcomer is an enemy till you know him to be a friend. Muḥammad slipped a cartridge into his rifle, Ḥussein extracted his riding-stick from the barrel, where it commonly travelled, and I took a revolver out of my holster. This done, Muḥammad galloped forward to the top of a mound; I followed, and we watched together the advance of the three who were rapidly diminishing the space that lay between us. Muḥammad jumped to the ground and threw me his bridle.

"Dismount," said he, "and hold my mare."

I took the two mares in one hand and the revolver in the other. Ḥussein had lined up beside me, and we two stood perfectly still

**Amurath to Amurath*, originally published by Macmillian in 1924, was republished by Gorgias Press Reprint Series, 2002.

while Muḥammad advanced, rifle in hand, his body bent forward in an attitude of strained watchfulness. He walked slowly,
alert and cautious, like a prowling animal. The three were armed
and our thoughts ran out to a possible encounter with the Benî
Hassan, who were the blood enemies of our companion. If, when
they reached the top of the ridge in front of us, they lifted their
rifles, Ḥussein and I would have time to shoot first while they
steadied their mares. The three riders topped the ridge, and as
soon as we could see their faces Muḥammad gave the salaam;
they returned it, and with one accord we all stood at ease. For if
men give and take the salaam when they are near enough to see
each other's faces, there cannot, according to the custom of the
desert, be any danger of attack. The authors of this picturesque
episode turned out to be the three men from Raḥḥâlîyeh. One of
them had lent a rifle to the boy who had guided us and, repent-
ing of his confidence, had come after him to make sure that he
did not make off with it. We pointed out the direction in which
he had gone and turned our horses' heads once more in the direction of Shetâteh.

Beyond Shetateh, they came upon the palace of Ukhaidir, the
finest example of Sassanian architecture and the little-known
archaeological site that Gertrude had come so far to find. She
immediately occupied her time with photographing and measuring, and stayed several days and nights despite the warnings of her crew.

One night I was provided with a different entertainment. I had
worked from sunrise till dark and was too tired to sleep. The
desert was as still as death; infinitely mysterious, it stretched
away from my camp and I lay watching the empty sands as one
who watches for a pageant. Suddenly a bullet whizzed over the
tent and the crack of a rifle broke the silence. All my men jumped
up; a couple more shots rang out, and Fattûḥ hastily disposed
the muleteers round the tents and hurried off to join a band of
Arabs who had streamed from the castle gate. I picked up a
revolver and went out to see them go. In a minute or two they

had vanished under the uncertain light of the moon, which seems so clear and yet discloses so little. A zaptieh* joined me and we stood still listening. Far out in the desert the red flash of rifles cut through the white moonlight; again the quick flare and then again silence. At last through the night drifted the sound of a wild song, faint and far away, rhythmic, elemental as the night and the desert. I waited in complete uncertainty as to what was approaching, and it was not until they were close upon us that we recognized our own Arabs and Fattûḥ in their midst. They came on, still singing, with their rifles over their shoulders; their white garments gleamed under the moon; they wore no kerchiefs upon their heads, and their black hair fell in curls about their faces.

"Ma'ashî," I cried, "what happened?"

Ma'ashî shook his hair out of his eyes.

"There is nothing, my lady Khân. 'Alî saw some men lurking in the desert at the 'asr" (the hour of afternoon prayer), "and we watched after dark from the walls."

"They were raiders of the Benî Ḍafî'ah," said Ghânim, mentioning a particular lawless tribe.

"Fattûḥ," said I, "did you shoot?"

"We shot," replied Fattûḥ; "did not your Excellency hear?—and one man is wounded."

Near the end of the expedition, on the west bank of the Tigris in the Tur Abdin, they came to the village of Ba Sebrina and Gertrude encountered a meeting of *aghas*, Kurdish aristocrats and leaders.

The âghâ of Sâreh belongs to one of the leading Kurdish families of these parts. I found him in an open space near the church, entertaining friends who had ridden over from a neighbouring village. They too were âghâs of the noble house, and they were tricked out in all the finery which their birth warranted. Their short jackets were covered with embroidery, silver-mounted

* Turkish police officer.

daggers were stuck into their girdles, and upon their heads they
wore immense erections of white felt, wrapped round with a
silken handkerchief of which the ends stuck out like wings over
their foreheads. They pressed me to accept several tame par-
tridges which they kept to lure the wild birds, and while we
waited for the priest to bring the key of the church, they exhib-
ited the very curious stela which stands upside down in the
courtyard. Meantime the village priest had arrived, and I followed him unsuspiciously into the church. But I had not stood
for more than a minute inside the building than I happened to
look down on to the floor and perceived it to be black with
fleas. I made a hasty exit, tore off my stockings and plunged
them into a tank of water, which offered the safest remedy in
this emergency.

"There are," said the priest apologetically, "a great many,
but they are all swept out on Sunday morning. On Sunday there
are none."

I confess to a deep scepticism on this head.

From *Visits of Gertrude Bell to Tur Abdin*,* describing her
adventures of 1909 and 1911, she tells of one archaeological
find of an unexpected nature.

The Babylonians, and after them the Nestorians and the Moslems, held that the Ark of Noah, when the waters subsided,
grounded not upon the mountain of Ararat, but upon Jûdî
Dâgh. To that school of thought I also belong, for I have made
the pilgrimage and seen what I have seen. . . .

In the high oak woods I forgot for a few hours the stifling
heat which had weighed upon us ever since we had left Môsul.
Each morning we had promised one another a cooler air as we
neared the mountains; each evening the thermometer placed in
the shade of my tent registered from 88° to 93° Fahrenheit [31–
34°C]. The heavy air was like an enveloping garment which it
was impossible to cast off, and as I walked through the woods I

*New Sinai Press, 2007, edited by Dale A. Johnson.

was overmastered by a desire for the snow patches that lay upon the peaks—for one day of sharp mountain air and of freedom from the lowland plague of flies. Sefinet Nebî Nûh, the ship of the Prophet Noah, was there to serve as an excuse.

Accordingly we set out from camp at four o'clock on the following morning. Kas Mattai and Shim'ûn in their felt sandals, raishîkî, a proper footgear for the mountaineer, Selîm, whom Providence had marked out for the expedition, 'Abdu'l Mejîd, a zaptieh from Zâkhô, who had been ordained as pointedly to walk upon flat ground, and the donkey. "As for that donkey," said Fattûh, "if he stays two days in the camp eating grass, Selîm will not be able to remain upon his back." He was Selîm's mount, and Selîm, who knew his mind better than any other among us, was persuaded that he would enjoy the trip. The donkey therefore carried the lunch. We climbed for two hours and a half through oak woods and along the upper slopes of the hills under a precipitous crest. But this was not what I had come out to see, and as soon as I perceived a couloir in the rocks, I made straight for it and in a few moments stepped out upon an alp. There lay the snow wreaths; globularia nudicaulis carpeted the ground with blue, yellow ranunculus gilded the damp hollows, and pale-blue squills pushed up their heads between the stones and shivered in the keen wind. Selîm had followed me up the couloir.

"The hills are good," said he, gathering up a handful of snow, "but I do not think that the donkey will come up here, nor yet 'Abdu'l Mejîd."

We returned reluctantly to the path and walked on for another half-hour till Kas Mattai announced that the Ark of Noah was immediately above us. Among asphodel and forget-me-nots we left the zaptieh and the donkey; Selîm shouldered the lunch-bags, and we climbed the steep slopes for another half-hour. And so we came to Noah's Ark, which had run aground in a bed of scarlet tulips.

Gertrude's research in Tur Abdin led to her re-evaluation of the architecture of that little-known area.

Into this country I came, entirely ignorant of its architectural
wealth, because it was entirely unrecorded. None of the inscriptions collected by Pognon go back earlier than the ninth century; the plans which had been published were lamentably
insufficient and were unaccompanied by any photographs.
When I entered Mâr Yâ'kûb at Salâh and saw upon its walls
mouldings and carved string courses which bore the sign manual of the Græco-Asiatic civilization I scarcely dared to trust to
the conclusions to which they pointed. But church after church
confirmed and strengthened them. The chancel arches, covered
with an exquisite lacework of ornament, the delicate grace of
the acanthus capitals, hung with garlands and enriched with
woven entrelac, the repetition of ancient plans and the mastery
of constructive problems which revealed an old architectural
tradition, all these assure to the churches of the Tûr 'Abdîn the
recognition of their honourable place in the history of the arts.

THE LOVER

In 1907, when she was thirty-eight, and happily occupied with a life of travel and study, Gertrude met the love of her life. Unfortunately, he was a married man.

Gertrude was in her prime, a supremely civilized and able woman with a rare grasp of world history and contemporary political debate, combined with a love of beautiful clothes. The center of attention at embassies and consulates throughout the Middle East, she had become a brilliant conversationalist and a confident storyteller. A famous traveler with her latest book just published, she was working hard with Sir William Ramsay in Binbirkilise in Turkey. Their ensuing book, *The Thousand and One Churches*, would become the standard work on early Byzantine architecture in Anatolia.

With less time to write letters, she kept a diary that she sent to her parents at regular intervals.

Making Her Way to Binbirkilise
From Her Diary, May 10, 1907

. . . We dropped down into the Konia plain. Got in about 12.30. . . . I washed and changed and went off to see the Doughty-Wylies.

Gertrude was asked to lunch by Dick and Judith Doughty-Wylie when she came to Konya to pick up her mail. She was tanned and wisps of her hair, escaping from her straw hat, had turned blonde. She exuded energy, and she talked volubly. She laughed a lot and made other guests laugh with her descriptions of the absentminded professor losing track of time and his luggage, dropping papers wherever he went, while Mrs. Ramsay ran along behind him with his Panama hat and a cup of tea. On one occasion Sir William Ramsay had turned to Gertrude and asked, "Remind me, my dear, where are we?" Dick Doughty-Wylie recalled this lunch: "GB walking in, covered with energy and discovery and pleasantness." Gertrude and he had left the table to discuss the Sufi philosopher and theosophist Rumi, whose tomb is at Konya. The Doughty-Wylies met and helped her several times at Konya. She invited them to visit her one day at Rounton.

Educated at Winchester and the Royal Military College in Sandhurst, Captain, later Lieutenant Colonel, Charles Hotham Montagu Doughty-Wylie VC, CB, CMG was the same age as Gertrude. Known as "Richard" or "Dick" to his friends, he was a quiet war hero with a chestful of medals. He had been severely wounded in the Boer War and again in Tientsin during the Chinese rebellion. He was the nephew of the traveler Charles Montagu Doughty who had written the sonorous *Arabia Deserta,* one of the books that Gertrude always carried with her when she went on expeditions.

A military photograph shows Doughty-Wylie thin and mustached, tanned, taller, broader, and more handsome than many of his contemporaries. He had enjoyed many affairs but married Judith only three years before meeting Gertrude. Judith had been widowed. She was ambitious, and appreciating Dick's need for breathing space, she had motivated his transfer to diplomatic work. In 1906, he was appointed the British military vice-consul at Konya.

*Konia, May 12, 1907, Letter to Chirol**

I wish you could drop down here for a few hours that we might have a good talk, but you would find me so preposterously sunburnt that you would scarcely recognize me.

*Sir Ignatius Valentine Chirol was a distinguished British journalist and traveler, a family friend who would later become foreign editor of the *Times*

Well, to Turkey. You know there is an English v. Consul [Dick Doughty-Wylie] here now, a charming young soldier with a quite pleasant little wife. He is the more interesting of the two, a good type of Englishman, wide awake and on the spot, keen to see and learn. . . .

Konia, from Her Diary

[I] lunched with the Wylies and spent the afternoon with them in their new garden. . . . They are dears, both of them. . . . [I] talked long to Captain DW of things and people.

May 1907

It makes me laugh to think I could ever have had the idea of leaving things to the Ramsays. They had arrived at Konia entirely without tents or camping possessions. "Nevertheless," writes Captain Wylie, "Ramsay was most eager to set off to join you at once—in the wrong direction. I lent him two tents and headed him off towards you.". . . Ramsay, bless him, is perfectly helpless in such matters as concern the management of a camp; and Lady Ramsay is completely helpless in everything, but one thing, which is that she is essential to his comfort. She is as deeply as she is ignorantly sympathetic about our doings. . . .

The good Ramsays have just been begging me to let them share the expenses, but I've persuaded them to leave things as they are. I don't want their time here to cost them a penny. It's an inestimable privilege and advantage to have Sir William to work with, and indeed I could not have ventured upon anything

---

of London. Gertrude had met him as a debutante in Bucharest in 1888, where he had become a friend of the Lascelles, the aunt and uncle with whom she was staying. Sixteen years older than the twenty-year-old Oxford graduate, he was highly amused by her independent mind, and she was soon in regular correspondence with him. Gertrude would write to her "Dear Domnul" all her life, often of the sufferings and dangers she did not mention to her parents, for fear of upsetting them.

at all without him. I think I can do the whole thing within the
sum I intended to pay.

While in Konya, Fattuh fell ill. The "Wylies," as she called
them at this stage, invited her with Fattuh to leave their tents
and stay at the consulate.

From the British Vice-Consulate, July 18, 1907

I am very much afraid I shall be delayed a few days. Fattuh is ill.
He gave his head a horrible blow on a low doorway two years
ago when he was with me, and he has been ill on and off ever
since. He suffers from acute pains in the head, and I fear there
must be something wrong. I cannot leave him in this state, and
had therefore determined to take him with me to C'ple to see a
very good doctor there. . . . Yesterday the authorities here said
they had no power to allow him to go to C'ple with me. . . . I
telegraphed at once to the Grand Vizier and to the Embassy asking for a special permit for him. . . . I would do a good deal for
Fattuh, and this is not much. It's a great alleviation to be staying
with the Wylies, they are dears, both of them.

Constantinople, July 26, 1907

I arrived last night—with Fattuh! . . . I can't leave Fattuh all
alone here till I am satisfied that he is out of the wood.

At home again, Gertrude began a scrapbook in which
Doughty-Wylie's latest heroic adventure figured large. In the
volatile mood engendered by the Young Turks' nationalist
rebellion, fanatical mobs had turned on Armenian Christians,
leaving corpses scattered over the countryside around Konya.
Donning his old uniform, Doughty-Wylie had collected a
posse of Turkish troops and led them through Mersin and
Adana, pacifying the murderous crowds. Wounded by a bullet, he went on patrol again with a bandaged right arm. For

this initiative, he was decorated both by the Queen and by the Turkish authorities. Gertrude's letter of congratulation was only one of many he received, but he answered hers. A year later they were in regular correspondence. Gertrude usually addressed her letters to Dick and Judith but sometimes to him alone.

Gertrude engineered a visit from Dick to Rounton. Concealing the fact that she had invited him, she wrote to tell Florence that he would be coming.

Holyhead, April 18, 1908

Captain Doughty suggests himself for two nights on Wednesday next. It's rather a bore but I can't say anything but do come for they were so exceedingly kind to me. He is very nice.

According to her diary, the Doughty-Wylies did visit the Bells at Rounton in 1908; she added no details.

In 1909, Gertrude was exploring the banks of the Euphrates and photographing and measuring the ruined palace of Ukhaidir. A new warmth entered the correspondence between the two of them as it shuttled to and fro between Mesopotamia and Addis Ababa, where Dick was now consul. Then, in spring 1912, he arrived in London to take up the appointment of director-in-chief of the Red Cross relief organization. He was without Judith, who was visiting her mother in Wales. As always when his wife was not with him, he stayed in his old bachelor flat on Half Moon Street. Gertrude decided immediately that she had to be in London, too, to give a lecture and see her cousins, and be fitted for a lot of new summer clothes. She shot up to town and launched herself into one of the happiest times of her life.

Her large circle of vivacious cousins and wealthy friends provided her with a perfect opportunity to absorb the weary soldier into her orbit. He met through her a more lively, stimulating group of people than he had ever known. In congenial groups, Gertrude and he went to exhibitions, museums, plays, the music hall, and concerts. He went to hear her lecture, something she did with style, her humor as much as her erudition carrying the audience with her. On a walk in the park or on the way to a restaurant, they would fall behind the others, absorbed in conversation. After dinner, too, they would draw apart, talking and laughing late into the night, veiled in the smoke from her ivory holder. Seeing Gertrude in her pearls and diamonds, her beautiful hair pinned up, and wearing one of her new French gowns, her family must have seen how pretty and flirtatious she could be.

This was becoming the most important relationship in her life. The flicker and pulse of sexual attraction between them grew stronger with each meeting. That summer she turned down an invitation to go on a scientific expedition to the Karakoram mountains in China, so that she could remain in London. It was easy, for a while, to forget the existence of Judith.

95 Sloane Street, London, February 6, 1913, Letter to Chirol

I must tell you I have given up the Central Asian plan, and written to tell Filippi*. The nearer I came to it, the more I could not bear it. I can't face being away from home for fourteen months. My life now in England is so delightful that I will not take such a long time out of it.

Judith was expected, and in due course she arrived in London. Gertrude left for Rounton and threw herself into gardening and studying, doing anything and everything to pass the time. The highlight of every day was the arrival of the post that might, and frequently did, bring letters from Dick.

There were few moments in Gertrude's life when she did not tell her parents the whole truth; if she hid something from

---

*Cavaliere Filippo de Filippi, author of many publications in Italian, English, and German, had invited Gertrude to join him in this scientific expedition to the Karakoram in 1913–14. In 1928, he became general secretary of the International Geographical Union.

them, it was always to shield them from anxiety. This time it was different. She knew that an affair with a married man would be completely unacceptable to them and to society in general. She began a chapter of duplicity by deciding to ask the Doughty-Wylies to Rounton at a time when she knew perfectly well that Judith was away. He would be just one of the crowd at a Rounton weekend house party. She did not intend to start a sexual relationship with him, just to continue the mutual delight of his attractive and attracted presence. She had her own sense of honor, one so inviolable that it would compromise the affair at every stage.

Florence, if she suspected anything, may have reflected that Gertrude at forty-four was not of an age when she could be told how to behave. So Dick came to Rounton for a few days in July 1913. After the day's excursion, the gallop across the fields, the noisy, cheerful dinner followed by card games, guests drifted upstairs in ones and twos while Gertrude and Dick sat by the fire, looking at each other. She must have let him know, obliquely, where her room was, because subsequent letters refer to their being together there, on the bed, and to a deeply intimate conversation they had. It is also clear that their night together went no farther—that at the final moment she pulled away. He left, pursued by her letters full of an agonized regret.

How did Gertrude remain a virgin so long? Twenty-three years had passed since her presentation at court when she was twenty-one, and twenty-one since her failed engagement to the legation secretary Henry Cadogan. With her green eyes, long auburn hair, and beautiful clothes, Gertrude was an attractive, feminine, confident, humorous, and energetic woman, but she had failed to find a man who interested her. Her character was too decided, her mind too sharp, and her critical sense too finely tuned to mix easily with less-developed personalities and intellects. She failed to hide a felt superiority to men who could not measure up to her father, and she was too much of a bluestocking for most of society. When Florence reprimanded her for traveling in a hansom cab alone with a "Captain X" in the year she came out, she wrote back that

Florence need not worry. "I discussed religious beliefs all the way there and very metaphysical conceptions of truth all the way back," and added disarmingly, "I felt sure you wouldn't like it, but you know, I didn't either!"

At an age when hopes of meeting a man she could love with all her heart had become unrealistic, she had found exactly the kind of man she had always been looking for. Dick was a man who would not be frightened by her intellect, a man with accomplishments the equal of hers. He was a brave soldier who could fight and hunt and quote poetry, who had read the great books of civilization, spoke foreign languages, who appreciated the theater and the National Gallery, who was equally at home in London and in foreign society, who was well traveled and knew the distinguished politicians and statesmen she knew herself. She had set her heart on a hero—and why not? She was, after all, a heroine.

His thank-you letter for the weekend at Rounton was deeply unsatisfactory to Gertrude, revealing that what had been a momentous weekend for her had been far less important to him. From London he thanked her for her letters but failed, as usual, to address her questions: "Wonderful letters, my dear, which delight me. Bless you. But there can be no words to answer you with. Well—let's talk about other things. . . ."

Dick, in his fond but confusing letters, never gave the slightest indication that he would leave his wife. It was only in letters to her dearest friend Chirol that Gertrude revealed the pain she was in. She knew there was no future for this relationship. She had hidden so long behind her lines of defense that she was caught unawares by his hold on her.

Sloane Street, London, October 30, 1913, Letter to Chirol

You know I am the more fortunate of two unfortunate people because I have had the opportunity to gather such delightful friends about me. But that only warms my heart more to the other unfortunate person, you understand.

Then came the hammer blow. He had accepted a post in
Albania, with the International Boundary Commission. "My
wife is in Wales. She'll come up when I wire to her and go with
me—till we see the hows and whys and wheres . . . I have
turned in to my old bachelor quarters in Half Moon Street, no.
29. Write to me there . . . while I am alone, let's be alone." He
signed the letter "Dick" for the first time. Then, a warning:
"Judith knowing you well and having always before seen your
letters would find it very odd to be suddenly debarred them and
on voyages our lives are at close quarters. . . . Of course call me
Dick in letters, and I shall call you Gertrude—there is nothing
in that . . . tonight I shall destroy your letters—I hate it—but it
is right—one might die or something, and they are not for any
soul but me. . . . If I can't write to you, I shall always think of
you telling me things in your room at Rounton . . . the subtle
book eludes, but our hands met on the cover." "The subtle book,"
she knew, was his metaphor for sex.

With the courage that characterized her entire life, she
accepted that she had broken the rules and that the rules were
on the side of the marriage vow. Gertrude had reached the cross-
roads of her life. She searched for escape and found it, as
always, in the desert. She decided that she would depart on a
long, hard expedition. He would have to focus on her and be
aware of the dangers she ran. She left six weeks after his own
departure followed by his letter—". . . you very clever and
charming person—and you in your desert." She resolved that
if she could not write him private letters, she would keep a
diary just for him. It would be the account of the adventures
and dangers she intended to search out, and she would send it
to him later, when she could do so.

Damascus, December 11, 1913, Letter to Chirol

I shall be glad to go. I want to cut all links with the world, and
that is the best and wisest thing to do. *The road and the dawn,
the sun, the wind and the rain, the camp fire under the stars,*

and sleep, and the road again—we'll see what they can do. If they don't cure, then I know of nothing that can. . . . Oh, Domnul, if you knew the way I have paced backwards and forwards along the floor of hell for the last few months, you would think me right to try for any way out. I don't know that it is an ultimate way out, but it's worth trying. As I have told you before, it is mostly my fault, but that does not prevent it from being an irretrievable misfortune—for both of us. But I am turning away from it now, and time deadens even the keenest things.

THE PRISONER

On the eve of his departure to Albania, Gertrude wrote to Doughty-Wylie of her plans to undertake an epic journey in one of the most dangerous parts of the desert. Dick was as worried as she could wish. He wrote back, "I am nervous about you . . . south of Maan and from there to Hayil is surely a colossal trek. For your palaces your road your Baghdad your Persia I do not feel so nervous—but Hayil from Maan—Inshallah!"*

Her destination would be Hayyil, the almost mythical city described by Charles M. Doughty, Dick's uncle, in his famous *Arabia Deserta,* the book that had accompanied her on all expeditions. She proposed to travel sixteen hundred miles by camel, taking a circular route south from Damascus to central Arabia, then east across the interior and the shifting sands of the Nefud, becoming the first Westerner to cross that angle of the desert. She would make her way to the Misma Mountains, a coal-black landscape with flint pinnacles as high as ten-story buildings. She would then descend into the plateau of granite and basalt at the heart of which the snow-white medieval city of Hayyil floated like a mirage. Her return journey would be north to Baghdad and west across the vast Syrian Desert, back to Damascus. Much of the journey would be through unmapped territory and areas where her caravan was likely to come under tribal attack.

It was as daunting a prospect politically as geographically. Britain was supplying arms and money to the chieftain Ibn Saud, allied to the puritan Wahhabi sect of Islam. The Ottoman

*God willing.

government supported the opposing dynasty of Ibn Rashid of
the Shammar federation, perhaps the cruelest, most violent
tribe of Arabia, centered on Hayyil. The trip would allow her
to provide the Foreign Office with detailed new information at
a critical moment, with both sides poised to strike to take control of the Arabian Peninsula.

She had already warned the British government that Ibn
Saud was better as a friend than as an enemy. She set out with
the ultimate intention of reaching Ibn Saud and making con-
tact with him in his stronghold of Riyadh.

Among the distinguished men who warned her against the
journey were Sir Louis Mallet, future ambassador to Constantinople; her old friend David Hogarth; and the Indian government's resident in the Persian Gulf, Lieutenant Colonel Percy
Cox, a name that would come to mean much to her later. Defiantly, Gertrude decided that she would go nevertheless.

Her first weeks in Damascus were taken up with organizing
the most elaborate caravan she had ever undertaken, hiring her
crew, buying gifts for sheikhs in the bazaars, and choosing
seventeen camels. She wired her father for an extra £400
($55,000 RPI adjusted), a not inconsiderable sum. She also vis-
ited the Rashid's sinister agent in the city, to whom she paid
£200 ($27,500), getting in return a promissory note that she
intended to cash in Hayyil to fund her return journey.

She had started keeping parallel diary entries. The first
would be a cursory memorandum written daily while the
memory was fresh. Reading these factual, ill-organized jot-
tings, full of Arabic words and phrases, gives a vivid picture of
Gertrude, tired and dirty after a day's march, her hair falling
out of its pins, scribbling away at her folding desk while Fattuh put up her bedroom tent, unpacked, and arranged her possessions. These notes contained positions of water holes and
Turkish barracks, routes through unmapped areas and other
information that she would pass on to the Foreign Office.
They were also the raw material for her upbeat letters home.

The second diary, with entries written a few days apart, was
a thoughtful and polished account of her journey and feelings,
kept solely for Dick—with the proviso that his wife might read

them—and portraying her as a shade less robust in her attitude to dangers and setbacks. She bundled up these diary entries and sent them to Dick when she arrived at an outpost or town big enough to have a post office. As she now had to avoid the Turkish soldiers who were looking out for her, she often had to carry her papers with her for weeks until she could send them.

She traveled on through all kinds of danger and difficulty but once again fell under the spell of the desert, terrifying and beautiful, with its roaring silence and jeweled nights.

The caravan left Damascus on December 16, 1913. The journey was marred by torrential rain and bitter winds. Not a week later came a tribal attack in which shots were fired, and they were nearly robbed of all their rifles and possessions. Not long afterward, her camp was invaded by Turkish soldiers who demanded permits she did not have. They arrested her faithful servant, Fattuh, and her guide, Muhammad al-Ma'rawi. She managed to persuade the local governor, the qaimaqam, to get them released but was ordered to telegraph for permits to travel before the caravan could leave. Unfortunately, the British ambassador in Constantinople, Sir Louis Mallet, was the very man who had warned her against making the journey. He told her that His Majesty's Government would disclaim all responsibility for her if she went farther. It was no more than she had expected, and she wrote in her diary that night: "Decided to run away." Before she left she was obliged to write a letter absolving the Turks from responsibility for her welfare.

———

The following extracts are taken from Gertrude's diary, which was written expressly for Dick. Since he spoke Arabic, Gertrude did not bother to translate every word.

January 16, 1914

I have cut the thread. . . . Louis Mallet has informed me that if I go on towards Nejd my own government washes its hands of

me, and I have given a categorical acquittal to the Ottoman
Government, saying that I go on at my own risk. . . . We turn
towards Nejd, *inshallah,* renounced by all the powers that be,
and the only thread which is not cut though is that which runs
through this little book, which is the diary of my way kept
for you.

I am an outlaw!

February 11, 1914

Yesterday . . . we began to see landmarks; but the country through
which we rode was very barren. In the afternoon we came to a
big valley, the Wadi Niyyal, with good herbage for the camels
and there we camped. And just at sunset the full moon rose in
glory and we had the two fold splendour of heaven to comfort
us for the niggardliness of the earth. She was indeed niggardly
this morning. We rode for 4 hours over a barren pebbly flat entirely devoid of all herbage. They call such regions *jellad.* In
front of us were the first great sand hills of the Nefud [al-Nafud].
And turning a little to the west we came down into a wide bleak
*khabra** wherein we found water pools under low heaps of
sand. The place looked so unpromising that I was prepared to
find the water exhausted which would have meant a further
westerly march to a well some hours away and far from our true
road. We watered our camels and filled the water skins in half
an hour and turned east into the Nefud. We have come so far
south (the *khabra* was but a day's journey from Taimah) in
order to avoid the wild sand mountains (*tu'us* they are called
in Arabic) of the heart of the Nefud and our way lies now within
its southern border. This great region of sand is not desert. It is
full of herbage of every kind, at this time of year springing into
green, a paradise for the tribes that camp in it and for our own
camels. We marched through it for an hour or two and camped
in deep pale gold sand with abundance of pasturage all about
us, through the beneficence of God. We carry water for 3 days

*Camping place.

and then drink at the wells of Haizan [Bir Hayzan]. The *Amir*, it seems is not at Hayyil, but camping to the north with his camel herds. I fear this may be tiresome for me; I would rather have dealt with him than with his *wakil*.* Also report says that he informed all men of my coming but whether to forward me or to stop me I do not know. Neither do I know whether the report is true.

February 13, 1914

We have marched for 2 days in the Nefud, and are still camping within its sands. It is very slow going, up and down in deep soft sand, but I have liked it; the plants are interesting and the sand hills are interesting. The wind driving through it hollows out profound cavities, *ga'r* they are called. You come suddenly to the brink and look down over an almost precipitous wall of sand. And from time to time there rises over the *ga'r* a head of pale driven sand, crested like a snow ridge and devoid of vegetation. These are the *tu'us*. At midday yesterday we came to a very high *ta's* up which I struggled—it is no small labour—and saw from the top the first of the Nejd mountains, Irnan, and to the W. the hills above Taimah and all round me a wilderness of sandbanks and *ti'as*. When I came down I learnt that one of my camels had been seized with a malady and had sat down some 10 minutes away. Muhammad and the negro boy, Fellah, and I went back to see what could be done for her but when we reached her we found her in the death throes. "She is gone" said Muhammad. "Shall we sacrifice her?" "It were best" said I. He drew his knife out, *"Bismillah allaha akbar!"* and cut her throat. . . .

We have a wonderfully peaceful camp tonight in a great horseshoe of sand, with steep banks enclosing us. It is cloudy and mild—last night it froze like the devil—and I feel as if I had been born and bred in the Nefud and had known no other world. Is there any other?

*The prince's representative.

February 15, 1914

We came yesterday to a well, one of the rare wells on the edge of the Nefud, and I rode down to see the watering. Haizan is a profound depression surrounded by steep sand hills and the well itself is very deep—our well rope was 48 paces long. They say it is a work of the . . . first forefathers, and certainly no Beduin of today would cut down into the rock and build the dry walling of the upper parts—but who can tell how old it is? There are no certain traces of age, only sand and the deep well hole. We found a number of Arabs watering their camels, the 'Anazeh clan of the Awaji who were camped near us. The men worked half naked with the passionate energy which the Arabs will put into their job for an hour or two—no more. I watched and photographed and they left me unmolested, though none had seen a European of any kind before. One or two protested at first against the photography, but the Shammar with me reassured them and I went on in peace. We go two days more through the Nefud because it is said to be the safest road and I am filled with a desire not to be stopped now, so near Hayyil. My bearings are onto Jebel Misma, which is but a few day's journey from Ibn al Rashid. I want to bring this adventure to a prosperous conclusion since we have come so far *salinum*—in the security of God.

February 16, 1914

I am suffering from a severe fit of depression today—will it be any good if I put it into words, or shall I be more depressed than ever afterwards? It springs, the depression, from a profound doubt as to whether the adventure is after all worth the candle. Not because of the danger—I don't mind that; but I am beginning to wonder what profit I shall get out of it all. A compass traverse over country which was more or less known, a few names added to the map—names of stony mountains and barren plains and of a couple of deep desert wells (for we have been watering at another today)—and probably that is all. I don't know what *tete* [offer] the Rashid people will make to me when I arrive, and even if they were inspired by the best will in the world, I doubt whether they could do more than give me a free passage to Baghdad, for their power is not so great nowadays as it once was. And the road to Baghdad has been travelled many times before. It is nothing, the journey to Nejd, so far as any real advantage goes, or any real addition to knowledge, but I am beginning to see pretty clearly that it is all that I can do. There are two ways of profitable travel in Arabia. One is the *Arabia Deserta* way, to live with the people and to live like them for months and years. You can learn something thereby, as he [Charles Doughty] did; though you may not be able to tell it again as he could. It's clear I can't take that way; the fact of being a woman bars me from it. And the other is Leachman's* way—to ride swiftly through the country with your compass in your hand, for the map's sake and for nothing else. And there is some profit in that too. I might be able to do that over a limited space of time, but I am not sure. Anyway it is not what I am doing now. The net result is that I think I should be more usefully employed in more civilized countries where I know what to look for and how to record it. Here, if there is anything to record the probability is that you can't find it or reach it, because a hostile tribe bars your way, or the road is waterless, or something of that kind, and that which has chanced to lie upon my path for the last 10 days is not worth mentioning—two wells, as I said before, and really I can think of nothing else. So you see the cause of my depression. I fear when I come to the end I shall not look back and say: That was worth doing; but more likely when I look back I shall say: It was a waste of time. . . . That's my thought tonight, and I fear it is perilously near the truth. I almost wish that something would happen—something exciting, a raid, or a battle! And yet that's not my job either. What do ineffective archaeologists want with battles? They would only serve to pass the time and leave as little profit as before. There is such a long way between me and letters, or between me and anything and I don't feel at all like the daughter of kings, which I am supposed here to be. It's a bore being a woman when you are in Arabia.

*Gerald Leachman, an officer famed in the desert for bravery and ill-temper, was murdered in Iraq in 1920. Gertrude Bell disapproved of him.

February 17, 1914

We were held up today by rain. It began, most annoyingly, just
after we had struck camp—at least I don't know that it was so
very annoying, for we put in a couple of hours' march. But the
custom of the country was too strong for me. You do not march
in the rain. It was, I must admit, torrential. It came sweeping
upon us from behind and passing on blotted out the landscape
in front, till my *rafiq* said that he should lose his way, there were
no landmarks to be seen. "No Arabs move camp today" said
he "they fear to be lost in the Nefud." And as he trudged on
through the wet sand, his cotton clothes clinging to his drenched
body, he rejoiced and gave thanks for the rain. "Please God it
goes over all the world" he said and "The camels will pasture
here for 3 months time." The clouds lifted a little but when a
second flood overtook us I gave way. We pitched the men's tent
and lighted a great fire at which we dried ourselves—I was wet
too. In a moment's sunshine we pitched the other tents, and then
came thunder and hail and rain so heavy that the pools stood
twinkling in the thirsty sand. I sat in my tent and read *Hamlet*
from beginning to end and, as I read, the world swung back into
focus. Princes and powers of Arabia stepped down into their
true place and there rose up above them the human soul conscious and answerable to itself, made with such large discourse,
looking before and after—. Before sunset I stood on the top of
the sand hills and saw the wings of the rain sweeping round
'Irnan and leaving Misma' light-bathed—Then the hurrying
clouds marched over the sand and once more we were wrapped
in rain. No fear now of drought ahead of us.

February 20, 1914

God is merciful and we have done with the Nefud. The day after
the rain—oh but the wet sand smelt good and there was a twit-
tering of small birds to gladden the heart!—we came in the
afternoon to some tents of the Shammar and pitching our camp

not far off we were visited by the old shaikh, Mhailam, who brought us a goat and some butter. Him we induced to come with us as *rafiq*. He is old and lean, gray haired and toothless, and ragged beyond belief; he has not even an *'agal* to bind the kerchief on his head and we have given him a piece of rope. But he is an excellent *rafiq*—I have not had a better. He knows the country and he is anxious to serve us well. And next day we rode over sand to the northern point of Jebel Misma'. Then Mhailam importuned me to camp saying there was no pasturage in the *jellad*, the flat plain below; and Muhammad al-Ma'rawi backed him for he feared that we might fall in with Hetaim raiders if we left the Nefud. But I held firm. Raiders and hunger were as nothing to the possibility of a hard straight road. For you understand that travelling in the Nefud is like travelling in the Labyrinth. You are forever skirting round a deep horseshoe pit of sand, perhaps half a mile wide, and climbing up the opposite slope, and skirting round the next horseshoe. If we made a mile an hour as the crow flies we did well. Even after I had delivered the ultimatum, my two old parties were constantly heading off to the Nefud and I had to keep a watchful eye on them and herd them back every half hour. It was bitter cold; the temperature had fallen to 27° [-2.8°C] in the night and there was a tempestuous north wind. And so we came to the last sand crest and I looked down between the black rocks of Misma' and saw Nejd. It was a landscape terrifying in its desolation. Misma' drops to the east in precipices of sandstone, weathered to a rusty black; at its feet are gathered endless companies of sandstone pinnacles, black too, shouldering one over the other. They look like the skeleton of a vast city planted on a sandstone and sand-strewn floor. And beyond and beyond more pallid lifeless plain and more great crags of sandstone mountains rising abruptly out of it. Over it all the bitter wind whipped the cloud shadows. "*Subhan Allah!*" said one of my Damascenes, "we have come to Jehannum."* Down into it we went and camped on the skirts of the Nefud with a sufficiency of pasturage. And today

*Quote means: "How great is God! We have come to hell."

the sun shone and the world smiled and we marched off gaily and found the floor of Hell to be a very pleasant place after all. For the rain has filled all the sandstone hollows with clear water, and the pasturage is abundant, and the going, over the flat rocky floor, is all the heart could desire. In the afternoon we passed between the rocks of Jebel Habran, marching over a sandy floor with black pinnacled precipices on either hand, and camped on the east, in a bay of rock with *khabras* of rain water below and pasturage all round us in the sand. We have for neighbours about a mile away a small *ferij* of Shammar tents, and lest there should be anyone so evil minded as to dream of stealing a camel from us, Mhailam has just now stepped out into the night and shouted: "Ho! Anyone who watches! come in to supper! . . . Let anyone who is hungry come and eat!" And having thus invited the universe to our bowl, we sleep, I trust, in peace.

February 24, 1914

We are within sight of Hayyil and I might have ridden in today but I thought it better to announce my auspicious coming! So I sent in two men early this morning. Muhammad and 'Ali, and have myself camped a couple of hours outside. We had . . . a most delicious camp in the top of a mountain, Jebel Rakham. I climbed the rocks and found flowers in the crevices—not a great bounty, but in this barren land a feast to the eyes. . . . Yesterday we passed by two more villages and in one there were plum trees flowering—oh the gracious sight! And today we have come through the wild granite crags of Jebel 'Ajja and are camped in the Hayyil plain. From a little rock above my tent I have spied out the land and seen the towers and gardens of Hayyil, and Swaifly lying in the plain beyond, and all is made memorable by *Arabia Deserta*. I feel as if I were on a sort of pilgrimage, visiting sacred sites. And the more I see of this land the more I realize what an achievement that journey was. But isn't it amazing that we should have walked down into Nejd with as much ease as if we had been strolling along Piccadilly!

March 2, 1914

What did I tell you as to the quality most needed for travel among the Arabs? Patience if you remember; that is what one needs. Now listen to the tale of the week we have spent here. I was received with the utmost courtesy. Their slaves, 'abds, slave is too servile and yet that is what they are—came riding out to meet me and assured me that Ibrahim, the *Amir's wakil* was much gratified by my visit. We rode round the walls of the town and entered in by the south gate—the walls are of quite recent construction, towered, all round the town—and there, just within the gate I was lodged in a spacious house which Muham-mad ibn Rashid had built for his summer dwelling. My tents were pitched in the wide court below. Within our enclosure there is an immense area of what was once gardens and corn-fields but it is now left unwatered and uncultivated. The Persian Hajj* used to lodge here in the old days. As soon as I was estab-lished in the *Roshan,* the great columned reception room, and when the men had all gone off to see to the tents and camels, two women appeared. One was an old widow, Lu.lu.ah, who is caretaker in the house; she lives here with her slave woman and the latter's boy. The other was a merry lady, Turkiyyeh, a Cir-cassian who had belonged to Muhammed al Rashid and had been a great favourite of his. She had been sent down from the *qasr†* to receive me and amuse me and the latter duty she was most successful in performing. In the afternoon came Ibrahim,‡ in state and all smiles. He is an intelligent and well educated man—for Arabia—with a quick nervous manner and a restless eye. He stayed till the afternoon prayer. As he went out he told Muhammad al-Ma'rawi that there was some discontent among the *'ulema*§ at my coming and that etc etc in short, I was not to

*The Muslim pilgrimage to Mecca, or a man who has participated in it.

†Palace.

‡Deputy to the absent emir.

§The Muslim religious scholars.

come further into the town till I was invited. Next day I sent my
camels back to the Nefud borders to pasture. There is no pasture here in the granite grit plain of Hayyil and moreover they
badly needed rest. I sold 6, for more than they were worth, for
they were in wretched condition; but camels are fortunately
dear here at this moment, with the *Amir* away and all available
animals with him. And that done I sat still and waited on events.
But there were no events. Nothing whatever happened, except
that two little Rashid princes came to see me, 2 of the 6 male
descendants who are all that remain of all the Rashid stock, so
relentlessly have they slaughtered one another. Next day I sent
to Ibrahim and said I should like to return his call. He invited
me to come after dark and sent a mare for me and a couple of
slaves. I rode through the dark and empty streets and was
received in the big *Roshan* of the *qasr*, a very splendid place with
great stone columns supporting an immensely lofty roof, the
walls white washed, the floor of white juss, beaten hard and
shining as if it were polished. There was a large company. We
sat all round the wall on carpets and cushions, I on Ibrahim's
right hand, and talked mostly of the history of the Shammar in
general and of the Rashids in particular. Ibrahim is well versed
in it and I was much interested. As we talked slave boys served
us with tea and then coffee and finally they brought lighted cen-
sors and swung the sweet smelling *'ud** before each of us three
times. This is the signal that the reception is over and I rose and
left them. And then followed day after weary day with nothing
whatever to do. One day Ibrahim sent me a mare and I rode
round the town and visited one of his gardens—a paradise of
blossoming fruit trees in the bare wilderness. And the Circassian, Turkiyyeh, has spent another day with me; and my own
slaves (for I have 2 of my own to keep my gate for me) sit and tell
me tales of raid and foray in the stirring days of 'Abd al Aziz,
Muhammad's nephew; and my men come in and tell me the gossip of the town. Finally I have sent for my camels—I should have
done so days ago if they had not been so much in need of rest. I
can give them no more time to recover for I am penniless. I

*Agar wood incense.

brought with me a letter of credit on the Rashid's from their agent in Damascus—Ibrahim refuses to honour it in the absence of the *Amir* and if I had not sold some of my camels I should not have had enough money to get away. As it is I have only the barest minimum. The gossip is that the hand which has pulled the strings in all this business is that of the *Amir*'s grandmother, Fatima, of whom Ibrahim stands in deadly fear. In Hayyil murder is like the spilling of milk and not one of the shaikhs but feels his head sitting unsteadily upon his shoulders. I have asked to be allowed to see Fatima and have received no answer. She holds the purse strings in the *Amir*'s absence and she rules. It may be that she is at the bottom of it all. I will not conceal from you that there have been hours of considerable anxiety. War is all round us. The *Amir* is raiding Jof to the north and Ibn Sa'ud is gathering up his powers to the south—presumably to raid the *Amir*. If Ibrahim chose to stop my departure till the *Amir*'s return (which is what I feared) it would have been very uncomfortable. I spent a long night contriving in my head schemes of escape if things went wrong. I have however two powerful friends in Hayyil, shaikhs of 'Anezah, with whose help the Rashids hope to recapture that town [Jof]. I have not seen them—they dare not visit me—but they have protested vigorously against the treatment which has been accorded me. I owe their assistance to the fact that I have their nephew with me, 'Ali the postman who came with me 3 years ago across the Hamad.

Yesterday I demanded a private audience of Ibrahim and was received, again at night, in an upper hall of the *qasr*. I told him that I would stay here no longer, that the withholding of the money due to me had caused me great inconvenience and that I must now ask of him a *rafiq* to go with me to the 'Anazeh borders. He was very civil and assured me that the *rafiq* was ready. It does not look as if they intended to put any difficulties in my way. My plan is to choose out the best of my camels and taking with me Fattuh, 'Ali and the negro boy Fellah, to ride to Nejef [al-Najaf]. The Damascenes I send back to Damascus. They will wait a few days more to give the other camels longer rest and then join a caravan which is going to Medina [al-Madinah]—10 days' journey. Thence by train. Since I have no money I can do nothing but push on to Baghdad, but it is at least consoling to think that I could not this year have done more. I could not have gone south from here; the tribes are up and the road is barred. Ibn Sa'ud has—so we hear—taken the Hasa,* and driven out the Turkish troops. I think it highly probable that he intends to turn against Hayyil and if by any chance the *Amir* should not be successful in his raid on [Jof], the future of the Shammar would look dark indeed. The Turkish Govt. are sending them arms . . . but I think that Ibn Saud's star is in the ascendant and if he combines with Ibn Sha'lan (the Ruwalla 'Anazeh) they will have Ibn Rashid between the hammer and the anvil. I feel as if I had lived through a chapter of the *Arabian Nights* during this last week. The Circassian woman and the slaves, the doubt and the anxiety, Fatima weaving her plots behind the *qasr* walls, Ibrahim with his smiling lips and restless shifting eyes—and the whole town waiting to hear the fate of the army which has gone up with the *Amir* against Jof. And to the spiritual sense the place smells of blood. Twice since Khalil was here have the Rashids put one another to the sword—the tales round my camp fire are all of murder and the air whispers murder. It gets upon your nerves when you sit day after day between high mud walls and I thank heaven that my nerves are not very responsive. They have kept me awake only one night out of seven! And good, please God! please God nothing but good.

March 6, 1914

We have at last reached the end of the comedy—for a comedy it has after all proved to be. And what has been the underlying reason of it all I cannot tell, for who can look into their dark minds? On March 3 there appeared in the morning a certain eunuch slave Sa'id, who is a person of great importance and with him another, and informed me that I could not travel,

*A strip of eastern Arabia adjacent to the Persian Gulf.

neither could they give me any money, until a messenger had arrived from the *Amir*. I sent messages at once to 'Ali's uncles and the negotiations were taken up again with renewed vigour. Next day came word from the *Amir*'s mother, Mudi, inviting me to visit them that evening. I went (riding solemnly through the silent moonlit streets of this strange place), and passed two hours taken straight from the *Arabian Nights* with the women of the palace. I imagine that there are few places left wherein you can see the unadulterated East in its habit as it has lived for centuries and centuries—of those few Hayyil is one. There they were, those women—wrapped in Indian brocades, hung with jewels, served by slaves and there was not one single thing about them which betrayed the base existence of Europe or Europeans—except me! I was the blot. Some of the women of the shaikhly house were very beautiful. They pass from hand to hand—the victor takes them, with her power and the glory, and think of it! his hands are red with the blood of their husband and children. Mudi herself—she is still a young woman and very charming—has been the wife of 3 *Amirs* in turn. Well, some day I will tell you what it is all like, but truly I still feel bewildered by it. I passed the next day in solitary confinement— I have been a prisoner, you understand, in the big house they gave me. Today came an invitation from two boys, cousins of the *Amir*'s to visit them in their garden. I went after the midday prayers and stayed till the *'asr*. Again it was fantastically oriental and medieval. There were 5 very small children, all cousins, dressed in long gold embroidered robes, solemn and silent, staring at me with their painted eyes. And my hosts, who may have been 13 or 14 years old—one had a merry face like a real boy, the other was grave and impassive. But both were most hospitable. We sat in a garden house on carpets—like the drawings in Persian picture books. Slaves and eunuchs served us with tea and coffee and fruits. Then we walked about the garden, the boys carefully telling me the names of all the trees. And then we sat again and drank more tea and coffee. Sa'id the eunuch was of the party and again I expressed my desire to depart from Hayyil and again was met by the same negative—Not till the

Amir's messenger has come. Not I nor anyone knows when the
messenger will come, neither did I know whether there were
more behind their answer. Sa'id came to us after the *'asr* and I
spoke to him with much vigour and ended the interview abruptly
by rising and leaving him. I thought indeed that I had been too
abrupt, but to tell you the truth I was bothered. An hour later
came in my camels and after dark Sa'id again with a bag of gold
and full permission to go where I liked and when I liked. And
why they have now given way, or why they did not give way
before, I cannot guess. But anyhow I am free and my heart is at
rest—it is widened.

March 17, 1914

I have not written any of my tale for these ten days, because of
the deadly fatigue of the way. But today, as I will tell you, I have
had a short day and I will profit by it. I did not leave Hayyil till
March 8. I asked and obtained leave to see the town and the
qasr by daylight—which I had never been allowed to do—and
to photograph. They gave me full permission to photograph—to
my surprise and pleasure, and I went out next day, was shown the
*modif** and the great kitchen of the *qasr* and took many pictures. Every one was smiling and affable—and I thought all the
time of Khalil, coming in there for his coffee and his pittance
of *taman*. It is extraordinarily picturesque and I make no doubt
that it preserves the aspect of every Arabian palace that has ever
been since the Days of Ignorance. Some day, *inshallah*, you shall
see my pictures. Then I photographed the *meshab* and the outside of the mosque and as I went through the streets I photographed them too. As I was going home there came a message
from my Circassian friend, Turkiyyeh, inviting me to tea at her
house. I went, and photographed Hayyil from her roof and took
an affectionate farewell of her. She and I are now, I imagine,
parted for ever, except in remembrance. As I walked home all
the people crowded out to see me, but they seemed to take noth-

*Reception room.

ing but a benevolent interest in my doings. And finally the halt, the maim and the blind gathered round my door and I flung out a bag of copper coins among them.

And thus it was that my strange visit to Hayyil ended, after 11 days' imprisonment, in a sort of apotheosis!

THE WAR WORKER

Baghdad, April 5, 1914, Letter to Chirol

. . . I should perhaps come back via Athens. I don't mind much either way, indeed I am profoundly indifferent. But I don't care to be in London much, and if there is no reason for hurrying, I shall not hurry. . . .

You will find me a savage, for I have seen and heard strange things, and they colour the mind. You must try to civilise me a little, beloved Domnul. I think I am not altered for you, and I know that you will bear with me. But whether I can bear with England—come back to the same things and do them all over again—that is what I sometimes wonder. But they will not be quite the same, since I come back to them with a mind permanently altered. I have gained much, and I will not forget it. This letter is only for you—don't hand it on to anyone, or tell anyone that the me they knew will not come back in the me that returns. Perhaps they will not find out.

Gertrude arrived back at Baghdad, mailed her diary for Dick Doughty-Wylie to Addis Ababa, and trekked wearily back across the Syrian Desert to Damascus. She had to have a period of convalescence with friends there before setting off again for London, arriving in a state of total depression. She would be awarded the Royal Geographical Society's Gold Medal for this journey, but nevertheless she considered that her expedition had been a failure. It had proved to be an impossible proposition to get to Riyadh and Ibn Saud. Doughty-Wylie was no nearer, and she didn't know when they would meet again. Her future seemed bleak and hopeless.

March 26, 1914, to Doughty-Wylie

[It] always leaves one with a feeling of disillusion. . . . I try to school myself beforehand by reminding myself of how I have looked forward . . . to the end, and when it came have found it—just nothing. Dust and ashes in one's hand.

In London, Dick had intended to bring the relationship with Gertrude to a close, but before he had been a month in Albania he was again writing to her every few days. Strangely, the months apart brought them closer than ever. Her letters to him had always been love letters, but now his to her became love letters too.

Finding himself in Addis Ababa without Judith, after a few months deprived of female company and perhaps drinking too much in the evening, Dick wrote Gertrude more passionate letters than ever before. Gertrude wrote love letters back, free from fear that what she said would fall into Judith's hands. The emotional tie between them was strengthening. "What wouldn't I give to have you sitting opposite in this all-alone house," he wrote, and finally came the words she had waited so long to hear: "You said you wanted to hear me say I loved you, you wanted it plain to eyes and ears . . . I love you—does it do any good out there in the desert? . . . Love like this is life itself."

Things were not going well between the Doughty-Wylies at New Year, when he wrote of "my wife's disappointment and of my relations too that I have not acquired more letters after my name" and wrote of "regret for things lost . . . and the dear love of you, all lost."

Gertrude was at Rounton when war was declared on August 4, 1914. She went out into the countryside, climbing on carts to urge the laborers and the men in the mines to do what she would have done had she been a man—join the army.

Country by country, most of the world slipped into war. A single shot in a remote European capital precipitated the mobilization of 65 million men and women, and would cause 38 million casualties. For the moment, all Gertrude could do was join the influx of well-born ladies into the workplace and take a genteel clerking job in a hospital at Lord Onslow's Clandon Park in Surrey, one of the many grand houses now occupied by the wounded. Rounton would soon follow and become a home for twenty Belgian convalescents. One weekend she called on friends, the St. Loe Stracheys, whose house was also a convalescent home.

Clandon Park, Surrey, November 17, 1914

One of their first [convalescents] was a coal black negro from the Congo. He succeeded in secreting a huge knife in his bed with him. His opening remark was: "*En Afrique pas de prisonniers.*" He drew his finger significantly across his throat and added: "*Mange.*". . . St. Loe observed mildly: "It is a curiously unexpected result of the war to have one's best bedroom occupied by a cannibal."

November 1914

I have asked some of my friends at the Red X to join me in the first suitable job abroad that falls vacant. . . . Arabia can wait.

After only three weeks at Clandon, she was asked to report to the new Red Cross office for Wounded and Missing Enquiries, situated in Boulogne. Given three days to get to France, Gertrude scribbled a message to her maid, Marie Delaire, at Rounton, demanding underclothes, watches, jackets, and her riding boots to cope with the mud.

The job of the Wounded and Missing Enquiry Department (the W&MED) was to try to answer the questions of families whose men had gone to war and whose letters had stopped. These men were either not yet known to be dead, too wounded to write, or had been taken prisoner. When Gertrude arrived in France, the office was only three weeks old and run by volunteers, including two of her childhood friends, Flora and Diana Russell.

Boulogne, November 25, 1914, to Doughty-Wylie

I had a hideous interview with the passport people at the Red Cross . . . age 46, height 5 foot 5½. . . . no profession . . . mouth normal . . . face, well . . . I looked at the orderly: "Round" she said.

November 1914

The cat and I are the only two not in uniform. . . .
     I think I have inherited a love of office work! A clerk was what I was meant to be . . . I feel as if I had flown to this work as one might take to drink, for some forgetting.

She saw at once that there was no system: the volunteers had begun the work when there was just a trickle of letters, but the trickle soon turned into a torrent. The recent Mons campaign had taken its toll of fifteen thousand British men killed, wounded, or missing, and yet the ladies were still trying to work from scribbled notes and from memory. The heiress who had lived her entire life for adventure now began to work as if her life depended on it. She created a database that the whole office could follow, put in place alphabetical card indexes and cross references, and weeded out the names that had been on the books for five months or more. These would remain in a file marked "Missing Presumed Dead" until verification, when their unfortunate families would receive the dreaded form from the War Office. From her knowledge of the straitened finances of working families at the ironworks, she understood what it would mean for these families to lose the breadwinner. She wrote to these families explaining their entitlements and how they could claim them.

November 26, 1914

It is fearful the amount of office work there is. We are at it all day
from 10 till 12.30 and from 2 to 5 filing, indexing and answering
enquiries. . . . The more we do, the more necessary it is to keep
our information properly tabulated. . . . I need not say I'm ready
to take it all. The more work they give me the better I like it.

She wrote home to complain that women were not allowed to
make inquiries at the hospitals but, undeterred, set up her own
channels through army chaplains and defiantly visited outsta-
tions and hospitals whenever she liked, talking to the men in
the wards. She asked Florence to send her a list of the Territorial Battalions and a London address book.

November 27, 1914

I sometimes go into our big hospitals and talk to the men. . . .
There are a good many Germans to whom I talk. Our men are
exceedingly good and kind to them and try to cheer them as far
as they can with no common language.

December 1, 1914

We have had the most pitiful letters and we see the most pitiful
people.

December 11, 1914, Letter to Chirol

There is a recent order, direct from Kitchener, that no visitor is
to go into hospitals without a pass. It's unspeakably silly. I
haven't yet had occasion to ask for a pass—I've been too busy—
but I don't suppose I should have any difficulty in obtaining one.
The reason given out is that spies get into the hospitals, question
the wounded and gain valuable information concerning the

position of their regiments! Anyone who has talked to the men in hospital knows how ridiculous that is. They are generally quite vague as to where they were or what they were doing.

From a Joint War Committee Report, Written by Gertrude

It should be appreciated at home that these enquiries from wounded men about their missing comrades are a most difficult part of our work. Men reach hospital from the trenches in such a nerve-racked condition that their evidence has to be checked and counterchecked by questioning other men, and thus every "enquiry case" may necessitate the catechism of four or five men.

As early as December 16, 1914, Gertrude wrote to her parents: "I've very nearly cleared away the mountain of mistakes which I found when I came. Nothing was ever verified, and we went on piling error on to error, with no idea of the confusion that was being caused. . . . If we are not scrupulously correct we are no good at all."

The efficiency of the Boulogne office was soon recognized, and Gertrude became the official head of department. She asked for, and was given, the task of responding to the inquiries. She replaced Form B101-82 sent by the War Office and its dreaded telegram—"Deeply regret to inform you that E. R. Cook British Grenadiers was killed in action 26th April. Lord Kitchener expresses his sympathy. Secretary, War Office"— with a more sensitive letter:

Madam,

It is my painful duty to inform you that a report has this day been received from the War Office notifying the death of Number 15296 Private Williams, J. D. which occurred at Place Not Stated on the 13th of November, 1914. The cause of death was Killed In Action.

Added to her anxieties about Doughty-Wylie were worries for her brother Maurice, who was now heading for the front. A lieutenant colonel of the Green Howards, he distinguished himself in the attack on German soldiers breaking through the Belgian border but was wounded a few months later and was invalided out in June 1917, almost totally deaf. He never regained his hearing.

One of the grimmest parts of her work entailed locating the graves of men hastily buried on the battlefield, whose relatives wanted to know whether there was proof of death. The Red Cross searchers would often find that the grave or pit containing the particular soldier they were trying to trace also contained a number of other bodies. Gertrude had recorded a grave containing ninety-eight men, of whom only sixty-six still wore their identity discs. Still suffering from depression, she took on more and more work, preferring to do it herself than delegate it to slower colleagues in the office.

December 27, 1914, Letter to Chirol

I hear that on Xmas Day there was almost the peace of God. Scarcely a shot was fired, the men came out of the trenches and mixed together, and at one place there was even a game of football between the enemies. . . . Strange, isn't it? . . . Sometimes we recover lost ground and find all our wounded carefully bound up and laid in shelter; sometimes we find them all bayonneted—according to the regiment, or the temper of the moment, what do I know? But day by day it becomes a blacker weight upon the mind. . . .

I feel tired . . . I'm too near the horrible struggle in the mud. It's infernal country, completely under water . . . you can't move for mud.

Boulogne, December 30, 1914

. . . There's no real forgetting and care rides behind one all the day. I sometimes wonder if we shall ever know again what it was like to be happy.

Undated Letter, to Chirol

When we are under a cross fire of artillery, we have about 50 casualties a day. . . . It's miserable up there now—continuous rain. . . . The roads beyond St. Omer are in an awful state. The cobbled pavement is giving way . . . and on either side of it is a slough of mud. The heavy motor transport, if it is pushed off the pavement into the mud can't be got out and stays there for ever.

Sir Robert Cecil, head of the British Red Cross, had at last persuaded the War Office to let him establish a communication line with regiments at the front. Major Fabian Ware and his team were to be the new recipients of the inquiry lists from the Red Cross office. The first of the team, a Mr. Cazalet, arrived in Boulogne on New Year's Eve with a bundle of papers to be sorted.

Boulogne, New Year's Day, 1915

We saw the New Year in after all. It happened this way. Yesterday morning there "débouchéd" in our office Mr. Cazalet, who is working with Fabian Ware out at the front. Mr. Cazalet brought a tangled bundle of letters and lists from which he had been working to compare with ours and to be put straight for him. We had 24 hours for the work before he returned to the front. It was just like a fairy story only we hadn't the ants and the bees to help us in a mountain of work. Diana ran out got a great ledger and proceeded to make it into an indexed ledger which we couldn't find here.

We only had two hours off from 7 to 9 to dine. . . . At 9 we went back to the office. By 9.30 everything was sorted out and I began to fill in the ledger, Diana keeping me supplied. We could not have done it if I had not prepared all that was possible beforehand. At midnight we broke off for a few minutes, wished each other a better year and ate some chocolates. . . . By 2 a.m. we were within an hour or two of the end so we came home to bed. I was back at 8.15 prepared the ordinary day's work . . .

returned to the ledger. By 12.30 it was finished with just an
hour to spare and I took it to Mr. Cazalet. It had been an exciting time but we won it and now this really important thing is
set going.

On the same day, Gertrude made a special visit to the Secunder-
abad Hospital for Indian residents and met Sikhs, Gurkhas,
Jats, and Afridis.

. . . The cooks [were] preparing Hindu and Muhammadan dinners
over separate fires, and the good smell of *ghee* and the musty
aromatic East pervading the whole. . . . Every man had the
King's Christmas card pinned up over his bed, and Princess
Mary's box of spices lying on the table beneath it.

Only to Chirol did she express the depth of her misery over
Doughty-Wylie and the trenches.

December 16, 1914, Letter to Chirol

I can work here all day long—it makes a little plank across the
gulf of wretchedness over which I have walked this long time.
Sometimes even that comes near to breaking point. I must talk
to you of this. I ought not to write of it. Forgive me. There are
days when it is still almost more than I can bear—this is one of
them, and I cry out to you. . . . My dear Domnul, dearest and
best of friends.

January 12, 1915, Letter to Chirol

They have put all the correspondence into my hands, Paris, Boulogne and Rouen. I am glad because the form in which we convey
terrible tidings—that is mostly what we have to convey—
matters very much, and when I have it to do, I know at least that
no pains will be spared over it. . . . I lead a cloistered existence

and think of nothing but my poor people whose fortunes I am following so painfully. . . .

The letters I receive and answer daily are heart-rending. At any rate, even if we can give these people little news that is good, it comforts them I think that something is being done to find out what has happened to their beloveds. Often I know myself that there is no chance for them, and I have to answer as gently as I can and carefully keep from them horrible details which I have learnt. That is my daily job.

My work goes on—quite continuous, very absorbing, and so sad that at times I can scarcely bear it. It is as though the intimate dossier of the war passes through my hands. The tales that come in to me are unforgettable; the splendid simple figures that live in them people my thoughts, and their words, brought back to me, ring in my ears. The waste, the sorrow of it all.

. . . Here we sit, and lives run out like water with nothing done. It's unbelievable now at the front—the men knee-deep in water in the trenches, the mud impassable. They sink in it up to the knee, up to the thigh. When they lie down in the open to shoot they cannot fire because their elbows are buried in it up to the wrist. Half the cases that come down into hospital are rheumatism and forms of frostbite. They stay in the trenches twenty-one days, sometimes thirty-six days, think of it.

In her short time at the W&MED, Gertrude came to understand trench warfare as few people did who had not themselves been on the front line. The British public were kept in the dark about the true numbers of casualties, while Gertrude had a clear view of the reality and of the duplicity that went on. It was the beginning of a disenchantment with government and authority that informed the attitude she held later in her life.

February 2, 1915, Letter to Chirol

They reckon the average duration of an officer at the front at about a month, before he is wounded. . . . The taking, losing and retaking of a trench is what it comes to; and 4000 lives lost over it in the last 6 weeks. Bitter waste. . . .

April 1, 1915, Letter to Chirol

The Pyrrhic victory of Neuve Chapelle showed more clearly than before that we can't break through the lines. Why they concealed our losses it is hard to guess. They were close on 20,000, and the German Casualties between 8 and 10,000.

It was only when Doughty-Wylie's letters arrived that her pain was briefly alleviated. Writing to her from Addis Ababa, his convoluted but increasingly loving messages had followed her from the desert to London and now Boulogne. Deprived of sex in Judith's absence, Dick could think of little else. "Tonight I should not want to talk. I should make love to you," he wrote. "Would you like it, welcome it, or would a hundred hedges rise and bristle and divide?—but we would tear them down. . . . You are in my arms, alight, afire. . . . But it will never be. . . ." He continued: "Women sometimes give themselves to men for the man's pleasure. I'd hate a woman to be like that with me. I'd want her to feel to the last sigh the same surge and stir that carried me away. She should miss nothing that I could give her."
  Gertrude wrote back letters full of infinite passion and longing.

Dearest, dearest, I give this year of mine to you, and all the years that shall come after it, this meagre gift—the year and me and all my thoughts and love . . . Dearest, when you tell me you love me and want me still, my heart sings—and then weeps with longing to be with you. I have filled all the hollow places of the world with my desire for you; it floods out to creep up the high mountains where you live.

Without warning, at the end of the year, Dick had sent the most unwelcome news. Judith, a former nurse, had also arrived in northern France to work in a hospital. Before long Gertrude had a letter from her, suggesting a meeting. Gertrude wanted to avoid Judith at all costs, but did not want to arouse her suspicions with a refusal. Gertrude was no dissembler. Asked the question, she would have told the truth. It seems from Gertrude's letter to Dick after the acrimonious meeting that Judith told her that Dick would never abandon his wife or his marriage.

> I hated it. Don't make me have that to bear. . . . You won't leave me? . . . It's torture, eternal torture.

Now, just as Gertrude was in the depths of despair, Dick wrote that he was coming home. He would reach Marseilles in February, visit Judith in France, then travel on to London. Gertrude should wait to hear from him and be ready to join him there. He could not stay long. He had volunteered for the front line "with joy" and was on his way to Gallipoli. They could have four nights and three days together.

It is a sad fact that the happiest romantic moments in Gertrude's life were also the most poignant and painful. The story of her passionate love for Dick, and of his for her, is the account of two people constantly separated, divided by her inviolable sense of honor as much as by convention and geography. The long-anticipated few days together at Half Moon Street passed, and still she had not consummated her love in the full physical sense. Her distraught letters to him afterward convey that she had not been able to overcome an inborn prudishness. She wanted to do so but could not stop herself from recoiling at the last moment, and he would not force himself on her. They met and parted, inconclusively, and she sent anguished letters after him to Gallipoli, consumed with regret, trying to explain her inability to consummate their union.

> Someday I'll try to explain it to you—the fear, the terror of it— oh you thought I was brave. Understand me: not the fear of consequences—I've never weighed them for one second. It's the fear of something I don't know. . . . Every time it surged up in me and I wanted you to brush it aside. . . . But I couldn't say to

you, Exorcise it. I couldn't. That last word I can never say. You
must say it. . . .

I can't sleep—I can't sleep. It's one in the morning. . . . You
and you and you are between me and any rest . . . out of your
arms there is no rest. Life, you called me, and fire. I flame and
am consumed. . . . Dick, it's not possible to live like this. When
it's all over you must take your own . . . Before all the world,
claim me and take me and hold me for ever and ever . . . Furtive-
ness I hate—But openly to come to you, that I can do and live,
what should I lose? It's all nothing to me; I breathe and think
and move in you. Can you do it, dare you? When this thing is
over, your work well done, will you risk it for me? It's that or
nothing. I can't live without you. . . . If you die, wait for me—I
am not afraid of that other crossing; I will come to you.

Increasingly desperate, tortured by regret and knowing he could
die at Gallipoli, Gertrude wrote Dick a passionate ultimatum:

March 7, 1915

I am very calm about the shot and shell to which you go. What
takes you, takes me out to look for you. If there's search and
finding beyond the border I shall find you. If there's nothingness,
as with my reason I think, why then there's nothingness. . . . Oh,
but life shrinks from it . . . but I'm not afraid. Life would be
gone, how could the fire burn? But I'm brave—you know it—as
far as human courage goes. . . . I'll do anything you ask and not
think twice of it . . . you may do anything you like with what is
yours—what's given is given, there is no taking back, no shadow
of it. And no reproach. I wish I had given more, except that more
of giving is still in my hand for you to take.

March 9, 1915

Oh Dick, write to me. When shall I hear? . . . I trust, I believe,
you'll take care of me—let me stand upright and say I've never

walked by furtive ways. Then they'll forgive me and you—all the people that matter will forgive. . . . But it's you who should be saying this, should be saying it now, not I. I won't say it anymore.

March 11, 1915

If I had given more, should I have held you closer, drawn you back more surely? I look back and rage at my reluctance.

March 12, 1915

I've had a few resplendent hours. I could die on them and be happy. But you, you've not had what you wanted.

But Dick had already told her that he could never leave Judith, who had threatened suicide if he left her, by using the morphia tubes available in the hospitals. In the archives of the Imperial War Museum there is a final letter from him to Judith's mother, Jean Coe, making clear that if he was killed she should go to her daughter at once in France and "see her through." Gertrude told him that she was not afraid of death, either, and also threatened suicide if he died.

When my heart quales I remember the morphia tubes and I know there is a way out. . . . If I can't sleep in your arms I'll sleep this way.

As Doughty-Wylie departed for Gallipoli, he found himself in a terrible dilemma. He could make his love for Gertrude plain and bring suffering to his wife, or he could support Judith and bring Gertrude unbearable pain. Both threatened suicide. Dick was exhausted by the conflict.

Having seen what Gertrude had achieved in Boulogne in only three months, Lord Robert Cecil brought her back at the end of March to organize the center of Red Cross operations in Pall Mall, London, where he asked her to combine all information about the wounded and missing on one record.

Gertrude, already fatigued in body and mind, set to work with a staff of twenty plus four typists. Even more work soon descended on her from the Foreign Office, which requested that the Red Cross should take on all the gathering and tabulating of information with regard to British prisoners. Her letters became fewer and terser.

Boulogne, March 22, 1915

Don't let anyone know I'm coming. I shall have no time and I don't want to be bothered with people.

Pall Mall, April 1, 1915, Letter to Chirol

I go nowhere and see no one, for I am at the office from 9 am till 7 pm. . . .

On April 26, 1915, predictably and agonizingly, she heard that Dick Doughty-Wylie had died a hero's death in Gallipoli. As she was neither kith nor kin to him, she had received no official letter. It is said that she heard this devastating news mentioned casually at a lunch party. She sat there ashen-faced, then quietly excused herself and left the table. Hardly knowing what she did, she made her way to the home of her half-sister Elsa. Her other half-sister, Molly, was to write "It has ended her life—there is no reason now for her to go on with anything she cared for."

The breakdown she suffered made it impossible for her to go into the office for many weeks. When she finally returned, she was pale and vulnerable. Her parents were deeply concerned about her, but she brushed off their suggestions that she should return to Rounton. Now that the love of her life was dead, she had no life other than work.

In July, Florence offered to come up to London to be with

her on the sad three-month anniversary of Doughty-Wylie's death. Gertrude wrote back:

> It's very dear of you, . . . but you mustn't do it. . . . Nothing does any good. . . .

August 5, 1915

> I could not possibly get away next week. I am having a horrible time, with a lot of new people, all to be taught and all making mistakes at every moment. There is no one in whose hands I could leave the office even for a day. It's being rather intolerable altogether. I hate changing and changes.

August 20, 1915

> I've been bitterly alone this month. It's intolerable not to like being alone as I used, but I can't keep myself away from my own thoughts, and they are still more intolerable.

Her friend from Oxford, Janet Hogarth Courtney, arrived in Pall Mall to share the burden of the Red Cross work with her and wrote: "I was greatly struck by her mental weariness and discouragement, little as she ever let either interfere with the work. But she would not, she said she could not, rest. The War obsessed her to the exclusion of every other consideration. . . . She would let no personal griefs lessen her capacity for doing. She faced a sorrow and put it behind her."*

One day Janet went in to work and Gertrude immediately drew her aside to tell her she had received a letter from Janet's brother, David Hogarth, now a lieutenant commander in the Royal Navy Volunteer Reserve at Cairo. He insisted that she join him at the Arab Bureau there. He wrote that anyone could

---

*Recalled by Janet Courtney in an article on Gertrude in the *North American Review,* December 1926.

trace the missing, but only Gertrude could map Northern Arabia. She would be leaving for Cairo within the week.

For hundreds of thousands of families, she had shone a light into the darkness and played a part in enabling them to bring closure to their losses, and get on with living. Her work for the W&MED was formally acknowledged as beyond value by HRH the Princess Christian and the other members of the War Executive Committee. Now the most exciting and rewarding part of her life was about to begin.

POSTSCRIPT

Toward the end of 1915, a woman veiled in black was seen to leave a wreath on Doughty-Wylie's grave at Gallipoli. Her identity has long been in doubt. According to one L. A. Carlyan:

> On November 17, 1915, a woman stepped ashore at V Beach, which had become the main French base. She is thought to be the only woman to have landed during the Gallipoli campaign. She left the River Clyde, now being used as a pier, walked through the castle . . . past the line of tottery walls and unearthed cellars that had once been Sedd-el-Bahr village . . . and began to climb Hill 141. On the summit she stopped at a lone grave fenced off with barbed wire, placed a wreath on the wooden cross and left. . . . Most likely she was Lilian Doughty-Wylie. . . . There is, however, a persistent story that it was his old friend Gertrude Bell, also in the area at the time.

Doughty-Wylie was killed on April 26, 1915.* Where was Judith on November 17? She had been posted to Saint-Valery-sur-Somme. It is most unlikely that either the army or the French hospital service would have seen fit to bring a widow into the war zone. Thirty-nine Victoria Crosses were awarded in all,

---

*The date of the landing is vague. Captain Eric Wheeler Bush, DSO, DFC, RN, author of *Gallipoli*, which was published in 1975, says that on the date Carlyan mentions boat landing was impossible because of serious storms.

including Doughty-Wylie's, and their widows would each have been entitled to the same consideration.

And where was Gertrude at this time? She was at 95 Sloane Street, packing her suitcase for Cairo, telling her father that she expected to arrive at Port Said on Thursday, November 25. On Tuesday, November 30—"this morning after my arrival"— she wrote that she had reached Port Said on the previous Thursday night after a terrible storm at sea.

Cairo is only a short train journey from Port Said. The days and nights of November 27, 28, and 29 are missing from her letters and diaries.

The Cairo Bureau was the intelligence base with specific responsibility for the Mediterranean Expeditionary Force sent to Gallipoli, and its staff included her great friend David Hogarth, her acquaintance Lawrence, Leonard Woolley, and Captain Hall. She was surrounded by friends. She would have had time to catch the express train to Port Said, board a transport ship just leaving with supplies for the Dardanelles, and take a lighter to V beach.

Gertrude's last letter to Florence before she left London suggests that she had put in a private request before she left.

I think it more than likely that when I reach Egypt I shall find they have no job that will occupy me more than a fortnight, and I may be back before Christmas. It's all vaguer than words can say. *As for any further journey nothing definite is said and I think the chances are strongly against it.* [Emphasis added]

THE INTRUSIVES

Three years before World War I, a chance meeting at an archaeological site in northwest Syria brought together two of the finest minds in the Middle East. Beginning with a purely social encounter, Gertrude Bell and Thomas Edward Lawrence began the intellectual duel that they were to continue all their lives. In an apocryphal comment on the argumentative Lawrence, Gertrude was to say that he "could ignite a fire in a cold room."

Urfa, May 18, 1911

I went there [Carchemish]—it was only five hours' ride—and found Mr. Thompson and a young man called Lawrence (he is going to make a traveller) who had for some time been expecting that I would appear.

May 23, 1911, Lawrence to His Mother

Miss Gertrude Bell called last Sunday, and we showed her all our finds, and she told us all hers. We parted with mutual expressions of esteem: but she told Thompson his ideas of digging were prehistoric: and so we had to squash her with a display of erudition. She was taken (in 5 minutes) over Byzantine, Crusader, Roman, Hittite, and French architecture . . . and over Greek folk-lore, Assyrian architecture, and Mesopotamian Ethnology

(by Thompson); prehistoric pottery and telephoto lenses, bronze
age metal technique, Meredith, Anatole France and the Octo-
brists . . . : the Young Turk movement, the construct state in
Arabic, the price of riding camels, Assyrian burial-customs,
and German methods of excavation with the Baghdad railway
(Thompson). This was a kind of hors d'œuvre: and when it was
over (she was getting more respectful) we settled down each
to seven or eight subjects and questioned her upon them. She
was quite glad to have tea after an hour and a half, and on going
told Thompson that he had done wonders in his digging in the
time, and that she thought *we* had got everything out of the
place that could possibly have been got: she particularly admired
the completeness of our note-books. So we did for her. She was
really too captious at first, coming straight from the German
diggings at Kalaát Shirgat. . . . Our digs are I hope more accurate, if less perfect. . . . So we showed her that, and left her
limp, but impressed. She is pleasant: about 36*, not beautiful,
(except with a veil on, perhaps). It would have been most annoying if she had denounced our methods in print. I don't think
she will.

To David Hogarth, Gertrude's friend and the chief archaeologist at Carchemish, absent on her arrival, Lawrence wrote
more flatteringly, "Gerty has gone back to her tents to sleep.
She has been a success: and a brave one."

The war began and T. E. Lawrence was sent as an army lieutenant to the new Arab Intelligence Bureau in Cairo, which
would be coordinating information arising from some sixteen
different departments of the British government from Khar-
toum to London and Delhi. Soon afterward, Gertrude—now
with the honorary title of Major Miss Bell—was sent to the
same office in Cairo, to master and document the intricacies of
Arab politics.

In many ways they were comparable figures. Both obtained
first-class honors in history from Oxford, and both were polyglots,

*She was forty-two at the time.

both were passionate archaeologists, and both had an innate affection for the Arabs. As her friend Janet Hogarth was to write, Gertrude "felt the desert with a poet's imagination; it drew her to its heart as it had before her drawn Doughty,* the solitary and the poet, and as it was later to draw Lawrence." She spoke Arabic far better than Lawrence, and was fluent in several other Middle Eastern languages. She was better traveled, and skilled in surveillance and cartography. Lawrence, lacking her wealth and therefore her status among the sheikhs of the desert, had not yet been accepted by them as an equal. What made her unique among the clever and well-traveled personnel of the Arab Bureau was not just that she possessed encyclopaedic knowledge of the tribes but that her information was so fresh—it was only eighteen months since she had returned to Britain from the Hayyil journey.

Cairo was full of friends and acquaintances who probably facilitated Gertrude's visit to Doughty-Wylie's grave at Gallipoli. There were David Hogarth; Leonard Woolley, the intelligence chief at Port Said; and Captain Hall, who was in charge of the railway. There was Aubrey Herbert, son of the Earl of Carnarvon, whom she had known for twelve years, his perfect Turkish a useful bureau tool. There was Sir Ronald Storrs, the most entertaining of the sparkling circle, an incomparable linguist who could reduce people of any nationality to helpless laughter in a matter of minutes.

And, of course, there was Lawrence, twenty-seven to Gertrude's forty-seven, a law unto himself and a source of constant aggravation to the military. Scruffy, brilliant, self-absorbed, he had a habit out of the office of wearing embroidered cloaks and waistcoats. The illegitimate son of an impoverished Irish baronet and the governess who cared for the children, he had taken their adopted name of Lawrence but would become successively Lawrence of Arabia, Aircraftman John Hume Ross, and Private Thomas Edward Shaw.

With the inspiring addition of the two new recruits, the Arab Bureau set its course to think and work beyond the failed

---

*The celebrated author of *Arabia Deserta*.

strategy of the British military to remove the Turks from Sinai, Palestine, and Arabia. In developing the notion that it was feasible to foster an Arab revolt against the Turks, they were working contrary to official policies. With the sense of a subversive mission, they gave themselves a name: "the Intrusives."

Gertrude, chain-smoking her way through their meetings, had a different point of view from the military. Disciplined modern warfare, she suggested, had failed on three fronts already. Her grasp of the situation and her persuasive clarity in presenting issues of enormous complexity led the way to realizing Lawrence's plan to "roll up Syria by way of the Hedjaz in the name of the Sherif . . . rush right up to Damascus, and biff the French out of all hope of Syria." Her knowledge of Arab methods of warfare was a novel addition to the collective determination of the bureau to find the way ahead. Probably the only one among them who had actually taken part in a *ghazu,* Gertrude would have discussed funding insurrection, cutting railway links, hijacking supplies, fostering terrorism, and provoking guerrilla warfare. In a radio broadcast of 1927,* Lawrence admitted that on the subject of the Arab Revolt he owed much to Gertrude.

It was hoped that a combination of intelligence gathering and analysis would produce a policy capable of setting the Arabs against the Turks, powerful allies of Germany. Gertrude was to identify the tribes, their affiliations and enmities, and map the desert tracks, the water holes and the ways through the mountains, calling on her meticulous diaries. Her letters home were fewer, and she never wrote of Bureau issues to her family: it was a secret office. On the other hand, she had begun her lifelong correspondence with people of political importance, many of whom she knew personally, such as Sir Robert Cecil, who had been the head of the Red Cross when she was working there and was now parliamentary undersecretary of state for foreign affairs.

---

*Interview by Elizabeth Robins, September 17, 1927.

Cairo, December 20, 1915, Letter to Sir Robert Cecil

Dear Lord Robert,

It is very nice to be able to write to you by bag for otherwise I could talk of nothing but the weather and my health, both of which are too good to call for any comment. They have set me to work here on Arabia, tribes and geography; we are going to bring out a sort of catalogue of the former, paying special attention to their numbers and political grouping, and a new edition of the map. Whether anyone will use them when they are done I don't know, but I am learning a great deal myself, which is delightful, and most amusing when the information is gathered from Arabs who happen to be here. I am getting hold of them gradually; they come up and sit with me by the hour, and I correct place-names and tribe-names in the course of conversation and hear about remote people and near people who were little but shadows before. Telegrams from Aden or Basrah bring fresh stuff—it is great fun as you can imagine. And we will end by producing something which, though it will be full of errors, will be a groundwork for the future. There is nothing else to be done at this moment; we are marking time, not very successfully I fear, in Mesopotamia, and waiting for the Turkish attack on the Canal. News from Syria is lamentably scanty and when it comes not of a very valuable kind. It looks as if they were going to tackle the Mesopotamian expedition before they come here, and as far as Egypt is concerned that is most fortunate, for until the last three weeks no preparations had been made to meet them, and the troops in this country were mostly details or raw and quite incoherent masses of Australians. It is almost incredible that we should have taken such a risk—quite incredible let us hope to the enemy. The negotiations with the Sharif have, however, been very skilfully conducted, and as long as we can keep him in play there is no fear of a big religious movement. He is the only person who could raise a *jehad*—the Turks, preaching at the instigation of the Germans, are as little likely to carry conviction this year as they were last year. The question is whether we *can* keep him in play. From all the information that comes in he seems to have acquired a very remarkable position in Arabia, but his strength is moral, not military, and if the Turks come down into Syria in force they may be able to put pressure upon him which he could not resist, and indeed it is not improbable that he would succumb to that ally of the Ottoman Government the "climate." Meantime we are hampered both by the French and by India, as you know. The Sharif, quite rightly as I think, refuses to consider the Arab question apart from the settled lands. He is right, because the desert is not self-supporting, and therefore whoever holds the markets in the cultivated provinces must ultimately control nomads and oasis dwellers. He has not shown himself unreasonable. We could probably come to terms, but never on the basis of relinquishing the whole of Syria—and the demands put forward recently by Picot extended French Syria from the Mediterranean to the Tigris. It would be wise to give the French a very long rope; when they come to consider the administration of such a Syria as that it is not improbable that they would find it a bigger business than they were prepared to undertake. But the weaving of long ropes takes time and it is time which is lacking. A serious Arab movement, if it were once to be set on foot, would turn them out of N. Africa just as easily as it would turn us out of Egypt. I think they will have to be content with the Alexandretta corner and Cilicia (good country and a good port) and of course the Lebanon which they will not forego—I think Beyrout also. The weakness of the argument is that the Arabs can't govern themselves—no one is more convinced of that than I—and when they come to us for help and counsel (as they will) the French will not regard it favourably. However, perhaps we need not look so far ahead, and the immediate necessity is to induce them to accept some compromise acceptable to the Arab party also, in face of the real danger that we may otherwise all founder together. As for the Indian difficulty, the retreat in Mesopotamia may help to bring the Indian Government into line. Mesopotamia is far less complicated a question than Syria; it is decades behind Syria in culture, and the Arab unionist movement has scarcely begun there. We shall not be able to annex either of the two provinces, Basrah or the Iraq, but no one will

object to our administration there if it is not graduated through
an Indian bureaucracy. Colonisation would have to be very
carefully and delicately handled. I could write a great deal on
that subject but I won't! You must have come to the end of your
patience and now that I think of it I wonder why I have assumed
that you would have any patience with my rather hasty opinions
on Near Eastern politics in general.

Cairo, January 3, 1916

. . . My tribe stuff is beginning to be pulled into shape. . . . I love
doing it. . . . I can scarcely tear myself away from it. . . . I'm getting to feel quite at home as a Staff Officer! It is comic isn't it.

Lawrence, on the other hand, was itching to leave mapmaking, to which he took a cavalier attitude. As he admitted in a
letter concerning his map of Sinai roads and wells, "Some of it
was accurate, and the rest I invented." One day, he feared,
nemesis was awaiting him: he would be told to find his way
about with nothing but a copy of his own map.

The Indian government, headed by the Viceroy, Lord
Hardinge, remained determined to extend its authority in Arabia and to annex Mesopotamia. Gertrude, who had first met
Hardinge nearly thirty years previously, was sent to Delhi on a
political mission to put the Intrusives' point of view.

Cairo, January 24, 1916

There is a great deal of friction between India and Egypt over
the Arab question which entails a serious want of co-operation
between the Intelligence Departments of the two countries and
the longer it goes on the worse it gets. It's absurd of course; we
are all well-meaning people trying to do our best, but they don't
realise what Arabia looks like from the West and I daresay we
don't realise how it looks from the East.

So I'm going—whether much good will come of it I don't

know, but it's worth trying at any rate and I shall learn a good deal for I hope they will let me dig into their Arab files and see what can be added from them to our knowledge. I think they will probably pay my journey, if not I shall go all the same because I think it's a good thing to do—in which case you will understand why my bank is called upon to honour a big cheque to the P & O Company. I expect you will approve of my proceedings as usual! We want to establish here a permanent Intelligence Bureau for the Near East, which shall endure after the war is over—it would be invaluable; but it could not work properly without the sympathy and help of India and that is the chief matter I wish to discuss with the Viceroy.

She was warmly greeted by the viceroy, who listened to her clear reasoning and sent her on to Basra, at that time the military center of activity in Mesopotamia as the army prepared to march north and drive the Turks out of Baghdad. He warned her that there would be considerable opposition on the part of intelligence and military staff to accepting a woman as an equal. She would be working at General Sir Percy Lake's military headquarters without title, job, or pay.

Hardinge wrote to Sir Percy Cox, the chief political officer, advising him to take Gertrude seriously. Had she read the letter she would have laughed. "She is a remarkably clever woman," he wrote, ". . . with the brains of a man."

She might have the honorary rank of major, but the military attitude to her arrival can be summed up by the remark of General Sir George MacMunn, the inspector general of communications in Mesopotamia, that she was a "little wisp of a human being, said to be a woman." In her letters home, Gertrude revealed how very tired she became of dealing with such misogyny and having to prove herself again and again.

Basra, March 18, 1916

. . . If I went away it wouldn't matter, or if I stay it wouldn't matter.

Basra, June 12, 1916

It's not easy here—some day I'll tell you about it. But the more difficult it is the more I feel I ought to stay.

With Hardinge's letter in mind, Cox decided to throw Gertrude in at the deep end. He arranged for her to have lunch with Generals Lake, Cowper, Money, and Offley Shaw, who had regarded her, until then, as just a little woman who had done a bit of traveling. That she surprised and impressed them is clear from her letter home.

Basra, March 9, 1916

To-day I lunched with all the Generals . . . , and as an immediate result they moved me and my maps and books on to a splendid great verandah with a cool room behind it where I sit and work all day long. My companion here is Captain Campbell Thompson, ex-archaeologist . . . delighted to benefit with me by the change of workshop, for we were lodged by day in Col. Beach's bedroom. . . . a plan which was not very convenient either for us or for him.

Gertrude was soon followed to Basra by Lawrence and Aubrey Herbert, on a brief visit from Cairo to bring an end to the siege of Kut, where eleven thousand British soldiers were stranded and starving. Lawrence and Herbert were authorized to offer the Turks up to £2 million ($189,000,000 RPI adjusted) to break the siege. It was a demeaning exercise and would fail.

Basra, April 9, 1916

This week has been greatly enlivened by the appearance of Mr. Lawrence, sent out as liaison officer from Egypt. We have had great talks and made vast schemes for the government of the universe. He goes up river tomorrow, where the battle is raging these days. . . . And who do you think is political officer? Aubrey! the ubiquitous Aubrey. Oh how glad I shall be to see him! One's extraordinarily lonely with no one of one's own. That's why even Mr. Lawrence was such a godsend. He speaks the same language at any rate.

Although Gertrude and Lawrence were never close personal friends, their occasional encounters as united colleagues sharing a mission to give the Arabs some degree of self-determination proved momentous. This visit from Lawrence gave the two nearly a fortnight together in which to talk on many aspects of the future of the Middle East. Judging from the date of those conversations, it seems to be that Lawrence was able to return to Cairo and convince General Edmund Allenby to lend his support to the Arab Revolt. The subversive intention of the Intrusives, to infiltrate the corridors of power to foster the new Arab world, was set in motion. In January 1917, Lawrence and Faisal, a son of the sharif of Mecca, began their triumphant march north with the Arab army. With the taking of Damascus, the Ottoman Empire finally came to an end. An armistice was signed, and in 1919 the Paris Peace Conference was convened at Versailles.

Awarded Commander of the British Empire (CBE), Gertrude was now based in Baghdad, working rather unhappily for A. T. Wilson, struggling in his role of acting civil commissioner. Promoted to Oriental secretary under Cox, she had found her duties restricted by Wilson once Cox had been posted to Tehran. She attended the Paris Peace Conference to battle for the peoples of the abandoned Turkish Empire in Mesopotamia, now without boundaries, identity, or government.

The chief contenders among the exhausted leaders assembling in Paris were President Woodrow Wilson for America, Prime Minister David Lloyd George of Britain, and Prime Minister Georges Clemenceau of France. But all eyes were on two international figures: Lawrence, sometimes in full Arab dress, sometimes in keffiyeh over his army uniform, appointed as adviser to the dignified and charismatic figure of Amir Faisal, son of Sharif Hussein. No one there could have been ignorant of the glorious story of Faisal's epic journey to Damascus at the head of ten thousand tribesmen, taking Aqaba and progressing north by means of just those terrorist tactics described by Gertrude in Cairo. Tribes taking over from tribes as they advanced, they finally marched into Damascus, where Faisal unfurled the flag of the Hejaz on October 3, 1918.

At last Lawrence was able to introduce Gertrude to Faisal. She sat for hours talking to the emir as he was having his portrait painted by Augustus John,* feeling increasing admiration and respect for him. He combined the air of command and the mystique she had expected but surprised her with his warmth, humor, and perfect command of French and English. A veteran warrior and thirty-three years old, Faisal captivated her as he had captivated Lawrence with his pensive air and melancholy expression. Gertrude and Lawrence resented the cavalier treatment of Faisal by the majority of the leaders at the conference. He had not been officially invited but had been sent by his father, Hussein, to speak for independent Arab government in the Middle East. Once in Paris, his representations were ignored despite Lawrence's best efforts. His predicament united Lawrence and Gertrude more closely than ever: they were now deeply involved as missionaries for the promise of independence that had been given to the Arabs in return for the triumphant tribal revolt against the Turks.

The Hotel Majestic, Paris, March 7, 1919

Meantime we've sent for Col. Wilson from Baghdad and Mr. Hogarth from Cairo—the latter at my instigation—and when they come I propose to make a solid bloc of Near Eastern, including Mr. Lawrence, and present a united opinion. They

---

*John had hired a studio in Paris to paint the portraits of key figures attending the conference.

have all urged me to stay and I think for the moment that's my business.

Paris, March 16, 1919

We had a very delightful lunch today with Lord Robert and T. E. Lawrence. . . . Lord Robert is, I think the salient figure of the Conference and T. E. Lawrence the most picturesque. I spend most of my time with the latter. . . .

Paris, March 18, 1919

I sat in Sir Arthur Hirtzel's* office all morning . . . huddled as near as I could get to the hotwater pipes and wrote some pages of comments on French complaints of our behaviour in Mesopotamia. Nothing more absurd than this document has met my eye—they really are an amazing people. T. E. Lawrence and I arranged to lunch together. As we were standing in the hall Lord Milner† came in. Said Mr. Lawrence "You go and ask him to lunch with us." So I, as bold as brass, invited him; he accepted and we had a delightful and most unofficial hour during which we got a good many useful things said. He also talked very interestingly . . . but as he bound us over not to quote him as an authority I won't go into details. We assured him that people who lunched with us always were indiscreet. It's Mr. Lawrence, I think, who induces a sort of cards on the table atmosphere.

Gertrude and Lawrence were among those invited to meet the French press at a dinner given by the editor of *The Times*, Henry Wickham Steed, and her great friend Chirol.

*Sir Arthur Hirtzel was an academic and senior adviser at the India Office.

†Lord Alfred Milner was the colonial secretary.

March 26, 1919

After dinner T.E.L. [T. E. Lawrence] explained exactly the existing situations as between Faisal and his Syrians on the one hand and France on the other, and outlined the programme of a possible agreement without the delay which is the chief defect of the proposal for sending a Commission. He did it quite admirably. His charm, simplicity and sincerity made a deep personal impression and convinced his listeners. The question now is whether it is not too late to convince the Quai d'Orsay and Clemenceau and that is what we are now discussing.

While Lloyd George supported the Arab right to self-determination through Faisal, M. Picot of France declared that British prearrangements with the Arabs were nothing to do with France and warned that if France were entrusted with the mandate for Syria, Faisal's claims would be ignored. Faisal left Paris deeply disappointed, and in due course Syria was put under French mandate. Faisal's betrayal was complete. With ninety thousand French troops in Syria, Arab nationalists defiantly elected Faisal king of Syria. His reign, so promising and well deserved, lasted only three months before the first experiment in Arab self-determination was stamped out by the French army boot.

Meanwhile, by July 1920, Gertrude was greatly concerned over the methods employed by her temporary chief, A. T. Wilson, in dealing with the Mesopotamian insurgencies. Interminable delays in the delivery of decisions over borders and policies fanned the disaffections, which "A.T." mishandled, overruling Gertrude's more diplomatic negotiations with the tribes and using punitive measures to put down uprisings. It was during this period that Lawrence angered Gertrude by his public criticism of the British administration in Iraq.

Baghdad, July 1920, Letter to Lawrence

What curious organs [the newspapers] you choose for self-expression! . . . However whatever the organs I'm largely in agreement with what you say.

June 27, 1920

What makes me furious is the rot that's served up to the British public about us.

September 5, 1920

The thing isn't made any easier by the tosh T. E. Lawrence is writing in the papers. To talk of raising an Arab army of two Divisions is *pure nonsense*. Except for officers, we haven't got the materials. Intermittently during the war we raised labour corps, with a considerable amount of pressure, up to 20,000 odd. Everybody admits that the drain on the agricultural population was more than it could stand. . . . You can't make them into an army under five years. . . .

I can't think why the India Office lets the rot that's written pass uncontradicted. T.E.L. again: when he says we have forced the English language on the country it's not only a lie but he knows it. Every jot and tittle of official work is done in Arabic; in schools, law courts, hospitals, no other language is used. It's the first time that that has happened since the fall of the Abbasids. . . .

We are largely suffering from circumstances over which we couldn't have had any control. The wild drive of discontented nationalism from Syria and of discontented Islam from Turkey might have proved too much for us however far-seeing we had been; but that doesn't excuse us for having been blind. . . .

Again I'm up against T. E. Lawrence. He says the Arab has character and needs intelligence. It's the exact contrary. He has plenty of intelligence, what he lacks is character; and that, if people only knew, is what a mandatory power is called on to supply. Can it be done?

September 19, 1920

The fact that we are really guilty of an initial mistake makes it difficult to answer letters like those of T. E. Lawrence. I believe them to be wholly misleading, but to know why they're misleading requires such an accurate acquaintance not only with the history of the last two years but also with the country and the people, apart from our dealings with them, that I almost despair of putting public opinion in England right. I can't believe that T.E.L. is in ignorance and I therefore hold him to be guilty of the unpardonable sin of wilfully darkening counsel. We have a difficult enough task before us in this country; he is making it more difficult by leading people to think that it's easy. How can it be easy when you're called upon to reconcile the views and ideals of a tribal population which hasn't changed one shade of thought during the last five thousand years, and of a crude and impatient band of urban politicians who blame you for not setting up universities. . . .

And T.E.L. talks of two Divisions as if they could be created tomorrow. Where's the money coming from?

Lawrence and Gertrude had been equally shaken and angered by the humiliation of Faisal and the disregard of all promises made to him in return for his delivery of victory to the Allies. Both yearned to assuage their sense of guilt for what had happened, and in March 1921, at the Cairo Conference, they were given a last chance to do so.

To Gertrude's great relief, Sir Percy Cox returned as high commissioner for Iraq in October 1920. Just five months later, Churchill—now colonial secretary—summoned Iraq's British officials to meet him for ten days in Cairo, from March 12, 1921. Lawrence was there as special adviser to the Colonial Office. Among the major figures assembling there were Cox and his party of six led by Gertrude, Air Marshal Hugh Trenchard, intelligence expert Sir Kinahan Cornwallis, Major General Sir Edmund Ironside, and A. T. Wilson. Churchill's essential task was to substantially reduce the taxpayers' £37 million ($2,374 billion RPI adjusted) bill for military control of the Middle East.

Gertrude began by taking Lawrence to task for some of his comments in the newspapers about the civil administration in Baghdad. Lawrence had written in *The Sunday Times* (August 22, 1920), for instance, "The people of England have been led in Mesopotamia into a trap from which it will be hard to escape with dignity and honour. Things have been far worse than we have been told, our administration more bloody and inefficient than the public knows." Gertrude confronted him with this, while acknowledging that mistakes had been made while A. T. Wilson had been acting civil commissioner.

Cairo, March 12, 1921

We arrived yesterday. . . . T. E. Lawrence and others met us at the station—I was glad to see him. We retired at once to my bedroom at the Semiramis and had an hour's talk, after which I had a long talk with Clementine [Mrs. Winston Churchill] while Sir Percy was closeted with Mr. Churchill.

But they were still great friends, still the old Intrusives, now major players in the Middle East and determined to see that Faisal had some kind of restitution for what he had suffered in Paris and Syria. The degree to which Lawrence and Gertrude had colluded is suggested in a subsequent letter of his: "GB swung all the Mespot. British officials to the Feisal solution, while Winston and I swung the English people." Churchill liked the fact that Faisal would give the British leverage over the Hejaz and was soon cabling home to stress what was for him the chief point: "Sharif's son Faisal offers hope of best and cheapest solution." As a Sunni ruler in a country with a

Shia majority, the emir's descent from the Prophet would be his trump card; but Churchill insisted that Faisal be elected, and that would have to be arranged by Cox and Gertrude.

The Intrusives had won the day: self-determination was going to become reality. Now it was up to Cox and Gertrude to mold Iraq into a nation, and Faisal into its king, while Lawrence grew more self-absorbed as the years passed, doubting that Iraq would "make good as a modern state." In August 1922, he enlisted in the RAF as Aircraftman Ross, after which he changed his name again, to T. E. Shaw, and joined the Royal Tank Corps.

In 1919, the year of the Paris Peace Conference, Lawrence's celebrity completely eclipsed that of Gertrude's, making it difficult to remember that up to then she was the more famous figure, lionized by the West, mobbed in the East. Fortunately, she could not have cared less. While she loathed publicity and warned her family not to give information about her to the press, Lawrence was both flattered and tortured by it. He reviled it but was spotted slipping into the back row of a cinema to watch a film feature about himself. His elevation to world status was largely due to the efforts of journalist Lowell Thomas, who wrote a fulsome biography of Lawrence and then toured the world giving lectures about his hero.

The bond between Lawrence and Gertrude remained strong, in spite of everything. He had, only half joking, suggested her as his replacement in 1918, in case he was killed in the Arab uprising, and he was to write to her sister Elsa, after Gertrude's death: "She stood out as the one person who, thinking clearly, saw the true ultimate goal of our work with the Arabs and, daunted by nothing, worked unsparing of herself toward it."

———

During this period, Gertrude wrote a collection of essays for an instruction manual for the newly appointed political officers arriving in the country, "The Arab of Mesopotamia." Written at the behest of the War Office, it contained a series of pieces on subjects ranging from the serious to the eccentric. Published anonymously, the book was generally assumed to have been written by a man. In answer to a question from her family, she said: "Why yes of course I wrote all the 'Arab of Mesopotamia.' I've loved the reviews which speak of the practical men who were the anonymous authors etc. It's fun being practical men isn't it. . . ."

Two of the essays from the manual follow:

The Arab Tribes of Mesopotamia

The cultivated delta watered by the Tigris and Euphrates is inhabited by Arab tribal confederations, more or less settled, who are immigrants from the Arabian deserts. Some have been established in Mesopotamia from a remote period, others have come in during the last two or three hundred years, but all are originally nomads of the interior wilderness. The unbroken drift of her peoples northwards is one of the most important factors in the history of Arabia. The underlying causes were probably complex, but chief among them must have been a gradual change in the climatic conditions of the peninsula, involving slow desiccation, together with the pressure of an increasing population on a soil growing steadily poorer. To the hunger-bitten nomad, the rich pastures of the Syrian frontier, the inexhaustible fertility of Mesopotamia, offered irresistible attractions, and opportunities for expansion were found in the weakness and political exhaustion of the neighbouring northern states, whether they were Turkish, Byzantine, Persian or yet earlier empires. The long records of Babylonia enable us to trace the process in its earlier historical phases, a study of existing conditions shows that until a recent period it was still going on, and if a forecast may be hazarded, it will not be arrested in the future, though the nature of the migration may be altered. Instead of devastating hordes, sweeping like locusts over cornfield and pasture, the surplus population of Arabia may find in a Mesopotamia reconstituted by good administration not only abundant means of livelihood but far-reaching possibilities of social and intellectual advance; and they will be received with welcome in a land of which the unlimited resources can be put to profit in proportion to the labour available.

The conversion of the wandering camel breeder and camel lifter into a cultivator of the soil, in so far as it has taken place in Mesopotamia, was an inevitable process. In their progress northward the tribes found themselves ultimately upon the limits of the desert; the wide spaces essential to nomadic existence no longer stretched before them, while the pressure of those behind forbade any return. They were obliged to look to agriculture as a means of livelihood. Thereby they lost caste with the true Badawin, yet, though these last would scorn to intermarry with tillers of the earth, shepherds and herdsmen of buffaloes, they are nevertheless of the same blood and tradition, and not infrequently fragments of very ancient and famous Arabian tribes are present among the cultivators upon the outer limits of Arabian migration. Thus in Mesopotamia the Bani Tamim, who are divided among various big tribal groups, were masters of the whole of Central Arabia before the time of the Prophet and still form a large part of the Oasis population— their first appearance in Mesopotamia dates from about the beginning of the Mohammedan era; and the Khazraj, now found chiefly on the Persian frontier, supplied by their martial exploits in the southern deserts much of the romantic stock in trade of the pre-Mohammedan poets.

It follows from the conditions under which settlement has been effected that the old tribes are often widely scattered along the edges of the cultivated land, large units which once ranged over extensive stretches of desert having been split up and thrust apart by the intrusion of others. For example, the Jubur, a tribe now only half nomadic, are found along the Tigris as far North as Mosul, as well as on the eastern frontiers, of Syria, and the Zubaid are divided between Mesopotamia and the volcanic districts east of Damascus.

The transition from a nomadic to a settled life is always a slow process and the very doubtful security offered by Turkish administration did not tend to hasten it. Except in the immediate neighbourhood of big towns, such as Baghdad and Basrah, tribal organization has not been relinquished, tribal law and customs hold good and tribal blood feuds continue to be a terrible scourge. A periodical reversion to tents is common and even the reed villagers are semi-nomadic, shifting frequently from place to place. The puzzled mapmaker may find his last addition to geographical knowledge removed, almost before his eyes, from the spot assigned to it in his survey and re-erected on another site. But the rising value of land tends to pin down these restless husbandmen and no sooner do they settle than their numbers increase out of all comparison with those of their hungry if prouder brethren who neither plough nor harvest the wilderness. The Muntafik confederation occupy an area which in round figures extends 65 miles from East to West and 50 miles from North to South, and number, at a rough estimate, not less than 200,000 souls, whereas the whole of the great Badawin group of the Anazah which peoples the Syrian desert from Aleppo to the sands of Central Arabia, can scarcely be reckoned at a higher figure.

The proximity of Persia and the existence in Mesopotamia of Karbala and Najaf, two of the most holy shrines of the Shiah sect, to which the Persians belong, with the resulting influx of Persian pilgrims, have brought the country much under Persian influences. Nomad Arabia belongs wholly to the Sunni half of Islam, yet the tribes settled in Mesopotamia have embraced, almost without exception, the Shiah faith. Those, however, who maintain purely nomadic habits, "people of the Camel" as they proudly call themselves, have kept as a rule to the desert doctrine and are almost invariably Sunni.

From the head of the Persian Gulf up to Qurnah tribal organisation has almost died out, except that many of the peasants working in the date gardens belong to the tribes of our staunch ally on the Persian side of the river, the powerful Shaikh of Mohammarah, who has in the past maintained the right to mobilise them for his own tribal operations. Above Qurnah the country, from Euphrates to Tigris for some distance along the banks of both rivers, is occupied by the Muntafik, a large and loose confederation of tribes of different origin, all of whom acknowledge, to a less degree or a greater, the over-lordship of the Sa'dun clan. These Sa'dun are sprung from a Mecca family closely related to the Sharif, a branch of which migrated to Mesopotamia towards the close of the Abbasid period, about the beginning of the 15th century. Themselves Sunnis and of the purest Sunni stock, they established their authority over the Shiah tribes and played a very considerable part in the stormy history of the land. In the case of one scion of the family who had rendered valuable service in Central Arabia, the Porte even tried the experiment of appointing him Wali of Basrah, but it quickly proved a failure and was abandoned.

Of late years their power as a ruling family has been gradually disintegrating owing to internal rivalries and dissensions and at present, though several of the leading members of the Sa'dun possess large estates in the Basrah Wilayet, they are able to exact but a small portion of their dues from their tribal tenantry and as tribal leaders in the field they are now of little account. Their family prestige is still, however, considerable.

The position of the Sa'dun clan, as affected by the outbreak of war between Turkey and Great Britain, has been a difficult one, for many of them own properties both in the territories in British occupation and in those at present controlled by the Turks; but except in the case of two or three irreconcilables their behaviour has on the whole been reasonable and intelligible, and there is little doubt that they will all come into the fold when they are satisfied that Turkish rule has vanished for ever from the Basrah Wilayet.

Some part of the Muntafik is still nomadic; the rest inhabit reed huts, villages, and even towns, cultivate the land and breed sheep, cattle, buffaloes and camels. Many of them who belong to the settled sections roam the desert in spring with their flocks and herds for the sake of pasturage.

The tribes of southern Mesopotamia are better armed than those above Kut and the Muntafik are well provided with modern rifles.

Above them, along the course of the Tigris almost up to Kut, lie two large and powerful tribes ranging from the river to the Persian Hills. Of these Al Bu Muhammed, a socially inferior and possibly non-Arab people, are rice-growers in the marshes

on either side of the Tigris and breed immense herds of buffaloes which are exported in great numbers to Syria. Like all
Marsh Arabs, they have maintained a semi-independence, and,
down to the youngest member of the tribe, they are well armed
with rifles. The second big group, that of the Bani Lam, have
occupied the country above Amarah for the last four or five
hundred years. Their Shaikhs claim descent from a famous pre-
Mohammedan tribe of Eastern Arabia, but, in spite of their pre-
tentions, none of the Badawin of the inner desert would regard
them as equals or intermarry with them. Their most prominent
Shaikh, Ghadhban, a great rebel against the Ottoman Government before the war, joined the Turks against us, but has now
reconsidered his position, and most of his house came to terms
with us as soon as we advanced up the Tigris. The Bani Lam are
cultivators, but none of them have entirely abandoned nomad
life. They inhabit tents and are generally on the move with their
herds from February to June. Their horses and camels are reckoned the best in Mesopotamia. They are good shots, especially
from the saddle.

Round Kut, both on the Tigris and on the upper part of the
great Hai canal, which flows out of the river southwards, the
Bani Rabi'ah bear sway, a tribe of ancient fame in Arabia. They
are a turbulent people, well-known robbers and disturbers of
traffic along the river, but not so efficiently armed as their neighbours to the South. Still less well provided with rifles and more
submissive to control are the two smaller tribes which cultivate
the Tigris banks up to Baghdad, the Toqah and the Zubaid,
while the inhabitants of the Euphrates marshes above Nasiriyah, though their reputation leaves much to be desired, have not
shown themselves ill disposed towards us.

Far down in the scale of civilization as these amphibious
dwellers in swamp and reed bed would seem to be, the amazing
quickness of the Arab in adopting himself to new conditions
and profiting by unexpected opportunities must never be forgotten. A child born yesterday in a reed hut or a black goat's hair
tent may well be found practising medicine or the law in Baghdad before the next quarter of a century is over, and, though his
father may prefer to abide by something more nearly resembling

the old customs, a solid balance at the bank will testify that he leads the simple life by choice and not of necessity.

The Star Worshippers of Mesopotamia

A curious phenomenon in Mesopotamia is the existence of a mass of people who have borrowed from all the races about them and have adopted customs belonging to all, and yet are totally isolated from them socially.

These are the Sabeans, known to some as the "Star Worshippers of Mesopotamia." Some writers have referred to them as "Saint John Christians," but this is a misnomer, because the "John" to whom they profess to adhere is certainly not a Saint, nor are they Christians in any sense of the word; they are the Sabeans mentioned in the Book of Job, though not the Sabeans mentioned in the Quran. During the time of the Mohammedan supremacy, however, they have accepted the interpretation that they are the Sabeans mentioned in the Quran, in order thus to protect themselves against persecution, since the Sabeans are mentioned in the Quran along with Christians and Jews as "People of the Book" and, therefore, to be reverenced.

The scientifically correct name of these people is the Mandæans. The word Mandæan in their own language means "disciple" and they refer to themselves as the "Disciples of John." Their language is Mandaitic, which belongs to the Semitic group of languages, and is a first cousin of Syriac. No printed literature exists, although a few of their manuscripts are in the hands of European scholars. The foremost Mandaitic scholar was Peterman, a German Orientalist, who about 60 years ago spent two years among the Sabeans at Suq-al-Shuyukh. They, of course, also speak Arabic, though never to my knowledge have they attended any Arabic Schools.

In the 17th century they numbered about 20,000 families, but at the present day their total does not exceed 3,000 souls. They exist only in Mesopotamia, a few living in Baghdad, and by far the great majority around Suq-al-Shuyukh. They are never to be found at a distance from running water inasmuch as the tenets of their religion demand their proximity to living water. The great decrease in population is due first of all to the persecution from the Mohammedan and then to internal strife; further many of their women have in late years been married to Mohammedans and thus the race is fast disappearing. They have three chief occupations, that of silver-smiths, canoe building and dairying. Their peculiar canoe is called the Mashhuf. Their silver work is justly famous for exquisite workmanship. It consists of black and silver wrought in cunning designs. The composition of this black substance, supposed to be antimony, is a secret of the trade with them. Of late years Arabs have been more tolerant towards them because of their ability as smiths and boat-builders, in neither of which occupations the Arab has any skill.

Their religion is a curious mixture of old Babylonian Paganism, of the Jewish Cult, of Christianity and Mohammedanism. From the Jewish religion they have borrowed sacrifices and purifications; from the Christian religion they have borrowed the observance of the first day of the week, Baptism, the Lord's Supper and the reverence for John the Baptist and from the Mohammedan religion they have borrowed polygamy.

Their great book, called the Sidra Rabba, contains their doctrines in rather fragmentary form, and gives evidence of a variety of authors, and a great number of contradictions. Even a glimpse of this book is very difficult to obtain, although many efforts have been made to secure a copy. Some years ago some travellers succeeded in stealing a copy, but representations were made to the Consul and the book was returned to the owners. I understand that a copy exists in the British Museum, together with a poor Latin translation which has never been completed. In 1904, through the friendship of their Chief Priest, I was allowed to purchase a copy for the sum of twelve pounds (Turkish), but on the condition that I should never sell the same. Even then, the next day there was a great demonstration by all the Sabeans and earnest endeavours were made by them to compel me to return the book. The copy in question is now being translated in America. A curious feature of this book is that half of each page is reversed to allow of the book's being placed over a narrow channel of running water and read by a Priest sitting on either side.

Another of their books is the "Book of Souls," two-thirds of which consist of prayers for the living and one-third of prayers for the dead. This book also contains a history of the death of Adam, who to them is one of the greatest Prophets.

A third book contains Liturgy for the Priests, and others contain marriage ceremonial, the life of John the Baptist, a treatise on astrology and various formulas for incantation and sorcery.

Their belief is that the world originated from what is called a "First Fruit," something like the Orphean theory of the world egg, and that the Great Lord brought forth life from this great egg, from which life again emanated another life who was Jesus Christ, but that the latter endeavoured to usurp the power of the former, and was therefore placed among the Planets as Mercury. They believe that the Heavens consist of the purest water, so hard that not a diamond can cut it, in which flow all the heavenly bodies as well as this earth. They also believe that the earth is surrounded on three sides by seas, but on the fourth there is a turquoise mountain, the reflection from which gives the blue colour to the sky. They further believe that the Queen of Darkness married Fire, and brought forth 24 sons, of whom 7 were the Planets including the Sun, 12 were the signs of the Zodiac and the remaining 5 are not known. These Planets are sources of evil to mankind. The Pole Star is situated at the very dome of Heaven and therefore they pray toward it, and for this reason they are called the "Star worshippers."

They practice Baptism, which by the pious among them is received every Sunday; they also observe a sort of Supper which apparently is an imitation of the Christian Communion.

They have places of Worship which, however, are only large enough to contain two or three Priests, and through these places of Worship run tiny streams of water over which prayers are said. There is no furniture in their Churches, save a shelf on which books and other articles are kept. Their priesthood is open to both men and women. The first grade is that of the noviatate, after which is the grade of Priest, thereafter a Bishop, and the highest official of the Church is the Chief Priest. The present

Chief Priest is named Shaikh Mahi and resides at Suq-al-Shuyukh. No priest may have the slightest blemish in his body and the consequence is that the Chief Priest is one of the most striking figures I have ever seen anywhere. A woman may attain to the rank of priesthood, but only on the condition that she marry a priest. It is against their religion for them to wear dark clothes, and for their women to wear anything blue.

One wonders how this curious growth will fare in the new soil of British administration. They are unquestionably pro-British, for the reason that they have always been anti-Turkish.

They never cut their hair, and both men and women may be called decidedly handsome, in fact so handsome that a Sabean can be at once recognised.

They were taken into the Army by the Turks, but were again excused because of the utter impossibility of meeting their religious demand to be always near running water.

THE NATION BUILDER

Gertrude, left idle in Basra while the army advanced north, suffered from lack of action and having no duties to carry out. She telegraphed Sir Percy Cox, asking when she might join him, and meantime cleared her desk and visited wounded Turkish soldiers. As the temperature rose to eighty degrees, she wrote to her stepmother and sisters to send her cotton and tussore dresses.

Basra, March 10, 1917

We are now hourly awaiting the news of our entrance into Bagdad. I had a letter from Sir Percy to-day, from the Front, full of exultation and confidence. I do hope I may be called up there before very long. It's a wonderful thing to be at the top of the war after all these months of marking time, and say what you will, it's the first big success of the war, and I think it is going to have varied and remarkable consequences.

We shall, I trust, make it a great centre of Arab civilisation, a prosperity; that will be my job partly, I hope, and I never lose sight of it.

In early April, she sent a two-word telegram to her parents, saying simply:

"Address Bagdad." She took a troop ship up the Tigris to Baghdad, a nine-day trip.

April 10, 1917

It's one of the new ships with electric light and fans and very comfortable, but I shall be glad to get to Baghdad where so many interesting things are happening. . . .

April 15, 1917

I'm free to admit that coming up this river gives one a whole-some respect for our lines of communication. . . . We passed Kut before sunrise but I got up to see it, poor tragic little place, with its shelled walls and shattered palm trees catching the first flush of day. It's quite empty still but we are going to clean it out and build it up as soon as possible. . . .

We anchored last night just above Ctesiphon. And today I know the river banks well for I've ridden up them more than once. Our big camps are the only unfamiliar objects. It's exactly 3 years today since I last set out from Baghdad across the Syrian desert on my way home from Arabia.

Baghdad, April 20, 1917

Such an arrival! Sir Percy made me most welcome and said a house had been allotted to me. I went off to see it and found a tiny stifling box of a place in a dirty little bazaar. It was abso-lutely empty—what furniture I had was with my heavy luggage and not yet landed and I hadn't even a boy as I had left my ser-vant to look after the heavy luggage. Fortunately, like a good traveller, I had not parted from my bed and bath. These I pro-ceeded to set up and further unpacked one of my boxes which had been dropped into the Tigris and hung out all the things to dry on the railing of the court. It was breathlessly hot. I hadn't so much as a chair to put anything onto and when I wanted water for washing I had to open my front door and call in the help of the bazaar. . . .

I dined with Sir Percy, armed myself with a loaf of bread for breakfast and returned to my empty house to sleep. By good luck my servant turned up late. . . . I confess however that after having done my hair and breakfasted on the floor I felt a little discouraged.

She set off in search of a better house by the river.

The first thing I stumbled onto was a rose garden with 3 summer houses in it, quite close to the Political Office and belonging foreby, to an old friend of mine, Musa Chalabi. I decided at once that this was the thing. But a kitchen had to built, a bathroom, sun blinds to be put up—a thousand things. I got Musa Chalabi to help me, and summoned in an old man . . . and after five days' work I'm in. . . . And my roses, I must tell you, are glorious. . . .

I'm going to have an exciting summer. . . . The rest for another time—I'm so busy.

Baghdad, May 11, 1917

This is how I pass my days: I'm out riding before 6, . . . a gallop in the desert and home through the bazaars. Occasionally I inspect an ancient monument on the way back. . . . A bath and breakfast and so to the office before 9. I'm there till after 7. . . . There's always just a little too much to do. I come back to dinner in my garden at 8 and I generally go to bed at 9.30.

May 17, 1917

Oh my dearest ones, it's so wonderful here—I can't tell you how much I'm loving it . . . I wonder what inheritance from Cumbrian farmers can have developed unexpectedly into so compelling an at-home-ness with the East?

May 17, 1917, Letter to Sir William Willcocks

I have grown to love this land, its sights and its sounds. I never weary of the East, just as I never feel it to be alien. I cannot feel exiled here; it is a second native country.

May 18, 1917

Nowhere in the war-shattered universe can we begin more speedily to make good the immense losses sustained by humanity. . . . It's an immense opportunity, just at this time when the atmosphere is so emotional; one catches hold of people as one will never do again, and establishes relations which won't dissolve. It is not for my own sake, but because it greases the wheels of administration—it really does, and I want to watch it all very carefully almost from day to day, so as to be able to take what I hope may be . . . a decisive hand in [the] final disposition. I shall be able to do that, I shall indeed, with the knowledge I'm gaining. It's so intimate. They are beyond words outgoing to me. What does anything else matter when the job is such a big one? There never was anything quite like this before. . . . It's the making of a new world.

————

The difficulties faced by the administration were formidable. Arabs spoke a common language but were not one people. Mesopotamia was not a country but a province of a derelict empire, not formally recognized as Iraq until full independence was gained in 1932. As the Turks had withdrawn northward, they had followed a scorched earth policy, smashing dams and destroying agriculture. Disease was spreading, and the one hospital in Baghdad was discovered to be in an indescribable condition. In spite of these and other massive problems, there was a noble determination on the part of Sir Percy Cox and his staff to do well for the people of the Basra and

Baghdad vilayets. It was this ambition above all that inspired Gertrude.

Self-determination remained a vague concept. To the Shia mujtahids, the religious representatives, it meant a theocratic state under Sharia law; to the Sunnis and freethinkers of Baghdad, it meant an independent Arab state under an emir; to the desert and mountain tribes, it meant no government at all.

The first overtures of the sheikhs and notables to the administration were made in the spirit of insurance, in the hope that the British would stay. Who was there, other than Gertrude, who would recognize and be recognized by so many of them, who could extend the traditional courtesies and interview them in their own language or dialect, who knew the differences between mujtahid, Sunni cleric, mufti, mukhtar, or mutawalli? As they were welcomed and reassured, enormous numbers descended on the secretariat. Gertrude, greeted as "Khatun" ("queen" in Persian and "noble lady" in Arabic) or "Umm al-Muminin" (Mother of the Faithful) would welcome them and usher them into the waiting room for Sir Percy, with a note explaining who they were, where they came from, and what they wanted.

Gertrude's most important political paper, the book-length *Review of the Civil Administration of Mesopotamia,* was written at the request of the India Office. It took nine months of her spare time and was a magnificent summary of the concerns that made this work the most important of her life. Giving a detailed insight into the work of the administration in establishing a functioning and prosperous land, it was received with great appreciation in London, particularly in Parliament where it was applauded by the House of Commons.

January 17, 1921

I've just got Mother's letter saying there's a fandango about my report. The general line taken by the press seems to be that it's most remarkable that a dog should be able to stand up on its hind legs—i.e. a female write a white paper. I hope they'll drop

that source of wonder and pay attention to the report itself. . . .
By the way, Mother need not think it was A.T. who asked me to
write it—it was the India Office, and I insisted, very much
against his will, on doing it my own way.

FROM *REVIEW OF THE CIVIL ADMINISTRATION OF MESOPOTAMIA*

Any administration . . . must bring to the task . . . singular
integrity and diligence, combined with a just comprehension of
the conflicting claims of different classes of the population. It
must also command the confidence of the people so as to secure
the co-operation of public opinion, without which so complex a
tangle could not be unraveled.

Reconstruction

A profound impression was produced among the tribes by the
rebuilding of Kut. This work, . . . an act of piety in memory
of those who had given their life in the defence of the town,
Arab as well as British, was undertaken immediately after the
occupation. . . . Houses were cleaned out as fast as possible and
disinfected, rubbish was carted away . . . the battlefields were
searched and the dead buried or re-buried. . . . The crowning
glory of the new Kut was an arcaded bazaar along the river
front. . . . Thus before the oncoming of winter the refugees were
lodged, and the town had become a more flourishing market
than it had been before its destruction.

Revenue

It was necessary to set up temporarily some sort of revenue and
fiscal administration. To this end it was decided to keep intact
the Turkish system, to which the people were accustomed, but
to free it from corruption and abuses and increase its efficiency.

The number of alien officials introduced was deliberately kept low. All other appointments were filled by the more honest of the ex-official people of the country, the large majority being Mussalmans. This would have been in any case inevitable, as the records of the departments were all in Turkish; the language of vernacular records and receipts, together with all other official business, was, however, changed to Arabic, a measure which satisfied local sentiment.

The initial difficulties in setting up civil administration in the occupied territories were greatly enhanced by the fact that, except for a few Arab subordinates, all the former Turkish officials had fled, taking with them the most recent documents and registers. . . . The British military authorities had at first no leisure to make any arrangements with regard to fiscal and revenue matters except in respect of customs, but towards the middle of January a Revenue Commissioner, Mr. Henry Dobbs, I.C.S., arrived in Basrah from India, and such records as had been left by the Turks were overhauled. They were mostly out of date and were lying mixed with masses of lumber on the floors of the Turkish offices. . . . The administration was confronted with the task of setting the whole of a strange and complicated system on its legs as quickly as possible. . . . Moreover, the exactions of the Turks before leaving, the confusion into which the administration had for some months been thrown, and the dislocation of trade by the stoppage of commerce with Baghdad on the one side and with India and Europe on the other, coupled with an unusually bad date season, had temporarily deprived the population of cash and credit.

Public Health

The sanitary condition of the towns made a notable advance during 1916. Latrines and incinerators were everywhere in use, butcheries and markets inspected, a successful campaign was carried on against flies and rats, and infectious diseases checked. In the villages of Qurnah, Qal 'at Salih and 'Ali Gharbi hospitals and dispensaries were served by the medical military officer of the station, usually with an Indian Sub-Assistant Surgeon, but at Suq, owing to the extreme shortage of medical staff, it was impossible to start regular medical work till 1917, and the absence of a dispensary was regarded by the inhabitants as a grievance, though no such institution would have been dreamed of in Turkish times. The readiness to submit to treatment in hospitals was very remarkable. The fame of the British doctors spread through the districts and patients came in from afar, willing to accept operation and even loss of limb when they were told that it was necessary. Among their other uses, hospitals and dispensaries provided a more convincing form of propaganda than any which could have been invented by the most eloquent preacher or the most skilful pamphleteer.

The people accepted inoculation and other precautions against plague, and were eager for vaccination.

Education

In the Baghdad Wilayat the Turkish educational programme was more comprehensive than at Basrah. It comprised a school of law, a secondary school, a normal school, a technical school, and 71 primary schools. The scheme, as set forth in the official Turkish Education Year Book, full of maps and statistics, might have roused the envy and despair of the British authorities of the Occupied Territories but for the knowledge that, provided a school were shown correctly as a dot on a map, the Turk cared not to enquire whether the pupils enrolled ever attended, or whether the system of education pursued in it was that of Arnold of Rugby or of Mr. Wopsle's great aunt. . . .

With the departure of the Turkish authorities in March 1917, the law, sultani* and technical schools ceased to exist as institutions, for nearly all the teachers were Anatolian Turks and left with the rest of Stambul officialdom, while in the case of the technical school the Turks blew up the machinery and burned the building. As to the primary schools, they were nearly all

*Turkish name for high schools.

looted by the mob. If it took rather longer to open some of the Baghdad schools than might have been expected, the delay may be attributed to the people themselves, who looted all the furniture and equipment of the schools and carried off the doors, windows and other portable fittings. . . .

The principal language taught was Turkish, Arabic being treated as a secondary language. The teachers were mostly Turks, often with only a scanty knowledge of Arabic; they were men of bad character, highly paid and incompetent. The school buildings were dirty and insanitary, and the schools hotbeds of vice to which respectable Arabs hesitated to send their boys. No one who was not of the Sunni sect was recognised as a teacher, and this, in a population predominantly Shi'ah, discouraged attendance. The registers were filled with fictitious entries. . . .

On these considerations it was decided that the medium of instruction should be Arabic throughout with English taught as a foreign language. . . . Primary text-books were carefully selected from the official primary text-books in use in Egypt, and class-room furniture was purchased from abroad.

The Law

This system of local justice was recognised by us to be a strong weapon on the side of order and good conduct. Just as it was the habit of the British Military Governors when hearing cases to call in the mukhtars, the headmen of the town quarters, and ask them to take part in the proceedings, so the Political Officers turned to the shaikhs of tribe and village and obtained their opinion. . . .

In one respect tribal custom, as administered by the majlis,* is not wholly satisfactory in our eyes. The tribesman regards the exaction of blood money payable to the relations of the murdered man as of greater moment than the punishment of the murderer, and is apt to be content with the fine without any further retribution.

*A court comprised of tribal elders to hear arguments and make rulings.

... In accepting tribal usage the Political Officer might find himself called upon to impose penalties which are foreign to British judicial tradition. Thus in cases of blood feud the tribes of the Euphrates almost invariably require the guilty party, in addition to the payment of blood money, to hand over a virgin to the family of the deceased, and they value this custom not only as a punishment, but also a safeguard, for, as they justly observe, the payment of fines does nothing towards allaying animosity, whereas inter-marriage provides a community of interests. . . .

Humanitarian Aid

The occupation of the Mosul Wilayat [where the Turks had held on, ten thousand people died of starvation in the winter of 1917–18] brought the British Administration into direct relations with the Kurds. . . . In no part of Mesopotamia had we encountered anything comparable to the misery which greeted us at Khaniqin. The country harvested by the Russians had been sedulously gleaned by the Turks, who, when they retired, left it in the joint possession of starvation and disease. The work of administration was at first little more than a battle with these formidable adversaries. . . . No sooner did the Kurds on both sides of the frontier hear that help was to be had, than they poured down the mountains, starving and typhus-stricken, to be brought slowly back to health, or else to die in our camps and hospitals. . . .

In the surrounding districts cultivation had for the last two years been completely suspended, and the population had been reduced by about 75 per cent of its pre-war figure. So severe was the famine that in some districts the inhabitants were living entirely on herbs and the few acorns which were left, and had been constrained to devour cats and dogs, and even in some cases human flesh.

Steps were taken at once to deal with the famine, grain was imported from Arbil, poor relief started, agriculture encouraged, and a measure of law and order secured.

Agriculture

On the Tigris from Samarra to the vicinity of Baghdad all cultivation had been destroyed. . . . What the Turks had not eaten
they had destroyed. Nearer Baghdad the rain and flood had
failed. This was the third bad season in succession, and stocks
of vegetable seeds, cereals, and, most important of all, fodder,
had been reduced to a minimum. . . . From Baghdad to Kut
there was no cultivation except on a few lifts and an area in the
Jaznah, where the ground was still moist from the flood of
1915. . . . The Turks had deliberately removed the tribes from
the river banks and forbidden agriculture. . . .

The chief duties of the Irrigation Directorate are flood protection, a heavy item with rivers which have a spring rise of 20 feet
or more, the control and conservancy of rivers and canals, the
provision of an adequate water supply at the heads of water-
courses, and the distribution of water as between different water-
courses. . . . Several canals have been re-aligned or extended, the
new lands commanded by them being eagerly taken up. An
important piece of work is now in progress between two of the
Euphrates channels which it is hoped will bring back into cultivation large tracts which have long lain barren.

. . . The necessity of controlling irrigation was at once apparent. . . . Canal clearance had also to be arranged. . . . By far the
most important irrigation work which claimed attention was
the great dam at the offtake of the Hindiyah channel from
the Euphrates . . . subject to destructive fluctuations. . . . British
engineers visited it in May 1917, and as the military irrigation
services extended . . . water flowed down the two loop canals in
time to permit the winter sowings of wheat and barley, and the
country on either side of the Hindiyah, after having lain barren
for several years, was in January 1918 covered with springing
barley. . . .

It would be difficult to estimate the proportion of the crop of
1918 which was due directly to the Agricultural Development
Scheme combined with the operations of the Irrigation Department, but the army was able to procure between 50,000 and
60,000 tons of grain from the spring crop, and the needs of the

civil population were supplied. . . . Not only was Mesopotamia safeguarded from famine, but by releasing the grain which had been stored against another lean year we were able to feed the Bedouin, and thereby to keep them in order, and to succour the Kurds on both sides of our frontier.

Oil

Abadan, the refinery of the Anglo-Persian Oil Company, was henceforth safe, and from being an object the protection of which was one of the primary duties of the Force, it assumed for the rest of the war the role of purveyor of crude oil, kerosene and petrol to every branch of His Majesty's services. The record of its work is one of which all those associated with it, as well as with the distant oil fields on which it depends, may well be proud.

From its tiny beginnings in Basra in 1915, the British administration grew in size as it settled into its role in Baghdad. Its remit extended over 150,000 square miles and some 3 million people. The secretariat remained small: Sir Percy Cox, Gertrude, and three other Cabinet-level officials. In total, there were five hundred executive staff including doctors, nurses, irrigation specialists, and agricultural researchers. The policies of the government were pursued throughout the country by a mere seventy Political Officers, each with a couple of Indian clerks, a sergeant, and a handful of riflemen. The income obtained by taxes grew tenfold during the five years. All of it was used to fund the medical, agricultural, veterinary, judicial, and other government services. The army, paid for by London, rebuilt and extended roads, railways, canals, ports, and public buildings, although the cost of this became a debt for the future government to pay off. Naturally, import and export trade collapsed in 1915 as the Turks retreated, but by 1919 it was more than four times greater than when they were in power.

Meanwhile, even the administrators were on iron rations. The food in the mess, where Gertrude ate during the working

week, was rationed and monotonous. A family friend of the
Bells, Colonel Frank Balfour, who later became Baghdad's
military governor, tells the story of joining her in the mess one
evening for dinner. When, for the fourteenth day running, the
meal consisted of bully beef, Gertrude surprised him by throw-
ing down her knife and fork in disgust and bursting into tears.

October 12, 1917

We are put to it to feed ourselves, and it is hard to feel Hercu-
lean on biscuits—We've had no butter all summer and when we
have it it's tinned. I've forgotten what potatoes taste like—the
meat is almost too tough to eat, chickens ditto; milk tinned—
how sick one gets of it! . . . When one's feeling rather a poor
thing one does hate it all. . . . Heaven send us a good harvest
next year.

The ferocious heat of Iraq was, perhaps, the main factor in the
breakdown of her health. Light as she made of it in her letters
home, she now frequently suffered from heat exhaustion, combined with overwork, cigarettes, and recurring malaria. Every
summer she had to repair to an officers' convalescent home for
a few days' recovery, and even in hospital she continued to
write position papers and draft a fortnightly diary for the government. Her red hair turned white, and she wrote home to
explain the extreme measures she used to get cool.

Baghdad, July 13, 1917

We have had a week of fierce heat, which still continues, temp
122 odd and therewith a burning wind which has to be felt to be
believed. On the worst nights . . . I drop a sheet in water and
without wringing it out lay it in a pile along my bed between me
and the wind. I put one end over my feet and draw the other
under and over my head and leave the rest a few inches from my
body. The sharp evaporation makes it icy cold and interposes a

little wall of cold air between me and the fiery wind. When it dries I wake up and repeat the process. This evening Sir Percy and I went out motoring at 7 but it was too hot. The wind shrivelled you and burnt your eyeballs. . . . My room in the office I shut up all day long and have it sluiced out with water 2 or 3 times a day. By these means I keep the temp at just under 100 [38°C].

Yes, that's what it is like.

When dresses had to be washed and ironed every day, she was in constant need of cool Western clothing. Her family sent her parcels of clothes, but there were never enough. She called in on a convent and explained her predicament.

Baghdad, June 14, 1918

The nuns are making me a muslin gown—it will be a monument of love and care. The essayages are not like any other dress-making I've ever known. I go in after riding before breakfast and stand in practically nothing but breeches and boots (for it's hot) while the Mother Superior and the darling dressmaking sister, Soeur Renée, hover round ecstatically and pin on bits of muslin. At our elbows a native lay sister bearing cups of coffee. We pause often while the Mother Superior and Soeur Renée discuss gravely what really is the fashion. Anyhow the result is quite satisfactory. Soeur Renée isn't a Frenchwoman for nothing.

Her highly pressurized life was complicated by her need for a maid, housekeeper, and dressmaker. Her stepmother, Florence, came up with a solution: Marie Delaire had been with the Bells since Gertrude hired her seventeen years previously. She came out to Iraq and served Gertrude devotedly for the rest of her mistress's life.

In October 1917, Gertrude was made a Commander of the Order of the British Empire, and a year later she was awarded the Founder's Medal of the Royal Geographical Society for her journey to Hayyil. In a glimpse of Gertrude during an at home given for forty or fifty Arab notables in Baghdad in 1919, she is described as entering the room in queenly style, "beautifully dressed as always" while everyone rose to their feet. She went around the room, shaking the hands of everyone in turn and saying a few appropriate words to each.

Since Cairo, she had been living in the East on her salary of £20 a month ($16,320 RPI adjusted equivalent to a salary of $88,000 income adjusted), and her generous private allowance had been piling up at home, unused. Since the two things she craved—good food and well-made European clothing—were unavailable, she responded to her father's letter about her allowance with the lack of financial interest that is the prerogative of heiresses that he should do whatever he wanted with the money. She was in the hospital when her father sent her a forty-ninth birthday present: a great emerald, which she pinned on her nightdress. A month later, Florence sent another parcel.

September 25, 1917

There arrived a jeweller's shop of brooches and pendants—the loveliest things—how could you reconcile it with your conscience, both of you, to run to such extravagance? I've never had so many brooches in my life. . . . Anyhow, bless you both; they are exquisite and I expect will excite the unbounded admiration of I.E.F.D. [Indian Expeditionary Force D]

So successfully put together and administered, so successful in its occupation until the end of the war, the British government of Mesopotamia was about to be undermined by interminable delays while it waited for international decisions on the position of the borders and its future in Iraq. Meanwhile, many strands of minority dissent, fanned into flames by Turkish agents, would grow into outright revolt. Waiting impatiently, Gertrude had to watch all progress slipping away in the teeth of growing anarchy. At this most difficult moment, Sir Percy Cox was sent to Tehran, leaving his former deputy A. T. Wilson as acting civil commissioner. He proved to be a boss whose high-handed tactics, punitive retaliation against dissidents, and preference for imperialist policies brought home to Gertrude the appalling truth: he had no sympathy for self-determination and would do his best to prevent it. He was built from a heroic colonialist mold, but his views placed him in the past. Gertrude, though eighteen years older, with her particular intelligence and her wholehearted dedication to the Arab cause, belonged to the future.

Six months after Cox's departure, A.T. disbanded the Baghdad branch of the Arab Bureau, under whose auspices Gertrude had been appointed, and effectively demoted her from Oriental secretary—a role equivalent to that of a Cabinet member—to political officer. At about this time, the League of Nations required her to write a paper, "The Political Future of Iraq," in which she made her feelings clear.

> I propose to assume . . . that the welfare and prosperity of Iraq is not incompatible with the welfare and prosperity of any other portion of the world. I assume therefore as an axiom that if, in disposing of the question of the future administration of Iraq, we allow ourselves to be influenced by any consideration whatsoever other than the well being of the country itself and its people we shall be guilty of a shameless act of deliberate dishonesty rendered the more heinous and contemptible by our reiterated declarations of disinterested solicitude for the peoples concerned.

A.T.'s refusal to consider Gertrude's suggestions of negotiation with dissidents and the punitive tactics he employed to put down uprisings resulted, inevitably, in increasing subversion. Sidelined, Gertrude put her views privately in letter form to her influential friends and acquaintances in London. The year of jihad in Iraq, 1920, is remembered as a failure of the British administration. It should be remembered that Gertrude had no part in the decisions to bomb villages or in the decisions

that led to military confrontations with tribes and the murder
of political officers on the borders.

January 17, 1919, Four Months After Cox's Departure

I might be able to help to keep things straight—if they'll let me. . . .
We are having rather a windy time over self-determination. . . . I
wish very much that Sir Percy were here.

December 28, 1919, Letter to Chirol

Sir P.C. is a very great personal asset and I wish the Government
would let him come back at once. The job here is far more
important than Persia.

January 12, 1920

I wish I carried more weight. But the truth is I'm in a minority of
one in the Mesopotamian political service—or nearly—and yet
I'm sure that I'm right.

February 1, 1920

We share the blame with France and America for what is
happening—I think there has seldom been such a series of hopeless
blunders as the West has made about the East since the armistice.

Baghdad, September 5, 1920

We are now in the middle of a full-blown Jihad, that is to say we
have against us the fiercest prejudices of a people in a primeval
state of civilization. . . . We're near to a complete collapse of
society—the end of the Roman empire is a very close historical

parallel. . . . The credit of European civilization is gone. . . .
How can we, who have managed our own affairs so badly,
claim to teach others to manage theirs better?

Baghdad, April 10, 1920

I think we're on the edge of a pretty considerable Arab nationalist demonstration with which I'm a good deal in sympathy. It
will however force our hand and we shall have to see whether it
will leave us with enough hold to carry on here. . . .

But what I do feel pretty sure of is that if we leave this country
to go to the dogs it will mean that we shall have to reconsider
our whole position in Asia. . . . And the place which we leave
empty will be occupied by seven devils a good deal worse than
any which existed before we came.

A.T. was made a Knight Commander of the Order of the
Indian Empire (KCIE) in May 1920. Gertrude commented to
her parents, "I confess I wish that in giving him a knighthood
they could also endow him with the manners knights are tra-
ditionally credited with!"

June 14, 1920

Meantime my own path has been very difficult. I had an appalling scene last week with A.T. . . . Most unfortunately I gave one
of our Arab friends here a bit of information I ought not, technically, to have given. It wasn't of much importance (Frank agrees)
and it didn't occur to me I had done wrong till I mentioned it
casually to A.T. He was in a black rage that morning and he
vented it on me. He told me my indiscretions were intolerable,
and that I should never see another paper in the office. I apolo-
gised for that particular indiscretion, but he continued: "You've
done more harm than anyone here. If I hadn't been going away
myself I should have asked for your dismissal months ago!" . . .
At this point he choked with anger.

July 4, 1920

The tribes down there [in the south of Iraq] are some of the most lawless in Iraq. . . . But I doubt whether we've gone the best way to make them appreciate the benefits of settled government. For months I and others have been telling A.T. that we were pressing them too hard. . . .

December 20, 1920

Rather a trying week, for A.T. has been over-worked—a chronic state—and in a condition when he ought not to be working, which results in making him savagely cross and all our lives rather a burden in consequence.

Just as Gertrude was considering whether she or A.T. should resign, there was light at the end of the tunnel. Sir Percy Cox was requested to return to Iraq. London had recognized that A.T.'s tactics were not working and that insurrection was growing worse. It was costing too much to run Iraq his way, flattening revolt to protect the infrastructure. It was the end of A.T.'s official career.

There was one final devastating argument over Gertrude's independence in making known her own views, as separate from A.T.'s. She wrote to people who were senior to him in the British government and India. A.T. was particularly incensed by her privileged private visit to the chief Shia family, the Sadr of Kadhimain, to visit the august mujtahid Sayyid Hassan. She entertained Arab nationalists to dinner in her own house, to keep the lines of communication open with potential leaders of a future Arab government. To her chief, this was tantamount to treason, although she was pursuing official London policy.

When A.T. left Baghdad, they parted in civilized fashion. As Gertrude said, "We shook hands warmly—you can't shake hands anything but warmly when the temperature is 115 [46°C]."

September 27, 1920

The night before he left he came in late to say goodbye. I told
him that I was feeling more deeply discouraged than I could well
say and that I regretted acutely that we had not made a better
job of our relations. He replied that he had come to apologise
and I stopped him and said I felt sure it was as much my fault as
his and that I hoped he would carry away no ill- feelings, a sentiment to which he cordially responded.

Sir Percy Cox passed through Baghdad on his way to London
in June 1920. He stopped off for a long discussion with Gertrude and left her his parrot to look after until his return to
Iraq in October, when he intended to set up a provisional Arab
government.

October 17, 1920

It's quite impossible to tell you the relief and comfort it is to be
serving under someone in whose judgement one has complete confidence. To the extraordinarily difficult task which lies before him
he brings a single eyed desire to act in the interests of the people of
the country.

November 1, 1920

Oh, if we can pull this thing off! rope together the young hot-
heads and the Shi'ah obscurantists, and enthusiasts like Ja'far,
polished old statesmen like Sasun, and scholars like Shukri—if
we can make them work together and find their own salvation
for themselves, what a fine thing it will be. I see visions and
dream dreams.

As the international powers were preparing their positions for the
forthcoming Paris Peace Conference, President Woodrow Wilson
made it clear that he expected the nations whose governments

had been eliminated by the war to be allowed to decide their own future. Sir Mark Sykes, a respected adviser to the British government, engineered a joint statement with the French to prove to President Wilson that they were aligned with his intentions and did not intend to colonize. Understanding little of the situation in Iraq, the government in London required A. T. Wilson to seek the opinions of the most respected members of the region stretching from Basra north to the Kurdish area. Wilson set about the task halfheartedly, as he was a firm believer in colonization. Before the consultation process even began, the Sykes Anglo-French Declaration was already causing trouble. Muslim religious leaders, the large Christian and Jewish communities, and the more sober secular leaders and sheikhs were petrified that a sudden withdrawal of the British administration and its supporting army would open all borders to their enemies. Bolshevik Russia, Ibn Saud's Wahhabis, and the vengeful Turks were poised to overwhelm Arabia.

Out of necessity, Gertrude had to take much of the responsibility for the conduct of the consultation, which involved inviting representatives from the major cities and religious groups to select a total of seventy-five nominees to answer three questions. Were they in favor of a single Arab state from Kurdistan to Basra? Should the state be headed by an Arab emir? Was there any preferred candidate for the role?

The responses, as expected by Gertrude, were hopelessly inconclusive except that there seemed to be unanimity about a new nation state covering the whole region. The exercise provoked vociferous responses from young would-be politicians including extremists who stated their views in the coffee shops, where public debate still takes place. They objected to the British presence, they fomented Sunni-Shia differences, and they ignored the interests of minorities. It fell to Gertrude to write a difficult document attempting to summarize the outcome of the exercise, to be sent to the Paris Peace Conference. She chose to enter the facts in great detail, describing the difficulties encountered and the conflicting wide-ranging opinions elicited. The document was entitled "Self-Determination in Mesopotamia."

Realizing that the document would be of no conclusive value, she took the initiative of consulting the most respected figure in Iraq, the elderly naqib of Baghdad, His Reverence Sayyid Abd ul-Rahman Effendi. The primate of the Sunni religious community, he was equally respected by the Shias. Her hour and a half spent with him is beautifully described below in an appendix she attached to the "Self-Determination in Mesopotamia" paper and sent to Paris.

Political Views of the Naqib of Baghdad

I went by appointment to see the Naqib on the morning of February 6th in order to bid him farewell, as I was leaving on the 8th for England. I arrived at the house earlier than he expected and was received by his son, Saiyid Hashim, with whom I sat talking several minutes before the Naqib came in. The Naqib has been living since the occupation in his house opposite the Takiyah of Abdul Qadir, of which he is the head, the house which he usually occupies on the river next to the Residency, having been taken as a billet, with his consent. His domestic arrangements are studiously simple. The room in which he receives visitors is on the first floor, with windows looking into a small garden court planted with orange trees. Hard, upright sofas covered with white calico, are ranged round the wall. In one corner of the room, by the window, where the Naqib sits, there is a small table covered with a white-cloth on which some book or pamphlet is always to be found. The walls are white washed and the room unadorned save by its spotless cleanliness. The Naqib is an old man bowed by years and somewhat crippled by rheumatism. His dress is a long sleeved robe, reaching to the feet, made of white linen in summer and black cloth in winter, and opening over a white linen under robe which is confined at the waist by the folds of a wide white band. On his head be wears a white turban folded round a red tarbush.

At his entrance Saiyid Hashim withdrew and the Naqib gave orders that no visitors were to be admitted. I then told him that I was leaving Baghdad rather earlier than I had intended as I had been summoned to Paris and I added that there were probably minor details, such as decisions as to frontiers where local knowledge might be called for. I instanced the question of the Mutasarrifliq of Dair from which place the ex-Rais Baladiyah had recently arrived with a request that the Mutasarrifliq might be attached to the Mesopotamian State, and I asked the Naqib for his opinion.

He replied that he had seen the man in question and was acquainted with his brother, who was an important citizen of Dair. Our visitors had been to the Naqib and had asked his advice on the future status of the district. A number of persons had however been present and the Naqib, characteristically unwilling to commit himself in public, had bidden the inquirer return on the following day when he himself would have had time to consider the matter. "He is waiting to see me now, and since we are talking confidentially I will tell you the answer I intend to give him. I shall say to him: 'My son, you will do well to come under the British Government, for the British are known throughout the world for justice and fair dealing.' But I will make clear to you," continued the Naqib, "what is in my thoughts. I do not like the French." (It must be understood that he is taking for granted that the French will control Syria up to the boundaries of the Mesopotamian State.) "Yes, I admire their learning and I delight in their cultured minds. But I do not like their Government. It is not concealed from us that the Muhammadan population of Algeria has suffered under their administration. These things are known. It is my desire to keep the French as far as possible from Baghdad. Khatun Sahib, I am speaking now for your ear only and I must pray you to forgive my words. I fear an inevitable conflict between the French and the British. For when the British have put their foot down, they do not lift it; what they hold they maintain. They will encounter the ambition and jealousy of the French and even if it meant a war of 50 years' duration they will not give way. I am a darwish: my concern is not with the things of this world. But I have a long experience of men and affairs, and I lay bare to you my apprehensions."

After embroidering this theme for some moments (for the Naqib is discursive in speech) he inquired, as is his invariable custom whenever I visit him, when we might expect the return of Sir Percy Cox. "Khatun," said he, "there are a hundred and a thousand men in England who could fill the post of Ambassador in Persia, but there is none but Sir Percy Cox who is suitable for 'Iraq. He is known, he is loved and he is trusted by the people of 'Iraq. He is a man of sober years. . . . Moreover he is a man of great standing in London. He will act as our spokesman. If the government wishes to know our thoughts he will be able to give the necessary information and his word will be accepted. I bear witness in God that if Sir Percy Cox had been in Baghdad we should have been spared the folly of asking the people to express their wish as to the future. It has been the cause of great unrest, and the agitation in the town is not yet allayed. You know that I have taken no part, and I forbade my family to meddle with the business. My son, Saiyid Mahmud, was the first to resign his appointment as delegate to the Majlis. I told him to have nothing to do with it. But many have come to me asking for my advice or pressing me to agree to their views. I replied. The English have conquered this country, they have expended their wealth and they have watered the soil with their blood. The blood of Englishmen, of Australians, Canadians, Moslems of India and Idolaters has drenched the dust of the 'Iraq. Shall they not enjoy what they have won? Other conquerors have overwhelmed the country. As it fell to them, so it has fallen to the English. They will establish their dominion. Khatun, your nation is great, wealthy and powerful: where is our power? If I say that I wish for the rule of the English and the English do not consent to govern us, how can I force them? And if I wish for the rule of another, and the English resolve to remain, how can I eject them? I recognise your victory. You are the governors and I am the governed. And when I am asked what is my opinion as to the continuance of British rule, I reply that I am the subject of the victor.

"You, Khatun," the Naqib was so kind to observe, "have an understanding of statecraft. I do not hesitate to say to you that I loved the Turkish government when it was as l once knew it. If I could return to the rule of the Sultans of Turkey as they were in former times, I should make no other choice. But I loathe and hate, curse and consign to the devil the present Turkish Government. . . .The Turk is dead; he has vanished, and I am content to become your subject.

"You are going to London; you will see and converse with the great and this is what you shall say. Let Sir Percy Cox return to the 'Iraq and let there be an end of military rule. It would be a great wrong if it should continue. I do not speak against the Commander-in-Chief. His nobility is apparent in his face. I have visited him; though it is not my custom, when Sir Percy Cox asked me to visit Sir William Marshall (the Naqib grappled somewhat unsuccessfully with the Commander-in-Chief's name) I consented. It would not have been fitting if I had refused. I also visited Maude. Your country owes Maude great praise, and we also owe him gratitude. He was beloved in Baghdad. But in the days of peace, power should be in the hands of statesmen and not of soldiers. You must keep an army in this country for the preservation of order, but the army must not govern. This is what you shall say: 'We wish to be governed by Sir Percy Cox. But do not say,' added the Naqib with some astuteness, 'even though it be true, that you yourself have become a Baghdadi and that your mind is wholly occupied with the welfare of the 'Iraq, for that will cause your words [to carry] less weight in London and we shall have the less profit from you.'"

After this word of warning, the Naqib returned to the theme of self-determination.

"What is all this talk," said he, "and what is its value? I trace it to America and I hear the voice of Wilson. Does Shaikh Wilson know the East, and its peoples? Does he know our ways of life and our habits of mind? You English have governed for 300 years in Asia and your rule is an example for all men to follow. Pursue your own way. Do not submit to guidance from Shaikh Wilson or from another. Knowledge and experience are your guides."

With this opening it was not difficult to draw the Naqib back to the discussion of recent events in Baghdad.

"Most of those who have spoken against you," said he, "are men without name or honour. Ramdi Pachahji is not of the slightest consideration; he is moreover possessed of the evil one (majnun). Who has ever heard of Ja'far Abu Timmam? He does not belong to the Ashraf of the town. But I tell you to beware of the Shi'ahs. I have no animosity against the Shi'ah sect," he hastened to assure me and I was careful to give no hint of my underlying doubts. "They love and respect me and I am regarded by them as their Shaikh. But turn your eyes on the pages of history and you will see that the salient characteristic of the Shi'ahs is their levity. . . . Idolatry and mutability are combined in them. Place no reliance upon them."

I then told the Naqib that we had a full list of those who had led the anti-British agitation, that, at the request of the Ashraf, it had been decided to arrest 6 or 7 of their members and that to the best of my belief the arrests had already taken place. He was stirred to the deepest interest and begged me to give him the names of those who had been arrested. I happened to have in my pocket a first and incomplete draft of the list of agitators, but I did not remember with precision which of these men were to be deported. At the head stood the names of 'Abdul Wahab al Naib and Shaikh Said, but these I omitted, as there was no intention of proceeding against them. The remainder of the names I read to the Naqib. There were only two of whom he had any knowledge. One of these two he knew too slightly to express any opinion about him; with the other, Shatur Chasibah, he was sufficiently well acquainted to pronounce with assurance that he was a rogue. I recollected that this man was not among those whom it had been intended to arrest and the Naqib asked me to give the Acting Civil Commissioner a message from himself to the effect that Shahir should not be allowed to remain in Baghdad. I then folded up the paper and said that all men were known to have made inflammatory speeches every evening in the coffee shops of the town, and that . . . they had undoubtedly done harm. There were, however, I added, two others who were still more harmful because they were men of high reputation. I alluded to 'Abdul Wabab al Naib and Shaikh Said. Owing to their position as Sunni divines it was not possible for us to take steps which would silence them effectually. The Naqib listened with attention and remained for a moment in thought. Finally he said:

"No, you cannot either imprison or deport them. The scandal would be too great. But if I know that I have the approval of Colonel Wilson, I will send for both of them and express to them my condemnation of their line of conduct. I know that they have been actuated by religious motives and that religious considerations have formed the substance of their arguments. On any point which touches religious interests, I speak with authority."

I thanked the Naqib warmly for this offer and said I had no doubt that Colonel Wilson would accept it with gratitude. A letter to this effect was despatched to the Naqib on the following day.

The conversation had now reached a point of such intimacy that I ventured, with apologies, to put a searching personal question to the Naqib. He, unintentionally, led up to it by speaking of the candidature of the Sharif, or of one of his sons, for the position of Amir of Mesopotamia.

"I am," he said, "a relative of the Sharif, I come of the same stock and I share the same religious opinions. You therefore understand that I am not actuated by difference of blood or of thought when I tell you that I would never consent to the appointment of himself or of his son as Amir. The Hijaz is one . . . the 'Iraq is one, there is no connection between them but that of the Faith. Our politics, our trade, our agriculture are all different. . . . The Hijaz is the holy land of Islam. It must remain a separate and independent state by which all Moslems can profit. Similarly with Jerusalem, which is a place of the highest sanctity to Moslems and also to Christians. . . . The rights of the Moslems and Christians alike should be guaranteed by the powers that all may reap advantage from their sacred shrine. As regards the government of Mesopotamia my detestation of the present Turkish administration is known to you, but I would rather a thousand times have the Turks back in the 'Iraq than see the Sharif or his sons installed here."

Upon this I said, "If for political reasons which we cannot at present foresee, it were necessary to put an Amir at the head of the 'Iraq State, would you, in order to avoid the selection of an Amir from Hijaz, accept the responsibility, with our help and support?"

My hand was lying upon the wooden arm of his sofa; he gave it two or three reproving blows with his fingers and leaning forward said laughingly, but with great emphasis: "How can you put such a question as that to me? I am darwish—does not my habit protect me?" He made the familiar gesture of shaking open his black robe. "It would be contrary to the deepest principles of my creed to become the political head of the State. In the time of my ancestor, 'Abdul Qadir, the Abbasid Khalifs were accustomed to consult him, as you and your colleagues consult me; but he would never have consented to take an active part in public affairs. Neither would I, nor any of his descendants consent to do so. This is my answer on the ground of religion, but I will also give you an answer based on personal reasons. I am an old man. This 5 or 6 years of life which remain to me I wish to spend in reflection and in study. When you came today I kept you waiting. I was busy with my books. They are my constant pre-occupation."

He broke off and I also kept silence for I was profoundly touched by his words. But he was yet dissatisfied with the reply he had given me and raising his voice he said slowly: "Not if it were to save 'Iraq from complete destruction would I alter what I have now spoken."

The interview had lasted an hour and a half and after a few words of excuse for my last question, excuses which he waved aside as needless, I begged permission to take my leave. Before he let me go he was so good as to express his personal affection for me and to remind me of our ancient friendship which, as he said, dates from several years before the war. I told him how greatly I valued it and thanked him for the confidence he had reposed in me by speaking so openly during the conversation which had just ended. He replied by asking me to regard him as a father, and saying that he hoped for an early renewal of our intercourse, he bade me go in peace.

THE KINGMAKER

In May 1885, when Gertrude was sixteen, a son was born in his father's castle at Taif in the deserts of the Hejaz and named after the flashing downstroke of the sword: Faisal.

He was the third son of the Hashemite Hussein ibn Ali, sharif of Mecca and self-proclaimed king of the Hejaz, the western region of the Arabian Peninsula. He was an aristocrat twice over. His father was of the bloodline of the Prophet Muhammad through his daughter Fatima. His mother, Hussein's first wife, was his father's cousin and therefore was also a descendant of the Prophet. Following hallowed tradition, Faisal was taken from his mother at seven days old and carried off to the black tents of the desert, to be brought up by a Bedouin tribe until he was seven years old. He never saw his mother again. She died when he was three. Gertrude had lost her mother at the same age.

The Sultan of the Ottoman Empire, Abdul Hamid, regarded the Hashemites with a mixture of suspicion and respect. He periodically rounded up the most powerful of the sharifs and ordered them to Constantinople, where he kept them in "honorable captivity" on frugal incomes, under the scrutiny of the sultan's sinister entourage of spies, guards, and black eunuchs. Sharif Hussein was held there for eighteen years.

In 1891, when he was six, Faisal was parted from his Bedouin foster family a year early and was taken with his brothers to join his father in a house on the Golden Horn crammed with the thirty-two women of his father's harem, with their suites and slaves. The political atmosphere of Constantinople was highly charged, with the city rife with secret societies, most of them reporting to the sultan. Initially a reformer, Abdul Hamid became paranoid, fomenting horrific massacres: he liked to ensure that his archenemies were dead by demanding that their heads be delivered to him in a box.

The sharif's household, large as it was, could afford meat only once a week. Discipline was severe: the *falaka* was still being used—a form of corporal punishment whereby a child's feet were bound together by rope and then a cane was used to beat the soles. On the other hand, Hussein saw that his sons were given a sound education by tutors.

In 1903, when Gertrude was enjoying her second world tour, the eighteen-year-old Faisal joined the Turkish army, patrolling the desert with the Turkish camel corps. A few years later, he was put in command of the Arab camel cavalry and instructed by the Turks to quell a rebellion of Arab tribesmen in Asir. Faisal and his brother Abdullah could not prevent the Turks from burning villages and were sickened by the mutilation of dead Arab rebels.

Six years later, the Sultan was deposed. In the reorganization Hussein gained the important title of emir of Mecca, the most holy city of Islam, with the very profitable supervision of the hajj, the annual pilgrimage. Faisal was to represent the constituency of Jidda in the Turkish parliament. At the outbreak of war in 1914, Hussein was ordered by the Turks to declare a jihad of all Muslims against Christians. The autocratic and courageous Hussein refused, saying that the Turks themselves had a Christian ally, Germany. He was supported in his refusal by an earlier approach from Lord Kitchener, suggesting that the Arabs and the British might become allies.

Now in a precarious position, Faisal was sent by his father to Damascus to propose a military uprising against the Turks in Syria. He communicated with his father in covert ways, by means of trusted retainers who carried messages to and fro in sword hilts, in the soles of their sandals, or written in invisible ink on wrapping paper. Faisal's friends in the Arab nationalists' political "clubs" could have betrayed him at any time, and he was particularly vulnerable as he was obliged to stay with the Turkish governor-general whenever he was in Damascus.

General Mehmed Jemal Pasha was suspicious of Faisal and
continually put him to the test. He would send for Faisal and
make him watch the public hangings of scores of his Syrian
friends. These brave men went to their deaths without making
any appeal to Faisal, who needed all his training in self-control
not to betray his disgust and anger. As T. E. Lawrence wrote
in *Seven Pillars of Wisdom*, "Only once did he burst out that
these executions would cost Jemal all that he was trying to
avoid, and it took the intercessions of his Constantinople friends,
chief men in Turkey, to save him." In January 1916, while Gertrude was in India talking to the viceroy, a second group of
Arab nationalists was being condemned. Jemal Pasha noted that
Faisal "moved heaven and earth" to save them. Those were
the only two times that Faisal let his feelings show. He knew
that one false step would have meant the end of the mission
for Arab independence.

Hussein now ordered Faisal back, to lead the Arab troops
raised by Faisal's brother Abdullah. Although Faisal believed
the time was not yet ripe, he extricated himself from Jemal
Pasha and on June 2, 1916, Hussein fired the shot that began
the Arab Revolt. He had given Faisal an impossible job: to pit
his few thousand ill-equipped troops against the twenty-two
thousand Turkish soldiers in the garrison of Medina. Having
learned the strength of the enemy with their battery of artillery, Faisal withdrew his troops into the desert and set about
raising a larger force of Bedouin.

A later strategy would isolate Medina from the rest of the
Turkish army, but, meanwhile, Faisal had gained the love of
his men, who called him Saiyidna Faisal ("our Lord Faisal")
and won their admiration for his courage. It would always be
remembered that when his tribesmen were reluctant to cross
an open stretch of land while being fired on from the walls of
Medina, Faisal laughed at them then walked his horse slowly
across the valley, never quickening his pace. From the far side,
he beckoned them to follow and they galloped after him.

Turkish revenge, directed against the Arab citizens of Awali,
was devastating. Lawrence wrote that they massacred "every
living thing within its walls. Hundreds of the inhabitants were

raped and butchered, the houses fired, and living and dead alike thrown back into the flames." The shock waves reverberated across Arabia and increased the hatred of the tribes for the Turks. Wherever Faisal led his tribes into battle, women and children were spared; and when the Turks would have slit the throats of their captives, Faisal would pay a pound a head for his prisoners to be captured alive.

Charismatic and patient in settling the private petitions of his tribesmen, Faisal was described by General Edmund Allenby as looking "the very type of royalty. . . . He combined the qualities of soldier and statesman; quick of vision, swift in action, outspoken and straightforward. . . . Picturesque, literally, as well as figuratively! Tall, graceful, handsome—to the point of beauty—with expressive eyes lighting up a face of calm dignity."

Notwithstanding his victorious leadership of the Arab Revolt, Faisal was ignored at the Paris Peace Conference as the Middle East was carved up between the British and French. Subsequently elected king of Syria by that country's nationalists, he was expelled by the French army in July 1920 and returned to the Hejaz a bitterly disillusioned man.

Knowing his history and having spent some hours in his company in Paris, Gertrude prepared for the Cairo Conference knowing exactly who she wanted for king of Iraq.

Christmas Day, 1920

I feel quite clear in my own mind that there is only one workable solution, a son of the Sharif and for choice Faisal; very very much the first choice.

———

At the Cairo Conference in March 1921, Cox, Gertrude, and Lawrence successfully convinced Churchill that Emir Faisal was the best candidate for king of Iraq. Not only was he a war hero and brave ally of the British during the revolt, but he presented the strongest hope for success and stability in Iraq.

Churchill asked whether the administration could deliver an election vote in favor of Faisal: "Can you make sure he is chosen locally?" Western political methods, he added, "are not necessarily applicable to the East, and the basis of the election should be framed." It was more than a recommendation; it was an order. Cox and Gertrude would have to see that Faisal came to power as the country's own choice, but he had to be seen to be elected independently of British wishes.

There now followed an inevitable delay while Churchill consulted with the Cabinet and obtained HMG's consent for Faisal to run as a candidate. Faisal was approached, and the French sounded out. Heavily occupied by their problems in Syria, from which they had expelled Faisal in July 1920, the French concurred on condition that he gave up all claims to Syria and all support for the Syrian nationalists. Faisal agreed and was ready to abandon his father's claims to Palestine in return for the throne of Iraq for himself and ruler of the newly created Emirate of Transjordan for his brother Abdullah.

Gertrude's self-determining Iraq was beginning to take shape. She and Cox had finally succeeded in persuading the most respected man in Iraq, the elderly naqib of Baghdad, head of the Sunni community, to undertake the formation of a provisional government. This would be followed by an elected parliament once Gertrude had devised a fair and representative voting system. The first job, however, was to pacify the country. Violence continued along the Euphrates and in the north, where RAF planes were bombing tribesmen who attacked British garrisons. Cox was determined to secure peace before taking another step, and he put down the disturbances with all the force he could muster. Gertrude hated the bombing and the burning but recognized that a nascent Arab government could not have coped with a raging insurgency.

How was she to deliver a form of democracy to a country so ignorant of national politics and comprised of so many factions? As she wrote:

The rank and file of the tribesmen, the shepherds, marsh dwellers, rice, barley and date cultivators of the Euphrates and Tigris, whose experience of statecraft was confined to speculations as to the performances of their next door neighbours, could hardly be asked who should next be the ruler of the country, and by what constitution.

Any simple majority voting system would have left great areas of the country unrepresented. Gertrude's efforts to resolve boundaries and develop structures for new governments had always been devoted to avoiding incompatible conjunctions of races and creeds. It was now her job to ensure that nobody suffered as a member of an oppressed minority in a country split by racial, religious, and economic differences. It was work after her own heart, and it would occupy her for months to come.

Baghdad, February 16, 1920

I'm acutely conscious of how much life has after all given me. I've gone back now, after many years, to the old feeling of joy in existence, and I'm happy in feeling that I've got the love and confidence of a whole nation. It mayn't be the intimate happiness which I've missed, but it's a very wonderful and absorbing thing—almost too absorbing perhaps. You must forgive me if it seems to preoccupy me too much. . . .

October 3, 1920

If you're going to have anything like really representative institutions you would have a majority of Shi'ahs. For that reason you can never have three completely autonomous provinces. Sunni Mosul must be retained as part of the Mesopotamian state in order to adjust the balance. To my mind it's one of the main arguments for giving Mesopotamia responsible government. We as outsiders can't differentiate between Sunni and Shi'ah; but leave it to them and they'll get over the difficulty . . . just as the Turks did, and for the present it's the only way of getting over it. The final authority must be in the hands of the Sunnis, in spite of their numerical inferiority; otherwise you will have a *mujtahid*-run state, which is the very devil.

November 3, 1920

The Shi'ahs complain that they are not sufficiently represented on the Council, wholly overlooking the fact that nearly all their leading men are Persian subjects and must change their nationality before they can hold office in the Mesopotamian state.

December 12, 1920

I'm entertained to find myself in the eyes of the Ministry of the Interior (and of the Arab Government) as the first authority on tribes. . . . I've worked at them for years. So it's really I who have settled the details of tribal representation. It's not only right in itself that the tribes should be represented but it's also essential for the safety of the National Government that the tribes should be associated with it. Moreover there's a strong feeling on the subject in advanced nationalist circles. All the same it's a bold step. The townsfolk and landowners who hate and fear the tribes (as the tribes hate and fear the townsmen) won't a bit like their gaining political status. It's the landless intelligentsia who want it and they are the backbone of the nationalist party. All the big landowners on the Council, from the Naqib downwards, will try to keep the tribes out.

Once the insurgent tribes had submitted, Cox granted a general amnesty. Churchill had wired London from Cairo: "Both Cox and Miss Bell agree that if procedure is followed, appearance of Faisal in Mesopotamia will lead to his general adoption." Now it was their responsibility to make it happen.

As a Sunni ruler in a country with a Shia majority, the emir's descent from the Prophet would be his trump card. The small committee that Gertrude, Cox, and the Iraqi ministers now formed set themselves to work out the timing and geography. Faisal should immediately be invited to Baghdad, but he would need to go to Mecca first, and have his candidature announced from the holy city, where his father was sharif. Support would grow as he progressed east. Now she was preoccupied with the business of making him welcome.

June 19, 1921

Here was Faisal arriving at Basrah on the 23rd. . . . On Thursday afternoon the Naqib . . . made a sound move. He informed the Council of Ministers that Faisal was coming and that they must make preparations to receive him properly and see that he was suitably lodged. Thereupon they appointed a reception committee of 5 ministers. . . .

Unfortunately, the committee caused so much controversy that the members almost came to blows. Gertrude attended the first meeting and, sighing, left it to its arguments and went about arranging the details herself. She called on the railway officials and had a train specially decorated for the emir. She arranged for a deputation of sixty notables to greet Faisal at the station, found competent servants for him, and arranged for the distribution of the new flags.

There remained the question of his lodging here which they proposed to solve by putting him into some rooms in the Sarai (the Government offices) which were now under repair . . . if they could be got ready in time. Public Works declared that it couldn't be done. Jafar telephoned to me in despair on Saturday morning; I telephoned to Public Works, made suggestions for covering bare walls with hangings and finally the thing was arranged . . .

Faisal arrived on Iraq on June 23, 1921. Charismatic and a natural orator, he was able to win over hearts and minds whenever he made a speech; he left most of Basra under his spell. With his entourage he then set off for Baghdad on a train covered

with flags. After innumerable delays, the train drew into the
station, a guard of honor presented arms, the crowd cheered,
and a band struck up. Faisal inspected the guard and progressed to the reception including the city's notables.

Sidi Faisal stood at the carriage door looking very splendid in
full Arab dress, saluting the guard of honour. Sir Percy and Sir
Aylmer* went up to him as he got out and gave him a fine cere-
monious greeting, all the people clapped. . . . Sir Percy began to
present the Arab Magnates, representatives of the Naqib. I hid
behind Mr. Cornwallis,† but Faisal saw me and stepped across
to shake hands with me. He looked excited and anxious—you're
not a king on approbation without any tension of the spirit—but
it only gave his natural dignity a more human charm. . . .

This morning on my way to the office I went to the Sarai and
gave my card to Faisal's A.D.C. He said would I wait a minute, the
Amir would like to see me; it was a little past seven, rather early
for a morning call. I waited, talking to the A.D.C. and presently
Faisal sent for me. They showed me into a big room and he came
quickly across in his long white robes, took me by both hands and
said "I couldn't have believed that you could have given me so
much help as you have given me." So we sat down on a sofa. . . .

Mr. Cornwallis came into the office later and I told him I had
called on Faisal. He said "That was quite right. All the way up
he had been hearing your praise and he gave me a message for
you in case he didn't see you to speak to to-day. I was to tell you
how grateful he was."

July 2, 1921

The next event was that evening's banquet in the Maude gardens. It was really beautifully done. The place lighted with electric lights looked lovely.

*Sir Aylmer Haldane, General Officer Commanding.

†Later Sir Kinahan Cornwallis, Faisal's personal adviser and soon a great
personal friend of Gertrude's.

Faisal carried on a little conversation in French with Sir Aylmer, but mostly he and I and Sir Percy talked across the table. . . . Faisal looked very happy and I felt very happy and so did Sir Percy. . . .

Then got up our great poet, of whom I've often told you, Jamil Zahawi, and recited a tremendous ode in which he repeatedly alluded to Faisal as King of the Iraq and everyone clapped and cheered. And then there stepped forward into the grassy space between the tables a Shi'ah in white robes and a black cloak and big black turban and chanted a poem of which I didn't understand a word. It was far too long and as I say quite unintelligible but nevertheless it was wonderful. The tall, robed figure chanting and marking time with an uplifted hand, the starry darkness in the palm trees beyond the illuminated circle—it hypnotized you.

The naqib followed the banquet with a welcoming dinner, a magnificent occasion on which Gertrude was seated at Faisal's right.

July 8, 1921

. . . It was a wonderful sight that dinner party. The robes and their uniforms and the crowds of servants; all brought up in the Naqib's household—the ordered dignity of it and the real solid magnificence and the tension of spirit which one felt all round one as one felt the burning heat of the night. For after all to the best of our ability we were making history.

July 20, 1921

. . . On Monday the Jewish community gave a great reception to Faisal in the Grand Rabbi's official house. . . . It was filled with rows of seats, with rows of notables sitting in them, the Jewish Rabbis in their turbans or twisted shawls, the leading Christians, all the Arab Ministers and practically all the leading

Moslems, with a sprinkling of white robed, black cloaked
'ulama*.... The speeches on these occasions are all set
speeches.... But yet they were interesting, because one knew
the tension which underlay them, the anxiety of the Jews lest an
Arab Govt should mean chaos and their gradual reassurance, by
reason of Faisal's obviously enlightened attitude.... Towards
the end he got up and spoke really beautifully; it was straight
and good and eloquent.... He made an immense impression.
The Jews were delighted at his insistence on their being of one
race with the Arabs....

Cox, though greatly relieved by Faisal's reception in Iraq and
by the Council having unanimously declared him king, knew
that a referendum must be held, so as to confirm Faisal as the
choice of the people. He and Gertrude had already framed the
question "Do you agree to Faisal as King and leader of Iraq?"
and printed the papers. They were circulated to a great number of tribal representatives including three hundred notables,
and only six weeks after Faisal's arrival, with all the papers in,
the referendum proved heavily in his favor. He was already
working with the naqib to form the first Cabinet; next he was
to be crowned in Baghdad.

Baghdad, July 27, 1921

I'm immensely happy over the way this thing is going. I feel as if
I were in a dream.... On our guarantee all the solid people are
coming in to Faisal, and there's a general feeling that we made
the right choice in recommending him. If we can bring some
kind of order out of chaos, what a thing worth doing it will be!

Before Faisal's official coronation came the tribal celebrations
in his honor at Ramadi. This would be his Bedouin coronation
and the culmination of the gains of the Arab fight for independence. For Gertrude, too, it was the most triumphant moment

*Muslim scholars of Sharia law.

of her life, the pinnacle of her long fight for self-determination for the Arabs. Although not the only Briton present, she would take the prime place among them as she stood on the dais beside Faisal, flanked by Ali Sulaiman, the powerful pro-British sheikh of the Dulaim, and her great friend Fahad Beg of the Anazeh.

For three weeks beforehand, temperatures had been over 115 degrees. Gertrude and her chauffeur had to leave at 4 a.m. to cover the seventy miles to Ramadi. Just before the halfway mark, she saw the cloud of dust that signaled Faisal's cavalcade ahead. A few miles before Fallujah they came to the tents of the Dulaim, and from that point on, the road was lined with tribesmen roaring their salute and waving their rifles above their heads, kicking up a fog of dust like drifting cliffs on either side. As Faisal's car drew ahead, they wheeled away and galloped on, to form a continuous wild cavalcade escorting him through Fallujah to Ramadi on the edge of the Syrian Desert.

Baghdad, July 31, 1921

Under the steep edge of the Syrian desert were drawn up the fighting men of the 'Anazeh, horsemen and camel riders, bearing the huge standard of the tribe. We stopped to salute it as we passed. Ali Sulaiman the Chief of the Dulaim and one of the most remarkable men in 'Iraq came out of Ramadi to meet us. . . . We . . . drove to the Euphrates bank where Ali Sulaiman had pitched a huge tent of ten poles—ie about 200 ft. long—with a dais at the upper end roofed with tent cloth and walled with fresh green boughs. Outside were drawn up the camel riders of the Dulaim, their horsemen and their standard carried by a negro mounted on a gigantic white camel; inside the tribesmen lined the tent 5 or 6 deep from the dais to the very end. Faisal sat on the high diwan. . . . He was supremely happy—a great tribesman amongst famous tribes and, as I couldn't help feeling, a great Sunni among Sunnis. . . .

Faisal was in his own country with the people he knew. I never saw him look so splendid. He wore his usual white robes with a fine black abba over them, flowing white headdress and silver bound 'aqal. Then he began to speak, leaning forward over the small table in front of him, sitting with his hand raised and bringing it down on the table to emphasize his sentences. The people at the end of the tent were too far off to hear; he called them all up and they sat on the ground below the dais, . . . 400 or 500 men. He spoke in the great tongue of the desert, which I had never heard him use before, sonorous, magnificent— no language like it. He spoke as a tribal chief to his feudatories. "For four years," he said, "I have not found myself in a place like this or in such company"—you could see how he was loving it. Then he told them how Iraq was to rise on their endeavours with himself at their head. "Oh Arabs are you at peace with one another?" They shouted: "Yes, yes, we are at peace." "From this day—what is the date?—and what is the hour?"—someone answered him. "From this day the 25th of July (only he gave the Mohammadan date) and the hour of the morning 11 (it was 11 o'clock) any tribesman who lifts his hand against a tribesman is responsible to me. I will judge between you, calling your shaikhs in counsel. I have my rights over you as your Lord."

A grey bearded man interrupted: "And our rights?" "And you have your rights as subjects which it is my business to guard."

So it went on, the tribesmen interrupting him with shouts of "Yes, yes," "We agree," "Yes, by God." It was like the descriptions of great tribal gatherings in the Days of Ignorance, before the Prophet, when the poets recited verse which has come down to this day and the people shouted at the end of each phrase: "The truth, by God the truth!"

When it was over Fahad and Ali Sulaiman stood up on either side of him and said, "We swear allegiance to you because you are acceptable to the British Government." Faisal was a little surprised. He looked quickly round to me, smiling, and then he said, "No one can doubt what my relations are to the British, but we must settle our affairs between ourselves." He looked at me again and I held out my two hands clasped together as a symbol of the union of the Arab and British Governments.

It was a tremendous moment, those two really big men who have played their part in the history of their time, and Faisal between them, the finest living representative of his race—and the link ourselves.

One after another Ali Sulaiman brought up his shaikhs, some 40 or 50 of them. They laid their hands in Faisal's and swore allegiance.

Gertrude was a frequent visitor at Faisal's apartments, coming and going as she chose and always ushered straight through the waiting room. There was an affection between them: he called her his sister. Knowing that he had never seen the great archway of Ctesiphon, she invited him to have breakfast there in the cool of the day, where they sat on fine carpets, drank coffee, and ate eggs, tongue, sardines, and melons.

Baghdad, August 6, 1921

It was wonderfully interesting showing that splendid place to Faisal. He is an inspiring tourist. After we had reconstructed the palace and seen Chosroes sitting in it, I took him into the high mounds to the South, whence we could see the Tigris, and told him the story of the Arab conquest as Tabari records it. . . . You can imagine what it was like reciting it to him. I don't know which of us was the more thrilled.

Faisal has promised me a regiment of the Arab army—the Khatun's Own. . . .

Oh Father, isn't it wonderful. I sometimes think I must be in a dream.

Baghdad, Two Days Before Faisal Was Crowned, August 21, 1921

That evening I had got so tired of sitting in the office that in spite of the heat I went out riding, and coming home along the river bank for coolness, I passed Faisal's new house up stream. . . . I saw his motor at the door so I left my pony with one of his slaves and went up onto the roof where I found him sitting with his ADCs. It was wonderful, the sun just set, the softly

luminous curves of the river below us, the belt of palm trees, and
then the desert, . . . the fading red of the sky. We all sat and talked.
Faisal uses no honorifics: "Enti, thous" he says to me—it's so refreshing after the endless "honours" and "excellencies,"—"Enti
Iraqiyah, enti badawiyah—you're a Mesopotamian, a Beduin."

With only days to go before the official coronation, a major
problem emerged. In the same letter, she wrote:

> Meantime . . . there's a breeze on. The Col. Office has sent us a
> most red-tapy cable saying that Faisal in his coronation speech
> must announce that the ultimate authority in the land is the
> High Commissioner. Faisal refuses and he is quite right. We are
> going, as you know, to drop the mandate and enter into treaty
> relations with Mesopotamia. Faisal says that from the first we
> must recognize that he is an independent sovereign in treaty
> with us, otherwise he can't hold his extremists. . . . My view
> was that, . . . in the end, there was no point in claiming an
> authority we could not enforce. . . . Faisal drafted an admirable
> statement which was telegraphed home, and Sir Percy a still bet-
> ter [one] which accompanied Faisal's. H.M.G. had said that, if
> Faisal didn't accept their view, the coronation must be delayed.
> It is fixed for Tuesday, the day after tomorrow, and the whole
> universe is assembling here for it. Sir Percy telegraphed firmly
> that in his opinion it could not be delayed and it is going on.

Faisal had always refused the mandate that the Colonial Office
wanted with Iraq. It was a difficulty that had never been
resolved until Cox had the idea of substituting a treaty, which
Faisal was more likely to accept. It fell to the judicial adviser,
Sir Nigel Davidson, in his role as counselor to the high commissioner, to explain the complexities and differences between
the two agreements:

> Substituting a treaty for the Mandate, that is to say, of exercising
> the Mandatory's powers and duties through a treaty with the
> government of the "Mandated Territory" was a stroke of genius.

It solved the difficulty of reconciling the fervid aspirations of the nationalists for complete and immediate independence with Great Britain's responsibilities to the League of Nations for securing (1) the financial stability, (2) the foreign relations, and (3) the adequate defence, of the new state. These responsibilities necessarily involved some measure of control until, in the judgment of the League, Iraq could be trusted to stand alone and be accepted as a member of the League. Unfortunately the term "Mandate" (particularly in the Arab translation) implied a subjection which was intolerable to the nationalist patriots and which the King could never afford to accept; but a treaty between "High Contracting Powers" in which one freely agreed to some limitations in its sovereign rights (as all treaties do) in return for financial, military and diplomatic assistance from the other, was a very different proposition and could be accepted without the stigma of "colonialism." It was on this basis that the constitutional monarchy of Iraq was established and achieved complete independence without further bloodshed or revolution.

Faisal was satisfied with the substitution of the treaty, and on August 23, was crowned in the carpeted courtyard of the Serai in Baghdad, in front of fifteen hundred guests: British, Arabs, townsmen, ministers, and local deputations.

Baghdad, August 28, 1921

We've had a terrific week, but we've got our king crowned and Sir Percy and I agree that we are now half seas over. The remaining half is the Congress and the Organic Law. . . .

Exactly at 6 [a.m.] we saw Faisal in uniform, Sir Percy in white diplomatic uniform with all his ribbons and stars, Sir Aylmer, Mr. Cornwallis and a following of ADCs descend the Sarai steps from Faisal's lodging and come pacing down the long path of carpets, past the guard of honour (the Dorsets, they looked magnificent) and so to the dais. . . . We all stood up while they came in and sat when they had taken their place on the dais. Faisal looked very dignified but much strung up—it was an agitating moment. He looked along the front row and caught my eye and I gave him a tiny salute. Then Saiyid Hussain stood up and read Sir Percy's proclamation in which he announced that Faisal had been elected King by 96% of the people in Mesopotamia, long live the King! with that we stood up and saluted him. . . . There followed a salute of 21 guns. . . . It was an amazing thing to see all 'Iraq, from north to south gathered together. It is the first time it has happened, in history.

Gertrude went straight back to the office afterward; it was only breakfast time. Then, and for the following days, crowds of representatives came to greet their new monarch and pay their respects to Cox and Gertrude. She described them in the same letter to her parents.

I . . . arranged for the deputations to pay their respects to [Sir Percy]. . . . It would be difficult to tell you how many people there were in the office at one and the same time. It was immensely interesting seeing them. . . . Basrah and 'Amarah came on Friday, Hillah and Mosul on Saturday; they were the big deputations. Of these Mosul was the most wonderful. I divided it into 3 sections: first the Mosul town magnates, my guests and their colleagues; next the Christian archbishops and bishops—Mosul abounds in them—and the Jewish Grand Rabbi. . . . The third group was more exciting than all the others: it was the Kurdish chiefs of the frontier who have elected to come into the 'Iraq state until they see whether an independent Kurdistan develops which will be still better to their liking. . . .

The Kurds came last and stayed longest. The Mayor of Zakho said that they hadn't had opportunity to discuss with Sir Percy the future of Kurdistan, what did I think about it? I said that my opinion was that the districts they came from were economically dependent on Mosul and always would be. . . . They agreed but . . . they must have Kurdish officials. I said I saw no difficulty there. And the children must be taught in Kurdish in the schools. I pointed out that there would be some difficulty

about that as there wasn't a single school book—nor any other—
written in Kurdish. This gave them pause and after consideration they said they thought the teaching might as well be in
Arabic, but what about local administrative autonomy? I said,
"Have you talked it over with Saiyidna Faisal—our Lord
Faisal?" "No," they said. . . . So I telephoned . . . and made an
appointment for yesterday afternoon.

Gertrude described for her family some of the personalities
who came to Baghdad to be presented to the king.

The Qadhi of Mosul is perhaps the most darling old man in the
whole of 'Iraq . . . looking very wise and very gentle. . . . 'Abdul
Latif Mandil . . . with the sharp fine features of the Arab of inner
Arabia [is] a great merchant. . . . One of the Christians was little
Mar Shim'un, archbishop and ruler of the Nestorians—he is 10,
poor little soul. The post goes in the family, from uncle to nephew,
for they are celibate, . . . and there he is in full canonicals and
great gold cross and chain, doomed to be an archbishop all his
days. Sa'id Beg [is] the religious head of the Devil Worshippers. . . . Qadir Agha of Shush deals with no world but this, but
he deals with it pretty thoroughly—in Kurdish, he has no other
tongue. He is huge man, and gigantically fat. He wears acres of
baggy striped trousers gathered round his waist on a string, the
jauntiest of fancy waistcoats. . . . He's worth seeing. . . .

I don't see how I'm ever going to tear myself away permanently from this country—do you? The only thing is I feel I'm
not being much good as a daughter and sister. Oh dear! it's per-
plexing. However we have a hard winter's work before us—
Congress and Organic Law—and I haven't much time to think
of anything else.

The week culminated in an invitation to Gertrude from the
king to discuss the design of the new national flag and his personal standard. His first Cabinet was formed; she had secret
reservations about three of the nine members and rejoiced that
it was no longer her decision.

Faisal's house on the river was ready, and he invited her to his first dinner there. Dressed exquisitely for evening, she floated up the Tigris on his launch. The people of Karradah recognized her as she passed, and they saluted her, smiling. In the distance they heard the drums of Muharram, when the Shias beat themselves with chains and mourn for Hussein, the grandson of the Prophet Muhammad. Her happiness is evident in every line of the letter she wrote to her father afterward, describing that evening.

September 11, 1921

Have I ever told you what the river is like on a hot summer night? At dusk the mist hangs in long white bands over the water; the twilight fades and the lights of the town shine out on either bank, with the river, dark and smooth and full of mysterious reflections, like a road of triumph through the mist. Silently a boat with a winking headlight slips down the stream, then a company of quffahs each with his tiny lamp, loaded to the brim with watermelons from Samarra. . . . And we slow down the launch so that the wash may not disturb them. The waves of our passage don't even extinguish the floating votive candles, each burning on its minute boat made out of the swathe of a date cluster, which anxious hands launched above the town. If they reach the last house yet burning, the sick man will recover, the baby will be born safely into this world of hot darkness and glittering lights. . . . Now I've brought you out to where the palm trees stand marshalled along the banks. The water is so still that you can see the scorpion in it, star by star; . . . .
. . . and here are Faisal's steps.

By 1921, so much had been achieved. An Arab king was on the throne, and a respected elder of Baghdad, the naqib, was prime minister. The country was in the hands of a Cabinet chosen from an array of representative Iraqis. There remained one sticking point, the mandate, still required by the League of Nations.

October 17, 1921

They are getting down to the treaty between the British and 'Iraq
Govts. Sir Percy told me he didn't anticipate any difficulty, and
when it is framed it will be an immense obstacle cleared from our
path. Faisal has been living in terror of it; he is afraid that the British Govt. may ask him to agree to terms which he can't get his
nationalists to accept, as the French Govt. did in Syria. Till that
nightmare has vanished he has no sense of security. I don't think he
has reason for anxiety. Sir Percy realizes very well what divergent
elements have to be reconciled, and as we've seen before, when Sir
Percy makes a pronouncement Mr. Churchill has to toe the line.

Months passed and Faisal still continued to refuse to agree to
the mandate or sign the treaty. Churchill finally sent a telegram ordering Cox and Faisal to London, where they knew he
would give them an ultimatum. In the confrontation, Iraq as
they knew it could cease to exist: the battle was within a hair-
breadth of being lost.

Cox, taking strength from the fact that he was close to
retirement, now used his personal authority. He replied to
Churchill that he saw no advantage in coming to London. He
proposed publishing the treaty in Iraq, as agreed with the
king, adding a rider that the mandate was their only point of
difference. The king could then show his people that he had
fought for the best terms possible. However, two more years of
debate concerning the mandate would follow before a resolu-
tion was finally reached.

In spite of problems over the mandate, it was one of the happiest times of Gertrude's life, partly because of her increasing
affection for the people she was dealing with.

September 17, 1921

Personally I'm a Sunni but it's no good pretending I don't feel
just as near to an old party like Saiyid Ja'far or a Shi'ah tribesman eating haricot beans.

September 25, 1921

I sometimes think how curious it all is, whether it's Fa'iq Beg or
King Faisal. People whose upbringing and associations and traditions are all so entirely different, yet when one is with them
one doesn't notice the difference, nor do they. Think of Faisal,
brought up at Mecca in a palace full of eunuchs, educated at
Constantinople, Commander-in-Chief, King, exile, then King
again; or Fa'iq, tending his palms and vines, and jogging into
Baghdad to seek out the best market for his dates—and both of
them run out to greet me with outstretched hands . . . as if I
were a sister. And I feel like a sister, that's the oddest part.

And Faisal, when I say I'm going home next summer replies
with asperity: "You're not to talk of going *home*—your home is
here. You may say you are going to see your father."

December 17, 1921, Letter to Col. Frank Balfour

You advised me once not to put my heart into it—of course I
can't do anything else. From Faisal downwards they've given me
a great deal more, in affection and confidence, than I've earned,
and if they were to break with me tomorrow I should remain in
their debt. Though they have immensely over-estimated my services they can't over-estimate my desire to serve them. Heart
and soul I've put into it; and I've had the reward in full measure.

Early in the new year she received a surprising gift.

February 2, 1922

I opened a parcel in the office the other day and out of it rolled
a large tiara. I really nearly laughed aloud—it was such an unexpected object in the middle of office files. But it's too kind of
you to let me have it—I had quite forgotten how fine it was. I
fear in wearing it I may be taken for the crowned queen of Mesopotamia.

March 30, 1922

I wear your diamonds as a necklace and my own in my hair.
They look very fine, I assure you, when I dine at the Palace!

On the anniversary of the coronation, Faisal held a formal ceremony at his palace on the Tigris. Gertrude, her now gray hair swept on top of her head, wore a cream lace evening dress pinned with her miniature orders, and her two Bell tiaras, one in her hair and one as a choker. The Residency party joined three or four hundred guests arriving in the courtyard. There they heard behind them the shouts and clapping of a demonstration by two extremist political parties.

The dissidents were gathering strength, but Faisal refused to allow any action to be taken against them unless the mandate was quashed. He also refused to sign the treaty while Britain continued to insist on the mandate.

The political procedure demanded that the king should now pass a vote of confidence in the Cabinet. Faisal, having no confidence in it, said so; and, not for the first time, the entire Cabinet resigned. It would not resume until September, which left the naqib in solitary and ineffectual charge as the anti-mandate insurrection spread. But now fate took a hand and provided Cox with a golden opportunity to break the impasse. The king developed acute appendicitis.

August 27, 1922

We have passed through the most troubled and dangerous 10 days. . . . In the evening [the king's] temperature was up, at 6 a.m. next day, five doctors, two English and three Arab, were debating whether an immediate operation was necessary, at 8 they decided it was and at 11 it was successfully over. Before it was done Sir Percy and Mr. Cornwallis spent an hour with him (this is deadly secret but it's part of history), represented to him that the political position had grown so grave that repressive measures were essential to save the country and begged him . . .

to give them permission to carry them out. He refused. He said
he would never be a party to measures which he was confident
would plunge the country into a rebellion that could not be suppressed. Until H.M.G. consented to adopt the methods for the
publication of the treaty suggested by himself and Sir Percy, he
could take no step. Sir Percy replied that that could not be for a
fortnight because it was a matter which had to be laid before the
[British] Cabinet and the Cabinet would not meet till the first
week of September. . . . We could not hold out for a fortnight if
we allowed the extremists to go on stirring up trouble.

But it was in vain and Sir Percy came back extremely sad that
he hadn't secured [the king's] co-operation—but resolved to go
on without it. Exactly what he was going to do I did not know
until . . . next day when he observed that the police were busy
arresting seven of the principal agitators in Baghdad, that the
two extremist newspapers had been closed down and the two
extremist parties abruptly ended.

We spent the morning in some anxiety. . . . We had troops
and armoured cars waiting outside the town gates, but they
were not needed. . . . The extremists collapsed. In the evening
an admirable communiqué in English and Arabic was published. . . . It is Sir Percy at his very best and you can't beat him.
Its effect was instantaneous. . . . Mr. Cornwallis had summoned
some 30 of the notables in the afternoon and read it to them.
They expressed themselves in no measured terms as delighted
with the action that had been taken, and not least delighted
were Nuri and Ja'far, those ardent Nationalists. . . .

Sir Percy has saved the situation and has given the King a loop-
hole through which he can walk when he is able to walk. . . . By
that time—his convalescence if necessary can be prolonged—we
shall have got a clear line from home, take it or leave it. Moreover
the moderates are lifting their heads sky high; Saiyid Mahmud's
party is swelling visibly and as soon as what has happened in
Baghdad becomes known in the provinces, the extremists will
have to build an ark if they want to escape from the political flood.

Any number of witnesses could testify that Faisal was uncon-
scious while Cox set his initiatives under way. When the king

recovered from his illness, he was deeply appreciative of Cox's actions, which relieved him from all blame in suppressing the insurgency. Cox then took the treaty to the naqib, handed him a pen, and—flustered and alarmed—he finally signed it. Cox also signed and, in compliance with the mandate, the Treaty of Alliance between Great Britain and Iraq provided for twenty years of British occupation in an advisory capacity. It was October 10, 1922.

Faisal proclaimed the treaty in a ringing speech that looked forward to "the continuance of the friendship of our illustrious ally, Great Britain, and to carrying out the elections for the convening of a Constituent Assembly to frame the Organic Law." It was also a step toward membership in the League of Nations as an independent country.

The king now ordered the preparation of elections to the Constituent Assembly to ratify the treaty and approve the constitution, after which the first parliament could be elected. Once again, Cox was called to London to review Britain's role in Iraq. He returned with an addendum to the treaty, a protocol that reduced Britain's involvement from twenty years to no longer than four more years from the ratification of peace with Turkey.

At the end of April 1923, Cox finally left Iraq. His last act of kindness to Gertrude was to sanction the cost of an additional drawing room to her summer house, in recognition of all the entertaining she did there for the good of the secretariat.

April 26, 1923

All this time rather tears the heart strings, you understand. It's very moving saying goodbye to Sir Percy. . . .

May 9, 1923

What a position [Sir Percy] has made for himself here! I think no Englishman has inspired more confidence in the East. He

himself was dreadfully unhappy at going—40 years' service is
not a thing one lays down easily.

February 13, 1924

I must tell you something very touching. . . . Sir Percy has sent
me a photograph of himself in a silver frame and across the corner he has written: "To the best of comrades." Isn't that the nic-
est thing he could possibly have written?

THE COURTIER

The new high commissioner for Iraq, Sir Henry Dobbs, took firm charge of Britain's responsibilities for security and foreign affairs. Elections now went ahead, with Faisal encouraging the population to go out and vote.

Once the constitution had been achieved, with an elected Cabinet and ministers responsible for their departments, the poignant truth was that Gertrude's own power and authority were diminished. After the treaty gave Iraqis the principal role in government, political and official decisions passed beyond her control. While Cox had been in charge, it had been routine for him to call on Gertrude throughout the week, to discuss policy and current events. Dobbs discontinued that habit, but he and his wife were on very friendly terms with Gertrude and frequently asked her to their house.

As she became less involved in office affairs, she devoted more and more time to archaeology. In August 1922, Faisal signed Gertrude's Law of Excavations, intended to protect the sites and historical treasures of Iraq. He appointed her honorary director of archaeology. Her tireless work to establish the Iraq Museum occupied her for the rest of her life (see "The Archaeologist").

Her devotion to the king and his well-being did not prevent her from a creeping disillusionment with his attitude over the nationalists and extremists who wanted Britain to leave Iraq. He refused again and again to suppress them. She feared that his obstinacy would cause Britain to pull out altogether, and that without its support, Iraq would break apart.

The following are extracts from a long letter Gertrude had written to her father over several days from May 18 to June 4,

1922. She had just returned to Baghdad from Jerusalem where
he had gone to meet her.

On Monday I went to tea with the King. I said that I had come
back with the conviction that we were the only Arab province
which was set in the right path and that if we failed here it
would be the end of Arab aspirations. He was most affectionate
and charming. . . . There may be difficulties in dealing with a
creature so sensitive and highly strung but his fine and vital
qualities and his wonderful breadth of outlook make up for
everything.

Mr. Cornwallis and I had a long talk. I told him I was very
unhappy over the King's indecisive attitude, his refusal to con-
tradict the statements of the extremist papers and the backing
he was giving to the most ignoble extremists. . . .

At 4.30 I went to tea with the King, determined to tell him
once and for all what was in my mind. I wish I could give you a
picture of it—the big, empty, shaded room with the electric fans
whirring; the King dressed in white robes with a fine white linen
kerchief bound round his head; the emotional atmosphere of
which he, with his acute perceptions, was fully conscious. For I
was playing my last card, and I told him so. I began by asking
him whether he believed in my personal sincerity and devotion
to him. He said he could not doubt it. . . . I said . . . that I was
extremely unhappy. I had formed a beautiful and gracious snow
image to which I had given allegiance and I saw it melting before
my eyes. Before every noble outline had been obliterated, I preferred to go; in spite of my love for the Arab nation and my sense
of responsibility for its future, I did not think I could bear to see
the evaporation of the dream which had guided me day by
day. . . . I would not wait until the villains in whom he put his
trust inevitably blackened me in his eyes.

On this theme we had a terrific discussion—during which he
kissed my hand at intervals, which is very disconcerting! . . . In
the end I got from him permission to publish an official contra-
diction of the newspaper reports . . . and when on leaving I
attempted to kiss his hand he warmly embraced me! . . .

I'm still *sous le coup* of this interview. Faisal is one of the

most lovable of human beings but he is amazingly lacking in
strength of character. . . . He veers with every breath.

June 6, 1922

I lunched with Mr. Cornwallis and heard that the King had
already gone back on one of the things I had urged him to do. . . .

Oh the King, the King! If only he would be more firm!

Did Gertrude appreciate the clever game that the king was playing? She had met her match in Faisal, whose political subtlety
was at least equal to hers. He had, after all, managed to get the
mandate turned into a treaty and get himself crowned in spite of
ultimatums from the British government, and he had kept the
British on his side while continuing to convince the extremists of
his independence. As a constitutional king he understood better
than Gertrude perhaps his duty to stand above politics. And
whatever Gertrude had said, she remained his dedicated friend,
trying to keep him on what she saw as the straight and narrow
while he disarmed her at every interview.

June 22, 1922

I went to tea with the King and had one of the most interesting talks
I've ever had with him. . . . I sat listening with breathless interest—
it was a contribution to history . . . but what I can't reproduce is the
psychology of it . . . his face narrow and eager between the folds of
his white kerchief, reflecting every turn of his thought with its wonderful mobility of feature; the shining eyes of the idealist, deepened
by sorrow and disappointment and yet no reproach in them.

July 16, 1922

. . . Perhaps the King does hold my hand more though he
embraces Mr. Cornwallis oftener—we compare notes.

July 20, 1922

Today the King ordered me to tea. He was at his best, wise and statesmanlike. . . . He is the most enchanting person, of that there is no doubt.

Gertrude had fought for an independent Arab nation for just as long as Faisal. It had been her inspiration in Cairo, Basra and Baghdad. She had been a lone voice in the days when she worked for A. T. Wilson; she had sat firm while Britain made repeated threats to withdraw from Iraq; she had nearly despaired during the insurrections of 1920; she had watched the years go by as the West procrastinated and the Turks put every obstacle in the way of defining a northern border for Iraq. Now, with so much behind her and so much achieved, she was tired and frail, indomitable of spirit but subject to bad health due to one of the worst climates in the world, no less than to her constant smoking.

One source of fun remained to her: court-making for the queen. Faisal had told Gertrude that after the debacle in Damascus in 1920, he had been cautious about bringing his wife and children with him to Iraq. In fact, his father Hussein had been holding Faisal's family in Mecca.

July 24, 1921

Faisal sent for me and we had a long talk. I asked him about his wife, who is his cousin, and said I thought she too ought to be encouraged to make a position and a court. He was rather shy about her—they are always embarrassed about their women, thinking that they are too ignorant to be presentable, but he agreed that we must make a beginning.

By 1924, settled into two palaces and with the Hejaz suffering increasing aggression from Ibn Saud and his Wahhabis, Faisal began to bring his family to Baghdad, beginning with his favorite and youngest brother, Zaid. After Zaid came the king's only son, twelve-year-old Ghazi, accompanied by his slaves. He immediately earned a place in Gertrude's heart.

August 20, 1924

The King is much excited because King Husain has at last released his only son, Ghazi, who has been kept at Mecca till now. The boy. . . is now at Amman and H.M. is sending Muhsin Beg across to fetch him.

She felt he needed good tutors and the company of men, but before she began on his entourage, she was required to help choose his clothes. The king now wore European dress most of the time and wanted his son to do the same.

October 7, 1924

The great event of Sunday was the arrival of the Amir Ghazi. . . . He is very little for his age. He has the long sensitive face of his father and charming manners, a shy dignity which is most engaging. The whole town turned out, more even than when Faisal came.

The next day I was called up to the palace to help to choose Ghazi's clothes. There was an English tailor from Bombay with patterns. So we chose his little shirts and suits, the tailor behaving like a tailor in Thackeray. He skipped about, pointed his toe and handed me patterns with one hand on his heart. Ghazi came in to be measured, half shy and half pleased.

October 8, 1924

I think the little Amir is going to be a great interest. The palace is all wrong, the wrong people there, and I do so want to get Ghazi's entourage properly constituted. I can't do much except mark time till Ken [Sir Kinahan Cornwallis] comes, but Sinbad

[Sir Harry Sinderson] has returned with his wife today and they will help me. As the King's personal physician Sinbad can have a good deal to say as to Ghazi's bringing up. He has been very much neglected in a household of slaves and ignorant women. He can barely read and write Arabic; but he is intelligent and twelve isn't so very old after all. I expect the women folk will come out now, after the break-up at Mecca. There are two daughters*—one of them must be nearly eighteen. Anyhow, having Ghazi will make a great difference to Faisal. It was too pretty to see them, the other day when I was sitting in H.M.'s garden, going off to pray hand in hand when the sunset prayers were called.

Meanwhile, Hussein had provoked Ibn Saud by appropriating the title of Caliph. In October, Ibn Saud attacked, Mecca fell, and King Hussein abdicated.

October 15, 1924

We are having fearful alarums and excursions over Mecca. The King had violent hysterics on Monday; on Tuesday he formally abdicated in favour of the Amir Ghazi—but only to Sir Henry. H.E. asked him where he was going, to which H.M. couldn't find an answer. His family, apparently, are sailing about the Red Sea like so many Flying Dutchmen. Sir Henry then advised H.M. to wait and see, so he withdrew his abdication for four days! I remember that in 1922 Ken Cornwallis had Faisal's abdication lying about in a drawer for a month.

Following the young emir came his mother, the queen, with Ghazi's three sisters, to live in the country villa at Harithiya. In accordance with family tradition, Faisal had married his first cousin, the emira Huzaima, who lived strictly in purdah with her daughters. The fact that the queen lived in seclusion would

*The third daughter, an invalid from birth, never appeared in public.

make the notion of a Western-style court impossible. Male visitors were entertained at dinners and receptions hosted by Faisal alone in the Baghdad palace, after which he would drive to Harithiya to spend the night with his family. Gertrude was one of the first to be received by the queen, who spoke only Arabic, although she understood a little English and French.

December 17, 1924

The Queen and all the family—not King Husain!—arrived yesterday. I haven't seen any of them yet but I dutifully telephoned this morning to ask after them.

December 23, 1924

She's charming, I'm so happy to say. She has the delicate, sensitive Hashimi . . . face and the same winning manner that he has. She had on a very nice, long tunicked brown gown . . . a long long string of pearls, . . . and a splendid aquamarine pendant. I saw the 2 eldest girls who are just like her, rather shy but not at all wooden and eager to be outgoing.

Gertrude asked the queen if she might invite Ghazi to tea, accompanied by his slaves, and was soon ordering him marvelous toys from Harrods.

December 14, 1924

The train and soldiers I had ordered for him from Harrods had arrived last mail and were presented, with great success. Especially the train. He loves all kinds of machinery and in fact was much cleverer about the engine than any of us. . . . We all sat on the floor and watched it running along the rails, following it with shouts of joy.

Gertrude was in charge of the clothes to be made for the queen, tunics and gowns suitable for the king's wife and her all-female receptions and tea parties. Out of doors, the royal women and their suites wore the traditional black silk veil, but when they visited the houses of their women friends or relations, the veils would be left with the maid at the door. Gertrude recommended the dressmaker-nuns who had made her own clothes before she had been joined by her maid, Marie, and brought them to Harithiya to introduce them. Later, Elsa and Molly would be dispatched to the London shops for suitable Western-style clothes for the queen and the daughters, only ever to be seen in private.

December 31, 1924

The King sent for me on Monday to discuss what arrangements should be made about the Queen's household. I was glad he consulted me for there were some terrible pitfalls ahead. He has acted on my suggestion that he should make the wife of his principal A.D.C., Jaudet Beg, mistress of ceremonies, as you might say—Chamberlainess it is in Arabic. Mme. Jaudet is of a very distinguished Circassian family, long settled in Baghdad and greatly respected. Miss Fairley, who is governess to the Amir Ghazi, is to teach the girls English and tennis and European behaviour. . . . She is a nice, good little girl and I am very much pleased that she has found a permanent place at the palace. I shall have to unteach them to call a napkin a serviette, which they will certainly do under her guidance.

So, once again, I'm busy court-making!

February 25, 1925

Yesterday I went up to the palace to take the King for a walk for the good of his health and found the girls having a music lesson and Ghazi having a writing lesson in his own little house. Ghazi had just developed a film in the developing box I had given him and was in a great state of glee, unimpaired by the fact that the figures of his sisters had the appearance of having been rocked in an earthquake at the time the pictures were taken. He is a dear little boy with charming manners; he makes a point of speaking English to me and here [enclosed] is his first letter in that tongue.

The young emir never failed to observe the traditional calls to prayer and presumably continued to do so even during his later school days at Harrow. For the loss of her son to an English public school, the queen would find it difficult to forgive Gertrude, on whose advice he was sent there.

Gertrude's health continued to deteriorate and, combined with the results of heat exhaustion, illness was a frequent problem.

March 29, 1923

I write from a bed of sickness from which however I am rapidly preparing to rise. It is nothing but a cold, with a touch of laryngitis which entirely extinguished my voice for two days. I caught it dining with the King on the 23rd. That night the Maude Bridge was swept away; and on Saturday the dykes burst 17 miles above the town on this bank and we now have 300 square miles under water. . . . Rather stupidly I yielded to curiosity on Sunday and rode out to see the waters. I found some officers of the Arab Army in need of a messenger so I galloped about getting things for them, and then I met the King and stopped and talked to him, so I stayed out too long. Then I had a dinner party . . . and behold no voice next day!

October 22, 1924

I have had a bad cold and a little fever too, which makes me miserable. However Sinbad and his wife are looking after me wonderfully.

The cold turned to bronchitis, unfortunately coinciding with the arrival of her half-sister Elsa and her husband, Vice Admiral Sir Herbert Richmond, visiting Baghdad on an official cruise in October 1924. Her other sister Molly's son George Trevelyan was also expected and would stay with Gertrude.

October 29, 1924

I've little to write about because I have been seeing so few people. The disappointment was that I was still in bed when George arrived and could not have him here. I was really crumpled up and Sinbad said I wasn't fit for company, so George went to the Residency. . . .

She had rapidly became so ill that Sinbad felt it necessary to visit her twice a day. The good-hearted Lady Dobbs not only invited George to stay at the Residency but lent her car to Gertrude so that as she improved she could drive the Richmonds around Baghdad and show them the sights.

November 5, 1924

Elsa is so delicious always and it has been so endlessly enjoyable to have her to talk to. . . . What with trying to be well and trying to work in the office and go about with the Richmonds, I've had as much as I could do. But it has been so heavenly having Elsa—I always feel when I am with her that there's no one in the world I love more.

She had always made light of her illness in letters to her parents, just as she had once made light of the dangers she had run when crossing the desert.

December 10, 1924

> You mustn't bother, darling Father, about my health. Sinbad
> says I have the most surprising power of sudden recovery, so
> much so that he sometimes feels inclined to accuse me of having
> been shamming! I know I was very much run down when Elsa
> first came, but in the ten days she was here I had recovered and
> I am now perfectly well.

The Richmonds had told Gertrude of the Bells' financial worries. The economic depression, combined with strikes, had hit
the family fortunes hard. Amalgamated with their competitors
Dorman Long by Gertrude's grandfather in 1901, the sale of
the shares and the chemical companies, together with the combining of the Bell rail interests with the North East Railway,
had once provided huge amounts of money into the family.
Gertrude's gift from her grandfather of £5000 ($752,000 RPI
adjusted) had funded her six-month expeditions into the desert. But now the Bell empire was on the point of collapse. The
share values of Dorman Long & Co., in which Sir Hugh Bell
and Sir Arthur Dorman owned the most stock, had begun to
fall. To boost the price of the shares, each had begun to buy
them up, but the decline of the company only accelerated.

> It's most tiresome that Dorman ordinary shares still don't pay. I
> wonder if you've got any of the big railway orders I read about
> in Reuters today. I have been very economical and I haven't had
> a new gown for eighteen months; I am feeling a little dingy this
> winter but I hope my bankbook looks brighter.

Added to personal financial and health worries, Gertrude was
preoccupied with the briefing of the League of Nations' Turkish Boundary Commission, which had arrived in Iraq both to
secure the strategic border of the armistice line to prevent
incursions by the Turks and to protect the oil fields. At the
dinner given in their honor in January 1925, she was the only
woman among fifty-eight guests and wore black velvet with
her orders and diamonds.

Now that her family had seen the frail state of her health for themselves, her father and stepmother redoubled their efforts to persuade her to return to England. Worn-out, she capitulated wearily to their demands.

"If I come home . . . I don't want to pay a round of visits on all my relatives and friends, but to be peaceful at Rounton. So will you [to Lady Bell] tactfully discourage other suggestions!"

In the summer of 1925, Gertrude finally returned to England, accompanied by her maid, Marie Delaire.

EPILOGUE

Florence wrote that Gertrude arrived home July 17, 1925, in "a condition of great nervous fatigue, and appeared exhausted mentally and physically." The doctors who were asked to see her, Sir Thomas Parkinson and Dr. Thomas Body, took the same view: that she required a great deal of care and ought not to return to the climate of Iraq. It was a serious warning—perhaps even more than that. Her old Oxford friend Janet Courtney was horrified by how thin and white-haired Gertrude had become since the portrait drawn by John Singer Sargent on her previous trip two years earlier. Her niece Pauline was to recall Gertrude at this time, always cold, always in a full-length fur coat, standing with her back to the fire smoking a Turkish cigarette in a long holder, the center of conversation.

Gertrude found her beloved father pained and harassed by the Bell financial misfortunes. Had she been told privately by the doctors that her heavy smoking had at last taken its toll and that she had only months to live, perhaps she might have spared him that knowledge.

On the other hand, something of significance certainly did pass between Gertrude and her stepmother in those last few weeks at Rounton, and it resulted in a closer bond between the two of them than had ever existed before. Perhaps Gertrude, finding that she now needed support and affection of the kind she had always half shrugged off, felt able to tell her stepmother what she had not been able to tell her father. Florence, with that unflinching contemplation of the verities of life and death natural to an experienced mother and grandmother, would have met Gertrude's revelation calmly and stoically, and perhaps conspired gratefully to keep Hugh in ignorance. They talked many times, and it was a changed Gertrude who set off once more for Iraq, writing to Florence of "this last summer" perhaps in more senses than one.

October 21, 1925

Darling Mother,

I must write a word to thank you for your letters of October 1st and 6th. I do so love to think that you liked me to come in to the library [at Rounton] in the mornings, even though I was interrupting you horribly. You know I feel as if I had never known you *really* before, not in all the years. It was perhaps because of the general crisis we were going through and my immense admiration for your courage and wisdom. Whatever it was I feel certain that I have never loved you so much, however much I may have loved you, and I am so thankful that we were together this last summer and that we both have the sense of its having been a wonderful experience.

In England she had caught up with her best friends and closest relations. Janet Courtney had suggested that Gertrude should stay in London and stand for Parliament.

August 4, 1925

You dear and beloved Janet,

No, I'm afraid you will never see me in the House. I have an invincible hatred of that kind of politics. . . . I don't cover a wide enough field and my natural desire is to slip back into the comfortable arena of archaeology and history. . . . I think I must certainly go back for this winter, though I privately very much doubt whether it won't be the last. . . .

Goodbye, my dear . . .

Did Gertrude mean her last winter in Iraq, or her last winter?

She left Rounton and went to the Bell house in Knights-bridge at the end of September to say her good-byes. As if alerted by Florence, a crowd of her friends and admirers came to wish her well.

95 Sloane Street

Darling Mother,

Before I go to bed I must tell you how I passed the day. It began at 9 by the welcome appearance of Pauline* just after I had breakfasted. At 10.15 Milly† appeared and accompanied me to all the places I had to go about tickets and reserved seats. I came in after one and went straight off to a lunch with Esme Dobbs at the Grosvenor Hotel. She *was* such a dear. As I left she said: "You must be a habit, like a drug or something which one can't do without once one has begun it." At 4.30 came Aunt Maisie.‡ Just as she went came Sir Percy Cox (complete with-out wife) and I had a delightful half hour alone with him. He was such a dear. Then came Domnul and very agreeable conversation *à trois* till Sir Percy left, and I had a quarter of an hour alone with Domnul till Mr. Montague Bell (Near East) appeared. By that time it was getting late and I only let him stay about twenty minutes for Marie was grappling with boxes and I wanted to see what she was doing. At eight I went to dine with the Amerys—Faisal and an A.D.C. and Madge Talbot§ the party. Mr. Amery was most encouraging and H.M. beaming—a successful evening. Now I'm going to bed, but not before I've told you that a library of beautiful books has arrived for me to read on the journey and that I love you more than words can say.

---

*Pauline Trevelyan, her sister Molly's daughter, now Mrs. John Dower.

†Gertrude's old friend, the Honorable Mildred Lowther.

‡Her father's sister, Lady Sheffield.

§One of the family of Mr. John Talbot.

She wrote a quick line to her father, who had helped her with train reservations.

> Dearest. Your letters were most useful and if you could contrive to make Mr. O'Connor (Enquiries Dept. of the Southern Railway) prime minister it would barely meet his deserts. He has secured me all my seats in crowded trains and is sending an omnibus at 9.45. I've told Mother about all my doings and the only thing I have to say to you is that I'm always and always your most loving daughter.

Gertrude embarked for the journey back with her cousin Sylvia Henley, who was to travel with her in stages and stay in Baghdad. Unfortunately, Sylvia reacted so badly to the Iraqi climate that she became ill and soon had to return to London. Marie came separately.

Baghdad, October 14, 1925

> It has been so wonderful coming back here. For the first two days I could not do any work at all in the office, because of the uninterrupted streams of people who came to see me.

She was delighted to see King Faisal again.

November 25, 1925

> We had the King and Zaid* to dinner, with Lionel Smith and Captain Holt. The King was as gay as could be and the final touch at dinner was some prunes oversoaked in gin. After two of them H.M. became uproarious and insisted that we should all eat two likewise. The effect was electric. Even the correct Captain Holt gave way to childlike fun.

*Zaid ibn Hussain, a younger brother of Faisal, an undergraduate at Balliol College, Oxford.

At the weekends she often joined the king and Ken Cornwallis
for shooting parties or a picnic and swimming in the Tigris.
She visited his new acquisition, a farm in the north, about
twenty miles from Khanaqin on the edge of the Persian mountains. She went there with a small party for Christmas 1925,
already suffering from a cold, and wrote to her parents:

December 30, 1925

. . . I had a terrific cold in the head last week and when I wrote
to you I had been indoors for two days, but I didn't tell you not
"wishing to trouble you." . . . On Sunday I put on more clothes
than I have ever worn before, and with a hot water bottle on my
knee, went up with the King and Ken and Iltyd* in a closed trol-
ley to Khanaqin. We got to the farm about sunset, found some
of the new furniture arrived and spent a happy time arranging
it, the King and I. I began then to feel very tired and went to bed
immediately after dinner. Next morning I felt rather bad; they
all came in to see if I wanted things and were in favour of not
going out shooting. However I shooed them off. . . . I felt rather
better and had them in before dinner to play a game of Bridge
with me in bed. But the next day I was pretty bad so Ken sent
for the very good local doctor only to find that he was spending
Xmas away and immediately, without telling me, telegraphed to
Baghdad for a doctor. By that time I wasn't taking much notice,
except that I had a general feeling that I was slipping into great
gulfs. Ken sat in my room all the afternoon reading. . . . Finally
at 6 arrived . . . Dr. Spencer! Sinbad was away. . . . He brought
with him a charming nurse, Miss Hannifan, who sat up with me
all night. They were both of them convinced that I had got pneumonia, but not a bit of it. Next morning it was clear that it was
no worse than pleurisy and a pretty general congestion. So they
delayed the departure of the morning train by an hour, thus do
we behave with our railway management, and took me down to
Baghdad. Ken is very useful on these occasions because he lifts

*Brigadier Sir Iltyd Clayton, a good friend of Gertrude's since 1919.

246

GERTRUDE BELL

you about so easily, and Iltyd is so useful because he talks so charmingly. They sat a good deal in my compartment and amused me. . . . An ambulance met me at the station and took me straight to hospital. . . . I have had a night nurse up to now, but I feel sure I shall not need her after tonight—Miss Isherwood, I like her very much too but Miss Hannifan is a nurse who almost makes it worth while to be ill. And lest you may think that I'm tottering about on the edges of graves, I may tell you that . . . all declare that if I hadn't the most remarkable constitution I should certainly have now been dangerously ill with pneumonia.

February 1926, Letter to J. M. Wilson*

It seems that I just didn't have pneumonia, chiefly through being made of steel springs. I spent Xmas Day in bed, with H.M., Iltyd and Ken nursing me when they weren't out shooting, and the next day I was so bad that they telegraphed for a doctor and a nurse. You need not mention these details to my family, to whom I have not retailed them.

One more thing—I can't bear the thought of leaving Baghdad and I put it out of my mind as much as possible. It makes me so miserable.

Gertrude was having to say good-bye to many of her friends in Iraq, now leaving for good. Lady Sinderson was moved to tears by the sight of Gertrude standing alone on the platform, waving, small and frail "like a leaf that could be blown away by a breath."

Increasingly lonely, often ill, Gertrude was devastated by the news of the death of her half brother Hugo, a clergyman in the Church of England, who died in February soon after returning to London from South Africa.

*J. M. Wilson, architectural adviser to the Ministry of Public Works; a former pupil of Sir Edwin Lutyens.

February 16, 1926

Darlingest Mother,

Thank you so much for your wonderful letter. It was good that I didn't have to wait for it long after the telegram. My mind has been so full of Hugo but the thing which comes uppermost is that he had a complete life. His perfect marriage and the joy of his children and then at the last his seeing you again—it was better so, if it had to be at all. I wonder if we should be happier too if we thought we were all to meet again. I never could bring myself to it even when I lost what was dearest to me. The spirit without the body would be as strange as the body without a spirit. One feels the lovely mind behind, but what one knows are the little gestures, the sweet smile, the expression of the mind. But it's no good wondering or thinking why one can't believe in the unbelievable: one just can't.

For the first time in her life, Gertrude had to think about money. With the May 1926 British General Strike only months away, and her family making drastic cuts in expenditure, she could not afford to resign her post as Oriental secretary and lose her salary along with the major part of her house rent, which was paid by the secretariat. Her parents had been worried about money since 1922, but when she had been with them, far from her preoccupations with Iraq, it had hit home how much their lives had been reduced. A month after Hugo's death, Hugh and Florence did what they had long been contemplating. They shut down Rounton Grange and moved to Mount Grace Priory, into the prior's small house set in the ruins of the Carthusian monastery, which stood on Hugh's property. Not only did Gertrude hate the idea of returning permanently to England with nothing to do, but she was unwilling to ask her father to support her financially. She worked on the annual report for the League of Nations and devoted herself to collecting and cataloging artifacts for the Iraq Museum.

June 16, 1926

I had a nice little ceremony on Monday when the King opened the first room of the museum. Today it was open to the public and as I came away at 8.30 this morning I saw some fifteen or twenty ordinary Baghdadis going round it under the guidance of the old Arab curator.

But the same day Gertrude wrote to J. M. Wilson:

My horizon is not at all pleasant. The coal strike hits us very hard; I don't know where we [her family and its fortunes] shall be this year. I have been caught in the meshes of the museum . . . and I can't go away leaving it in its present chaos. So I shall probably stay here through the summer and when I come back, come back for good. Except for the museum, I am not enjoying life at all. One has the sharp sense of being near the end of things with no certainty as to what, if anything, one will do next. It is also very dull, but for the work. I don't know what to do with myself of an afternoon. . . . It is a very lonely business living here now.

Griefs, loneliness, and a sense of frustration added to a depression that is clear to see in her letters home.

May 13, 1926

I think it is extremely unlikely that I can afford to come back and out again this summer—it's a very expensive business.

May 26, 1926

I hope you won't think I'm wrong in saying that I can't go away and leave all my antiquities unarranged and unguarded. . . . It isn't because I don't immensely want to see you and Father, but

I know you will understand that it means a very great deal to leave everything that I have been doing here and find myself rather loose on the world. I don't see at all clearly what I shall do, but of course I can't stay here for ever. . . . I'm not at all necessary in the office.

Her father wrote to Gertrude urging her to come home. In return she wrote:

Baghdad, June 2, 1926

I do understand that things are looking very discouraging and I am dreadfully sorry and unhappy about you. But I don't see for the moment what I can do. You see I have undertaken this very grave responsibility of the Museum. . . . I had been protesting for more than a year that I must have a proper building; this winter one fell vacant and they gave it to me, together with a very large sum of money for fittings, etc. Then first I had to reroof it and next I was held up at least 2 months by the floods. . . . Now all the very valuable objects—they run into tens of thousands of pounds and incidentally they would never have been taken out of the ground if I had not been here to guarantee that they would be properly protected—have been transferred pell-mell into the new building and there is absolutely no one but I who knows anything about them, since J. M. Wilson left. . . . It's a gigantic task. . . . But I can't resign from my post as Oriental Secretary. . . .

   Except for Museum work, life is very dull. . . .

June 16, 1926

. . . It is too lonely my existence here; one can't go on for ever being alone. At least, I don't feel I can.

Gertrude had told Domnul, some years previously, that death was no longer a thing she feared, that it had been robbed of its sting.

I wonder . . . what it will be like after, if there's any sort of an "after."

———

On Sunday, July 11, 1926, having joined the usual afternoon swimming party, Gertrude returned home exhausted by the heat. She went to bed, asking to be woken at 6 a.m.—or, perhaps, not to be disturbed until then. Perhaps she had said something unusual to Marie or was looking very ill. In any case, her maid was worried about her and decided to check on her during the night. Gertrude was asleep, a bottle of pills beside her. Whether there were any overt signs of suicide, whether the bottle was empty, and whether Marie called the hospital or waited are not known. What is known is that on the previous day, she had sent a note to Ken Cornwallis, asking if he would look after her dog, Tundra, "if anything happened to me."

Her death certificate, made out by the director of the Royal Hospital in Baghdad, stated that she had died from "Dial poisoning." Dial was the name for a preparation of diallylbarbituric acid, or allobarbital, used at the time as a sedative and later discontinued partly because of its frequent use in suicide attempts. Dr. Dunlop wrote that her death had taken place in the early hours of July 12. It was a couple of days before her fifty-eighth birthday.

Cornwallis did not look after Tundra. Florence and Hugh must have asked Marie to arrange the dog's passage to England. Tundra arrived at Mount Grace, where the Bells soon received a remorseful letter from Cornwallis, explaining that he had been unwell at the time of Gertrude's death and had not realized the significance of her letter.

In her *Letters of Gertrude Bell*, Florence wrote that Gertrude's death brought "an overwhelming manifestation of sorrow and sympathy from all parts of the earth, and we realized afresh that her name was known in every continent, her story had crossed every sea." A legendary personality had emerged from the Gertrude that her family had known. One of the first letters to arrive from Iraq was from her friend Haji Naji, who wrote: "It was my faith always to send Miss Bell the first of my fruits and vegetables and I know not now where I shall send them."

In London there was a memorial service for her at St. Margaret's Church in Westminster. In a condolence telegram, King George V wrote to Hugh and Florence that "the Queen and I are grieved to hear of the death of your distinguished and gifted daughter, whom we held in high regard. The nation will with us mourn the loss of one who by her intellectual powers, force of character and personal courage rendered important and what I trust will prove lasting benefit to the country and to those regions where she worked with such devotion and self-sacrifice."

The Colonial Secretary Leo Amery paid her the rare tribute of a statement in the House of Commons. Sir Valentine Chirol wrote a moving portrait of her for *The Times*, stating that she was "perhaps the most distinguished woman of our day, in the field of Oriental exploration, archaeology, and literature and in the service of the Empire in Irak [sic]." T. E. Lawrence wrote a brilliant if characteristically cranky letter to Hugh from India. Seeking anonymity and isolation, he had enlisted in the RAF as Aircraftsman Shaw and obtained a posting far afield. He had not known of Gertrude's death until George Bernard Shaw's wife had sent him Florence's compilation of her letters.

In a condolence letter to her father, written on November 4, 1927, Lawrence wrote:

I think she was very happy in her death, for her political work— one of the biggest things a woman has ever had to do—was as finished as mine. That Irak state is a fine monument; even if it only lasts a few more years, as I often fear and sometimes hope. It seems such a very doubtful benefit—government—to give a people who have long done without. Of course it is you who are unhappy, not having Gertrude any more, but there—she wasn't yours really, though she did give you so much.

Her letters are exactly herself—eager, interested, almost excited, always about her company and the day's events. She kept an everlasting freshness; or at least, however tired she was, she could always get up enough interest to match that of anyone who came to see her. I don't think I ever met anyone more civilised, in the sense of her width of intellectual sympathy. And she was exciting too, for you never knew how far she would leap out in any direction, under the stimulus of some powerful expert who had engaged her mind in his direction. She and I used to have a private laugh over that—because I kept two of her letters, one describing me as an angel, and the other accusing me of being possessed by the devil—and I'd show her first one and then another, begging her to be charitable towards her present objects of dislike.

However, you won't want to know what I think; her loss must be nearly unbearable, but I'm so grateful to you for giving so much of her personality to the world. . . .

David Hogarth; Salomon Reinach, the editor of the *Revue Archéologique*; Leonard Woolley of the British Museum; and hundreds of sheikhs, British officers, and Iraqi ministers added their commiserations. In Baghdad, King Faisal and his Cabinet designated one of the rooms in the museum the "Gertrude Bell Room," and Henry Dobbs wrote on behalf of her friends there to say that they had commissioned a brass plaque, to be put up in the Iraq Museum:

GERTRUDE BELL

Whose memory the Arabs will ever hold
In reverence and affection
Created this Museum in 1923
Being then Honorary Director of Antiquities for the Iraq
With wonderful knowledge and devotion
She assembled the most precious objects in it
And through the heat of the Summer
Worked on them until the day of her death
On 12th July, 1926
King Faisal and the Government of Iraq

In gratitude for her great deeds in this country
Have ordered that the Principal Wing shall bear her name
And with their permission
Her friends have erected this Tablet

At the time of her death, King Faisal was absent from Iraq.
His brother Emir Ali was acting as regent. He immediately
ordered a military funeral for her. She was buried the same
afternoon in the cemetery outside Baghdad. Her body was
driven in a "Health Service motor car" to the British cemetery
from the Protestant church, her coffin draped with the Union
Jack and the flag of Iraq and decked with wreaths from Faisal's family, the British High Commission, and many others.
The cortege drove slowly through streets lined with soldiers of
the Iraqi army and was followed on foot by the regent, the
prime minister, the high commissioner, and other state officials both civil and military. Enormous crowds had assembled
from across the country to watch her coffin pass by and to pay
her silent homage—Islamic leaders side by side with Jewish
merchants, effendis alongside the poor and ragged. It was reported in the newspapers that "the whole population of the
capital participated in the procession of burial." At the cemetery gates young men of the High Commission, openly griev-
ing, shouldered the coffin to its resting place. The British army
chaplain performed the burial rites, and senior British officials
scattered handfuls of soil over it. Surrounded by "a huge con-
course of Iraqis and British"—including Sir Henry Dobbs and
the entire British staff, the Iraqi Cabinet, and many tribal
sheikhs—the coffin was laid in the plain stone tomb. Word
had spread across the desert with mystifying speed, and the
tribes had been pouring into Baghdad all afternoon: first the
Howeitat and Dulaim, then sheikhs from near and far.

Sir Henry Dobbs wrote:

She had for the last ten years of her life consecrated all the
indomitable fervour of her spirit and all the astounding gifts of

her mind to the service of the Arab cause, and especially to
Iraq. At last her body, always frail, was broken by the energy of
her soul.

Her bones rest where she had wished them to rest, in the soil
of Iraq. Her friends are left desolate.

But let us not mourn, those who are left, even those who were
nearest to her, that the end came to her so swiftly and so soon.
Life would inexorably have led her down the slope—Death
stayed her at the summit.

July 13, 1926, The Times editorial

Some power in her linked the love of the East with a practical aim
that became a dominating purpose. . . . That she endured drudg-
ery, was never dismayed by continual disappointment and never
allowed her idealism to turn to bitterness, shows a strength of
character rare indeed among those of the English for whom the
East has become a passion. She was the one distinguished woman
among them and her quality was of the purest English mettle. . . .
Miss Bell has left the memory of a great Englishwoman.

The many obituaries paid tribute to the fact that, thanks to
her, Iraq was better governed than it had been for five hundred
years, calmer, more prosperous, and evidently more contented,
with the British and the Arabs working together in friendly
collaboration. *The Times of India* obituary offered a masterly
summing-up of her character and work. While the British
appreciated Gertrude as an author, traveler, and archaeologist,
it said, they remained to the end ignorant of the "astonishing
position she had built up for herself in Iraq, a position which
has made her responsible, more than any other single individ-
ual, for the shape and appearance of modern Iraq as it stands
today."

She had persuaded the British government to take on the
financial risks of Iraq, and she had convinced Iraqi leaders that
it meant well by them, and that there would be no return to
colonial methods. Her grand design was "the creation of a

free, prosperous and cultivated Iraq, the mainspring for a revival of Arab culture and civilization. . . . It was Gertrude who advocated day in day out the granting of as complete a measure of local autonomy as was compatible with some British hold on the country—not . . . on the score of expediency, but on that of the natural right of the Arab race to a 'place in the sun.'"

But for those who loved Gertrude most, Florence's words remain unforgettable. She wrote, "In truth the real basis of Gertrude's nature was her capacity for deep emotion. Great joys came into her life, and also great sorrows. How could it be otherwise, with a temperament so avid of experience? Her ardent and magnetic personality drew the lives of others into hers as she passed along."

Index

Note: Page numbers in *italics* refer to maps.

'Abdul Qadir, 55
Acropolis, 43
aghas (Kurdish aristocrats), 100–101
agriculture in Mesopotamia, 186–87
Al Arab newspaper, xxxviii
al-Askari, Ja'far Pasha, 24
Albert Medal of the Royal Society of
    Arts, xxix
Alexander, the Great, 91, 92
Allenby, Edmund, 159, 207
al-Ma'rawi, Muhammad, 117,
    119, 124
Al-Mutanabbi, 14
Alpine Journal, 29, 30
Alps, 26
al-Said, Nuri Pasha, 24
Amurath to Amurath (Bell), xii,
    xxxiii, xxxiv, 99–100
Anglo-Persian Oil Company, 187
antiquities work of Bell, xix, xxxii,
    xli. *See also* archaeological work
    of Bell
Anti-Suffrage League, xxxiii, 20
Arab Bureau. *See* Arab Intelligence
    Bureau
Arabia Deserta (Doughty), 106, 115,
    121, 124
Arabian Diaries, 1913–1914
    (O'Brien, ed.), xii
Arabian Nights, 128, 129
Arabic language
    and Bagdad Public Library (Salam
      Library), 9–10

Bell's difficulties with, 3, 4–5, 7
Bell's fluency in, 9, 152
and Bell's political paper, 182
and Bell's relations with Arabs, xiv,
    6–7, 8, 68
and Lawrence, 152
lessons in, 63
poetry in, recited by Bell, 68
Arab Intelligence Bureau, xii, xl,
    151–66
    and Arab Revolt, 153, 159
    Bell's assignment to, 151
    and Bell's demotion, 191
    Bell's role in, 153
    and correspondence of Bell, 153
    and the Intrusives, 153, 159
    Lawrence's criticism of, 162–64
    mission of, 153
    and self-determination for Arabs,
      155, 159, 162, 166, 191
Arab Revolt, 78n, 153, 159, 206, 207
Arabs and Arab culture
    and Balfour Declaration, xvi,
      xviii, xxxviii
    and Bedouin etiquette, xiv
    Bell's affection for, 152, 223
    Bell's expertise about, 71–72, 152
    Bell's relations with, xiv–xv
    and Cairo Conference, 164–165
    diversity in, 179
    and English women, 23, 75
    Lawrence's affection for, 152
    lines of heredity in, xiv

Arabs and Arab culture (*cont.*)
  and provisional Arab government, xl
  and raids, 76–78
  and siege of Kut, xiii,
    xxxvi–xxxvii, 158–59
  tents of, 68, 98–99
  and tribal call-to-arms, 77–78
  tribal organization in, xv
  See *also* self-determination of
    Arab people
Arab Tribes of Mesopotamia, The
  (Bell), xii, 166–75
archaeological work of Bell, xxxiv,
  40–57
  acquisitions for museum, 42–43,
    54–56, 247
  in Asia Minor, 96
  Assyrian artifacts, 54
  Babylonian artifacts, 54, 55, 102–3
  in Binbirkilise, 47–50
  Byzantine sites, xii, 41, 81
  credentials for, 40, 41
  and desert expeditions, 71, 102–3
  and Director of Archaeology
    appointment, 42, 52, 54, 229
  and field books, xi
  and Gertrude's Law of
    Excavations, 229
  and looting, 42
  and palace of Ukhaidir, xxxiii,
    xxxiv, 41–42, 50–52
  and *Prolegomena* entry, 42
  protection of sites and treasures, 52
  training in surveying and
    mapmaking, xxxiii
  See *also* Iraq Museum
archive of Bell's works, xi
Ark of Noah, 102–3
Armenians, xxxiii
Ashur, 82, 83
Asia, 83–84, 95–96
Asia Minor
  archaeological work of Bell in, 96
  expedition through Syrian Desert
    to (1905), 63, 76–81

  expedition to (1907), 81–82
  scarcity of resources in, 70
Asquith, Herbert, 20, 22
Assaf, 90
Assyrian artifacts, 54
Atatürk, Mustafa Kemal, xliii
Athens, 43
athleticism of Bell, 26
At the Works (F. Bell), xi, 19
awards. See honors awarded to Bell

Baal, Temple of, 74
Babylon, xix, xl, 82
Babylonian archaeological artifacts,
  54, 55, 102–3
Baghdad, xxxvii
  and Bell's fluency in Arabic, 9
  Bell's home in, xxxvii, 178
  Bell's travels to, xxxiii, xxxv
  and British administration, 187
  and expedition of 1911, 84
  and expedition of 1913–14, 89
  heat in, 188–89
  and influenza pandemic, xxxix
  insurrection in, 201–2
  naqib of, 197–203, 208, 213, 222,
    225, 227
  school for girls in, 21
  women and social observances
    in, 25
  women's club in, 24
  women's emancipation in, 24
  women's hospital in, xl, 21
  and World War I, xxxvii
  See *also* Iraq Museum
Baghdad Public Library (later Salam
  Library), xli, 9–10
Balfour, Arthur James, xvi
Balfour, Frank, xxxiii, 188, 224
Balfour Declaration, xvi,
  xviii, xxxviii
Barre des Écrins ascent of Bell, 28
bazaars, 81
Bedouins
  and coronation of Faisal, 214–17

and Damascus government, 21
language of, 6, 7
and *rafiq's* role in desert
    expeditions, 65
Beirut, xxxiv
Bell, Ada (aunt), xxvii, xxx
Bell, Ada (sister), ix–x
Bell, Florence (née Cubitt), xxvi, 247
    appointed Dame Commander of
        the Order of the Indian
        Empire, xxxix
    and Bell's education, x–xi
    on Bell's emotional depth, 255
    and Bell's failing health, 241–42
    and Bell's romance, 110–11
    and Bell's service in Baghdad, 189
    and British Red Cross, xxxiv
    and correspondence, xxiii, 67, 105
    death of, xliv
    and Doughty-Wylie's death,
        146–47
    and family vacations, 27
    financial difficulties of, 239
    and mountaineering of Bell, 33
    move to Mount Grace Priory,
        xliii, 247
    and pageant, xliv
    and social work, 19
    and women's suffrage, 18, 20
    At the Works (F. Bell), xi, 19
    and World War I, xxxv
Bell, Gertrude
    athleticism of, 26
    awards (*see* honors awarded
        to Bell)
    background of, ix
    birth of, xxvi
    childhood of, xi
    competencies of, 21 (*see also*
        languages spoken by Bell)
    death of, xliv, 250–54
    education of, ix, x–xi, xxviii
    expeditions of (*see* desert
        expeditions of Bell)
    family life desired by, xx, 63

health issues of, xxxviii, 30,
    188–89, 237–39, 240, 241,
    245–46
intelligence work of (*see* Arab
    Intelligence Bureau)
interests of, 26, 63
legacy of, xix
nation building of (*see* Faisal I; Iraq)
romantic relationships (*see*
    Cadogan, Henry; Doughty-
    Wylie, Charles Hotham
    Montagu "Dick")
undervalued status of, 18
will of, xlii
Bell, Hugh (father)
    in Baghdad, xl
    and baronetcy, xxxii
    and Bell companies, xxxi
    and Bell's failing health, 241–42
    and Bell's final trip to Iraq, 244
    and Bell's romance, 110–11
    birth of, xxv
    bond with Bell, xi
    and Cadogan's relationship with
        Bell, 11, 19
    capitalist perspectives of, 19
    and correspondence, xxiii, 67, 105
    death of, xliv
    and death of father, xxxii
    and death of first wife, ix–x
    and Doughty-Wylie's death, 146
    and family vacations, 27
    financial difficulties of, 239,
        241, 247
    and Forth Bridge Railway
        Company, xxvii
    health issues of, xxxiii
    in Italy, xxix
    Lord Lieutenant appointment
        of, xxxii
    marriage of, xxvi
    move to Mount Grace Priory,
        xliii, 247
    and Parliament elections,
        xxix, xxxiv

Bell, Hugh (father) (*cont.*)
   and Rounton Grange, xxxii
   and Sydney Harbour Bridge, xliii
   travels with Bell, xxx, xxxi, xxxiii,
      xxxix, xl, xli
   and women's suffrage, 18, 19
Bell, Hugo (brother), xxvii
   death of, xliii, 246–47
   marriage of, xli
   ordained as priest, xxxiii
   travels with Bell, xi, xxxi, xxxiii, 8
Bell, John, xxviii
Bell, Lizzie (great-aunt), xxix
Bell, Margaret (grandmother), xxviii
Bell, Maria (Mary Shield; mother),
   ix, xxv, xxvi, xxvii
Bell, Mary (Molly; sister), xi, xxvii,
   xxxii, 146, 236
Bell, Maurice Hugh Lowthian
      (brother), xxvii, xxviii, xxix
   and baronetcy, xliv
   and the Boer War, xxx, xxxi
   and death of mother, ix
   move to Mount Grace Priory, xliii
   travels with Bell, xi, xxx
   and World War I, xxxv, xxxvi,
      xxxviii, 137–38
Bell, Sir Isaac Lowthian, xxv–xxvii
   and Albert Medal of the Royal
      Society of Arts, xxix
   and Bell companies, xxxi
   death of, xxxii
   and family fortunes, xix
   monetary gifts to
      grandchildren, xxxii
   and Mount Grace Priory, xxx
Bell, Thomas (great-grandfather), xxv
Bell Brothers, xxv, xxx
Beni Hassan tribe, 76
Beni Sakhr tribe, 65, 66, 77–78
Bibliothèque Nationale de France,
   41, 44
Binbirkilise, 42, 46–50, 70, 71, 82
Bin Bir Kilisse site, 47
Boer War, xxx, xxxi

Bolshevik army of Russia, xvi,
   xxxviii, 196
Bonar Law's Conservatives,
   xxxv–xxxvi, xli
books published by Bell, xi. *See also*
   publications of Bell
Britain
   and Arab leadership, xv
   and Bell's expertise in state
      affairs, 63
   Bell's honorary rank in military,
      151, 157
   and Constantinople, 97
   fame of Bell in, 71
   and France, xxxii
   Mandate of (*see under* Iraq)
   and Mosul district borders, xliv
   and parliamentary elections, xxxiv
   Poor Laws of, 19
   and post World War I decision
      making, xv–xvi
   property laws of, 19
   and suffrage for women, xxxiii,
      xxxviii, 18–20, 22
British Archaeological Expedition to
   Iraq, xlv
British Museum, xlii
British School of Archaeology in
   Iraq, xliv, xlv
Browne, Edward G., 12
Burma, 8
Byzantine archaeological sites, xii,
   41, 81

Cadogan, Henry, xxix, 11–12, 19, 111
Cairo, Arab Bureau in. *See* Arab
   Intelligence Bureau
Cairo Conference, xl, 164–65, 207
camels, 68, 85–86, 89, 119
caravans, 75
Carlyan, L. A., 148
castle of Ukhaidir. *See* palace of
   Ukhaidir
Cecil, Sir Robert, 139, 145–46,
   153–57

Chalabi, Musa, 179
Chirol, Sir Ignatius Valentine, xx,
    xxviii, xxxiii, 70
  Bell's correspondence with, 107n
  on Bell's personal qualities, xix
  and Bell's romance, 106, 110,
    112–14, 140, 146
  and death of Bell, 251
  and Hayyil expedition, 132
  and Iraq's nationhood, 192
  relationship with Bell, 106–7n
  and World War I, 139, 140–42
Churches and Monasteries of the Tur
    Abdin, The (Bell), xii, 84
Churchill, Winston, xxxi, xxxv, xl
  advocacy for evacuation of Iraq,
    xiv, xv
  and Cairo Conference, 164–65
  and Faisal as king of Iraq,
    207–8, 210
  Middle East role of, xli
  sightseeing with, 40
  and Treaty of Alliance, 223
  and World War I, xxxvi
Cilician plain, 69
Clarence steelworks, ix–x
Clayton, Gilbert, xxxvi
Clemenceau, Georges, 159
climbing of Bell. See mountaineering
    of Bell
clothing of Bell
  in Baghdad, 189, 190
  for desert expeditions,
    66–67, 79
  for dress occassions, 27, 67
  and feminine refinement, xix
  for mountaineering, 27, 31–32
  tiara given to Bell, 224–25
Commander of the Order of the
    British Empire (CBE), xxxviii,
    159, 189
Conference of Lausanne, xlii
Constantinople, 97, 204–5
Cornwallis, Sir Kinahan, 165, 212,
    219, 230, 231, 245, 250

correspondence of Bell, xx
  and the Cairo Bureau, 153
  dating of, 67
  and desert expeditions, 67, 71, 87
  diary entries made in lieu of,
    67, 105
  and Hayyil expedition, 116–17
  and intelligence work of Bell,
    xii–xiii
  Lawrence on, 251–52
  and mountaineering of Bell, 29
  preservation of, 67
  recipients of, xxiii
Cossacks, atrocities committed
    by, xxxvii
Courtney, Janet Hogarth, xx,
    147–48, 241, 242
Cox, Sir Percy, xxxiii, xxxvi, xxxvii
  amnesty granted by, 210
  and Arab leadership, xv
  and Bagdad, xl, 176, 177, 187
  and Bell's competence, 158
  civil commissioner role of, xxxviii,
    164, 179–80, 194, 195
  departure of, 227–28
  and Faisal as king of Iraq, 219–20
  and Florence's dinner for
    Faisal, xliv
  on Hayyil expedition, 116
  and insurrection in Iraq, 192, 194
  and Iraq's nationhood, 166
  naqib on leadership of, 199–200
  retirement of, xlii
  and Tehran assignment,
    xxxviii, 191
  and Treaty of Alliance, xli, 218–19,
    222, 225–27
  and treaty with Ibn Saud, xlii
critics of Bell, xiv
Ctesiphon, 82

Daja Tribe, 68
Damascus, xxxiv
  and Druze, 21
  and expedition of 1911, 84–85

Damascus (*cont.*)
  and expedition of 1913–14, 86
  French occupation of, xl
  and Hayyil expedition, 116, 117
  interactions with local
    government, 21
  Islamic population of, 80–81
  lawless element countered in,
    86–87
Darius, 92
Darwin, Charles, ix
Davidson, Sir Nigel, 218
Dead Sea, 64
Delaire, Marie, xxxi, xxxix, 189,
    240, 250
Denison Ross, Sir Edward, xxx, 12,
    13–14
depression of Bell, 248
  and Hayyil expedition, 120,
    132–33
  and World War I, 138
dervish, Bell's violent encounter
    with, xiii
Desert and the Sown, The (Bell), xi,
    xxxii, xxxiii, 63, 94, 98–99
desert expeditions of Bell, xiii, xxx,
    58, 59–104
  1900 expedition, 62, 72–76
  1905 expedition, 62, 63, 76–81
  1907 expedition, *60–61*, 81–82
  1909 expedition, *60–61*, 82–84, 99
  1911 expedition, *58*, 84–85
  1913–1914 expedition, *58*, 85–90
    (*see also* Hayyil expedition)
  and age of Bell, 59
  and archaeological work of Bell,
    71, 102–3
  and astronomy, 89
  Bell's love of, xiii, 76
  and caravans, 75
  challenges associated with,
    68–69, 81
  clothing for, 66–67, 79
  correspondence of Bell from, 67,
    71, 87

  and dangerous encounters, 86–87,
    99–100
  dressing for, 66–67
  enthusiasm of Bell for, 53
  and etiquette of the desert, 65–66,
    67–68
  and expertise developed by Bell,
    71–72
  and fame of Bell, 71
  fatigue experienced due to, 89, 90
  and guns, 77, 99–100
  and historical reflections, 83–84
  and horses, 71, 76, 79
  and hotels, 63–64
  and language acquisition, 8
  lawless element countered in,
    86–87
  learning curve associated with,
    65–67
  maps for, 66
  and Noah's Ark, 102–3
  and palace of Ukhaidir, xxxiii,
    xxxiv, 41–42, 50–52, 82, 84,
    99–100
  provisions for, 89
  rafiq's role in, 65, 123
  and recruitment of Fattuh, xxxii
  and servants, 69 (*see also* Fattuh)
  and Shakespeare's works, 14
  and tents, 68, 79–80, 98–99
  through Syrian Desert to Asia
    Minor (1905), 45–47
  and tribal call-to-arms, 77–78
  and Turkish officials, 72–73, 76,
    87, 117
  watchmen assigned to Bell, 81
  and water, 85
  weather conditions during, 79,
    84, 90
diaries of Bell, xx
  in Bell archive, xi
  and fatigue of travel, 90
  and Hayyil expedition, 116
  in lieu of correspondence, 67, 105
  publication of, xii

Dickens, Charles, ix, xliv
Dobbs, Sir Henry, xlii, xliv, 182, 229,
    252, 253–54
Dorman Long & Co., xxx, xxxi,
    xliii, 239
Doughty, Charles M., 106, 115, 121
Doughty-Wylie, Charles "Dick,"
    xxxiii, xxxvi, 86
  background of, 106
  Bell's correspondence with,
    109, 117
  death of, xxxv, 146, 148
  diaries written for, xii
  and Hayyil expedition, 115,
    116–17, 132
  mourning of Bell for, 146–47
  romantic relationship with Bell,
    105–14, 133, 135, 142–46
  and Turkish officials, 87
  visit to grave of, 148–49, 152
  and World War I, 145
  and Young Turks' nationalist
    rebellion, 108–9
Doughty-Wylie, Judith, 105, 109,
    113, 133, 142–43, 145, 148
Druze, 21, 72–74, 76–78, 79, 94
Dughan, Khalil, 5

Edward VII, king of Great Britain,
    xxxi, xxxiv
Egypt, 156
Elizabeth, queen of Romania, xxviii
epigraphy, 41
Euphrates River, xii, xxxiii, 41,
    83, 99. See also Amurath to
    Amurath (Bell)
expeditions. See desert expeditions
    of Bell

Faisal I, King of Iraq, xxxvii, xli,
    165–66
  appendicitis attack of, 225–27
  and Arab Revolt, 159–60, 206, 207
  and archaeological work of Bell,
    xlii, 42, 229

  background of, 204–7
  on Bell's committment, xiii
  and Bell's final trip to Iraq, 244–45
  and Bell's fluency in Arabic, 9
  Bell's relationship with, 160, 212,
    217–18, 230–32
  and British Mandate, 218–19,
    222–23, 225–27, 231
  and the Cairo Bureau, 159
  and Cairo Conference, 164–65
  and constitution of Iraq, xlii
  and coronation ceremonies,
    214–17, 218, 219–20
  death of, xliv
  and death of Bell, 252–53
  deposed, xl
  as descendant of the Prophet,
    204, 210
  and end of the Ottoman
    Empire, 159
  European dress of, 233
  and extremists and nationalists,
    162, 205–6, 218, 223, 225, 226,
    229, 230
  family of, 25, 232–37
  Florence's dinner for, xliv
  and insurrection in Iraq, 227
  and Iraq Museum, xliv
  and Iraq National Assembly, xliii
  as king of Iraq, xli, 207–27
  as king of Syria, xl, 162, 207
  and Paris Peace Conference, 160,
    162, 207
  and self-determination for
    Arabs, 162
  and Treaty of Alliance, xli, xliii,
    218–19, 222–23, 225–27, 231
Faisal II, King of Iraq, xlv
Fallujah, 89, 215
fame of Bell
  in Britain, 71
  and death of Bell, 250–51
  and desert expeditions, 71
  and Lawrence, 166
  for mountaineering, 28, 29

fame of Bell (*cont.*)
  and publications of Bell, 94
  in Syria, 76
family life desired by Bell, xx, 63
Fattuh (servant), xxxiii
  Bell's appreciation for, 70–71
  and dangerous confrontations, 51,
    85, 99–100
  and donkey, 103
  and expedition of 1909, 82
  and expedition of 1911, 84, 85
  and expedition of 1913–14, 87,
    88, 116, 117, 127
  health issues of, 108
  and Lloyd George, 70
  recruitment of, xxxii, 69–70
feminine refinement of Bell, xix
Ferdinand, Franz, xxxv
finances of Bell, xli, 41, 190, 247, 248
Finsteraarhorn ascent of Bell, 26, 28,
  29–30, 34–38
FitzGerald, Edward, 12
fleas, 80, 102
France
  and Britain, xxxii
  Damascus occupied by, xl
  and Syrian mandate, xiv, 78n,
    162, 208
  and travels of Bell, xxx, xxxix
  and World War I, xxxvii, 134–35
French Alps, 28
French language, 10
Fuhrer, Heinrich, 28, 30, 32–33,
  36–38
Fuhrer, Ulrich, 26, 28–30, 32–34,
  35–38

Georges-Picot, François, 78n
George V, king of England, xxxiv,
  xliii, 251
Germany
  German language, 3, 10
  travels of Bell to, xxxiv
  and World War I, xxxv, xxxvii,
    xxxviii, xxxix

Gertrude's Law of Excavations, 229
Gertrudspitze (Gertrude's Peak),
  xxxi, 29
Ghazi, king of Iraq, xliv, xlv, 233–37
Gill Memorial Award, xxxiv
Green Howards Battalion, xxxv

Hafiz, poetry of, 4, 11–17
Haifa, 21
Haldane, Sir Aylmer, 24
Hall, Captain, 149, 152
Hamid, Abdul, 204–5
Hamlet (Shakespeare), 14, 122
Hardinge, Charles, xxviii, 156,
  157, 158
Hayyil expedition, xxxiv, xli, 71, 87
  artifact acquisitions, 53
  Bell detained in, xii, xxxiv, 89,
    128–30
  and Bell's correspondence, 116–17
  Bell's understanding of Arab tribes
    following, 152
  dangers associated with, 115–16
  and depression of Bell, 120,
    132–33
  difficulties of travel to, 115–16,
    117–24
  and expedition logistics, 116
  and financial concerns, 126–27,
    128, 129
  and Founder's Medal of the Royal,
    xxxviii, 189–90
  Muslim women of, 20–21
  and photography of Bell, 130
  and regional tensions, 115–16,
    117, 127
  return from, 130–31
health issues of Bell
  from heat in Iraq, 188–89
  in later life, 237–39, 240, 245–46
  mountaineering injuries, 30
heat in Iraq, 188–89
Hebrew language, 3, 10
Henley, Sylvia, xliii
Herbert, Aubrey, xiii, 152, 158–59

Herodotus, 44
hillsides, structures built into, 48
Hindustani, 3, 8, 10
Hirtzel, Sir Arthur, 161
Hittite archaeological sites, xii, 49, 81
Hogarth, David, xxx, 40, 43, 72, 147–48
 and Bell's travels, xxxvi
 and the Cairo Bureau, 149
 and death of Bell, 252
 and grave of Doughty-Wylie, 152
 on Hayyil expedition, 116
 and Lawrence, 151
honors awarded to Bell
 Commander of the Order of the British Empire (CBE), xxxviii, 159, 189
 Founder's Medal of the Royal Geographical Society, xxxviii, 189–90
 Gill Memorial Award of the Royal Geographical Society, xxxiv
 Gold Medal of the Royal Geographical Society, xxxv, 132
 Prolegomena entry, 42
horseback riding, 64, 68, 71, 76, 79
House of Rashid, 72
Howeitat, 77
humanitarian aid, 185
Hussein, Saddam, xv
Hussein ibn Ali, King of Hejaz, xxxvii, xliii, 160, 204–6, 232, 234

Ibn Hadhdhal, Sheikh Fahd Beg, 22
Ibn Rashid, Muhammad, 116, 125, 128
Ibn Saud, xxxi, xxxiv, xliii, 132, 232
 and Hayyil, xli
 and Mecca, xliii, 234
 power of, xviii
 and regional tensions, 115–16, 128
 treaty with, xlii
 and World War I, xxxvii

incarceration of Bell, xii, xxxiv, 89, 128–30. *See also* Hayyil expedition
India
 and Egypt, 156
 and English women, 23
 and language acquisition, 8
 and Queen Victoria, xxvii
Industrial Revolution, 18
influenza pandemic, xxxix
intelligence work of Bell, xii–xiii, xxxvi. *See also* Arab Intelligence Bureau
Intrusives, 153, 159. *See also* Arab Intelligence Bureau
Iraq
 Bell on political future of, 191
 Bell's diminished role in, 229
 Bell's role in founding of, ix, xiii–xiv, 254–55
 British administration of, 155–56, 162–66, 176–97, 218–19, 222–23, 225–27, 229
 and British School of Archaeology in Iraq, xlii, xliv, xlv
 Cabinet of, 214, 221, 222, 225, 226, 229
 constitution of, xlii, 229
 Cox's civil commissioner role in, xxxviii, xl, 164, 179–80, 194, 195
 declared a republic, xlv
 elections in, xlii, 208–9, 214, 229
 enemies of, xvi
 extremists and nationalists of, xiv, 162, 194, 196, 218, 225, 226, 229, 230, 231
 Faisal as king of, xli, 207–27
 friends of Bell in, 20
 heat in, 188–89
 independence of, xiv, 179
 insurrection in, 190–94, 201–2, 208
 in League of Nations, xliv
 and Mosul district borders, xliv

Iraq (cont.)
    provisional government in, 208
    stability in, xv, 207
    and Treaty of Alliance, xli, xliii,
        218–19, 222–23, 225–27
    and treaty with Ibn Saud, xxxvii
    tribal population of, xv, 210
    women's emancipation in, 24
    See also Baghdad; Mesopotamia;
        self-determination of Arab
        people
Iraq Museum, xlii, 52–57
    artifact acquisitions for, 42–43,
        54–56, 247
    Babylonian Stone Room of, 43, 57
    Bell's devotion to, 57, 229, 248–49
    as Bell's legacy, xix
    building for, 56
    closure of, in wartime, xlv
    and death of Bell, 252–53
    first room opened, xliii
    and Gertrude Bell Principal Wing,
        xliv, 248, 252
    looting of, xlv
    and plaque, xliv, 252–53
    reopening of, xlv
Iraq National Assembly, xliii
Iraq Petroleum Company, xliv
Ironside, Sir Edmund, 165
Islam and Islamic societies
    and Bell's Hayyil expedition,
        125–26
    in Damascus, 80–81
    and death of Bell, 253
    and education, 184
    and the Hijaz, 202–3
    and King Hussein, xliii
    and Koran, 4
    and political relations, 97
    and self-determination for
        Arabs, 180
    and Sharia law, 180
    Shia, 180, 184, 196, 209–10
    Sufis, 11–12, 13
    Sunnis, 180, 184, 196, 209–10

    Wahhabis, xliii, 115–16, 196, 232
    women of, 20–21, 22, 23–24, 25
Italy, travels in, xxix, xxx, xxxiv, 3, 7

Japan, 3, 9
Jebel Druze, 72–74, 78, 86–87
Jerusalem, xviii, xxx, xxxviii, 3, 64
Jews and Judaism
    and Balfour Declaration,
        xvi, xxxviii
    and death of Bell, 253
    and Faisal as king of Iraq, 214
    in Palestine, xvii–xviii
    and Rages, 91
    in Syria, xvii–xviii
    and Zionism, xvii
Jordan, xlii, 64

Kadhimain, 54
Kaimmakam, 88
Kara Dagh, 70
Karbala, xii
Kiosk, Yildiz, 97
Kirkuk, 56
Kish (archaeological site), 43, 55, 56
Kitchener, Lord, 136, 205
Koran, 4
Kuntze (climber), 29
Kurds and Kurdistan, xvi, 185,
        220–21
Kut, siege of, xiii, xxxvi–xxxvii, 158

Lady Margaret Hall, Oxford,
        x, xxviii
Lake, Sir Percy, 157
Langdon, S. H., 55
languages spoken by Bell, xxix, xxx,
        3–10
    and Asia Minor, 96
    and Bagdad Public Library (Salam
        Library), 10
    and desert expeditions, 63
    difficulties experienced in
        acquisition of, 5
    effort devoted to, 63

and range of Bell's abilities, 21
and translations by Bell, xi
See also Arabic language
Lascelles, Florence (cousin), xxviii
Lascelles, Gerald, xxix
Lascelles, Lady Mary (aunt), xxviii,
    xxix, xxx, 11
Lascelles, Sir Frank (uncle), xxviii,
    xxix, xxxix, 11
Laurence, Alec, 22
Lawrence, T. E., xxxiv, xxxvii, xlii
    and archaeological work, 52
    background of, 152
    and Bell's travels, xxxvi
    and the Cairo Bureau, 149, 152,
        158–59
    and Cairo Conference, 165
    compared to Bell, 151–52
    criticism of British administration
        in Iraq, 162–64, 165
    and death of Bell, 251–52
    on Faisal, 206
    fame of, 166
    on giftedness of Bell, xviii–xix
    and Iraq's nationhood, 166
    mapmaking of, 156
    and Paris Peace Conference,
        159–61
    relationship with Bell, 166
    Seven Pillars of Wisdom, xlii, 206
    on Turkish massacres, 206–7
    and Turkish siege of Kut, xiii, 158
    upon meeting Bell, 150–51
    and World War I, xxxvi–xxxvii,
        xxxviii
Leachman, Gerald, 121
League of Nations, xxxix, xl,
    xlii, xliii
    annual report for, 247
    and British Mandate, 218, 222
    Iraq's membership in, xliv
    and "The Political Future of Iraq"
        (Bell), 191
    and Turkish Boundary
        Commission, 239

Lebanon, 7
legacy of Bell, xix
Letters of Gertrude Bell, The (Bell),
    xliv, 250
Lloyd George, David, xxxvii, xli
    and Fattuh, 70
    and Paris Peace Conference, 159
    and suffrage for women, 20
London, 22, 82

MacDonald, Ramsay, xlii
Macmillan Company, xli
MacMunn, Sir George, 157
Mallet, Sir Louis, 87, 116, 117–18
Malta, 7
Mandæans, 172–75
maps and mapmaking, xxxiii, 66,
    82, 156
Marius (mountain guide), 27, 30–31
Marshall, Horace, 3–4
Mâr Yâ'kûb at Salâh, 103–4
Massignon, M., 50
Mathon (mountain guide), 27,
    30–31, 32
Matterhorn ascent, 30, 32
Mecca, xliii, 65, 211, 233
Medina, 127, 206
Meije ridge ascent of Bell, 26–28,
    30–31
Mesopotamia
    agriculture in, 186–87
    artifacts from, xix
    Bell's political paper on, 180–87
    education in, 183–84
    famine in, 185
    humanitarian aid, 185
    and independence of Iraq, 179
    law in, 184–85
    public health in, 182–83
    as racial melting pot, xv
    reconstruction of, 181
    revenue options in, 181–82
    status of, 179
    Syria compared to, 155
    travels of Bell to, xxxiii, xxxv

Mesopotamia (*cont.*)
  tribal population of, xv, 210
  See also Iraq; self-determination of
    Arab people
military service of Bell, xiv
Mill, John Stuart, 18, 21
misogyny, 157
Montagu, Sir Edwin, xvi
Mont Blanc, 28
Morkill, Frances, xli
Morris, William, ix
mountaineering of Bell, xxx, xxxi,
    26–39
  Barre des Écrins ascent, 28
  clothes for, 27, 31–32
  and fame of Bell, 28, 29
  on family holidays, 26–27
  Finsteraarhorn ascent, 26, 28,
    29–30, 34–38
  Gertrudspitze (Gertrude's Peak), 29
  and guides, 27, 28, 29, 30–31, 32
  injuries sustained in, 30
  Lauteraarhorn-Schreckhorn
    ascent, 29
  Matterhorn ascent, xxxii, 30, 32,
    38–39
  Meije ridge ascent, 26–28, 30–31
  Mont Blanc ascent, 32
  and reputation of Bell, 28
  Schreckhorn traverse, 26, 28, 32
  training in, 28–29
  Urbachthaler Engelhorn ascent,
    29, 32–34
  and women mountaineers, 27
Munich, Germany, xxxiv
Musée de Cluny, 41

Nabataean ruins of Petra, 65–66
Naji, Haji, xiii, 20, 251
Namrüd, 98
naqib of Baghdad, 197–203, 208,
    213, 222, 225, 227
National Portrait Gallery, London, 18
Nestorians, 102
Newcastle University, xi

Nightingale, Florence, 19
Nimrud, Abu, 7
Noah's Ark, 102–3

O'Brien, Rosemary, xii, 94
office work of Bell, xiii
Oriental secretary assignment, xiv, xl,
    xlii, 53, 159, 191, 247, 249
Ottoman Empire, xxxiii, 88–89,
    115–16, 159
Oxford University, xxviii

Palace and Mosque at Ukhaidir, The
    (Bell), xii, xxxiv, xxxv
palace of Ukhaidir, xxxiii, xxxiv,
    41–42, 50–52, 77, 82, 84,
    99–100
Palestine, xvi, xvii–xviii, xxxviii, 7
Pankhurst, Christabel, 20
Paris Peace Conference, xxxix,
    159–62, 195–96, 207
Parliament, British, xliv, 18–19,
    180, 242
Pasha, Jemal, 206
Persia, xxviii, 59, 91–94
Persian language, 3, 4, 7, 10, 11, 12
Persian Pictures (Bell), xi, 90
"Personhood," 18
Petra, Nabatean ruins at, 65–66
photographic memory of Bell, 68
photography of Bell
  and archaeological work of Bell,
    xi, 41
  and desert expeditions, 67,
    120, 130
  equipment for, xi, 67
  and etiquette of the desert, xxxi
Poems from the Divan of Hafiz
    (Bell), xi, xxix, xxx, 11–17
poetry of Bell, 11–17
"The Political Future of Iraq"
    (Bell), 191
politicians, Bell's perspective on, xiv
Poor Laws of Britain, 19
Princeton Expedition, 96

Principles of the Manufacture of Iron and Steel (Bell), xxviii
Prolegomena, 42
property laws of Britain, 19
publications of Bell, xi–xii, xx
  Amurath to Amurath, xii, xxxiii, xxxiv, 99–100
  Arab Tribes of Mesopotamia, The, xii, 166–75
  Churches and Monasteries of the Tur Abdin, The, xii, 84
  Desert and the Sown, The, xi, xxxii, xxxiii, 63, 94, 98–99
  Letters of Gertrude Bell, The, xliv, 250
  Palace and Mosque at Ukhaidir, The, xii, xxxiv, xxxv
  Persian Pictures, xi, 90
  Poems from the Divan of Hafiz, xi, xxix, xxx, 11–17
  "The Political Future of Iraq," 191
  Principles of the Manufacture of Iron and Steel, xxviii
  Review of the Civil Administration of Mesopotamia, xii, xxxix, xl, 180–87
  Safar Nameh: Persian Pictures, xxix
  "Self-Determination in Mesopotamia," 196–97
  Thousand and One Churches, The, xi–xii, xxxiii, 42, 46, 47, 81, 105
  Vaulting System at Ukhaidir, The, xii
  Visits of Gertrude Bell to Tur Abdin, 102
public health, 182

Qadir, 'Abdul, 54
Qallat Semaan, 59
Queen's College, x

Rages, 91–92
Ramadi, 85, 215

Ramsay, Sir William Mitchell, xxxiii, 42, 48–49, 81–82
  absentmindedness of, 106, 107
  archaeological work of, xii
  and ruins of Binbirkilise, 47
  writing partnership with Bell, 105
  See also Thousand and One Churches, The
Rashid dynasty, xli
Red Cross, xxxiv, xxxv, xxxix, 134–42, 145–46, 147
Reform Bill of 1832, 18
Reinach, Salomon, xxxii, 40–41, 44–45, 96, 252
Review of the Civil Administration of Mesopotamia (Bell), xii, xxxix, xl, 180–87
Revue Archéologique, 40
Richmond, Admiral Sir Herbert, xxxiii, 238
Richmond, Elsa (nee Bell), xi, xxi, xxvii, xxxiii, 146, 236, 238
Robinson Library at Newcastle on Tyne University, 67
romantic relationships of Bell, 11–12. *See also* Cadogan, Henry; Doughty-Wylie, Charles "Dick"
Rosen, Friedrich, 3, 59, 63
Rosen, Nina, 3, 59, 63
Rounton Grange, xxxii
  Bell's departure from, xliii, 247
  and Bell's romance, 110
  demolished, xlv
  gardens of, xxxiv
  and World War I, 134
  and World War II, xlv
Royal Geographical Society, xxxiii
  Bell elected to, xii, xxxiv
  and death of Bell, xliv
  Founder's Medal of the Royal awarded to Bell, xxxviii, 189–90
  Gill Memorial Award awarded to Bell, xxxiv

Royal Geographical society (*cont.*)
  Gold Medal awarded to Bell, xxxv, 132
  time spent working at, 82
Royal Photographic Society, xi, 41
Russell, Diana, 135
Russell, Flora, 135
Russia, xvi, xxxviii, 196

Sabeans, 172–75
Sackville-West, Vita, xliii
Safar Nameh: Persian Pictures (Bell), xxix
safety, Bell's attitude toward, xiii
Saint-Germain Museum of National Antiquities, 40
Salam Library (formerly Bagdad Public Library), 9–10
Salkhad, 72, 77
Salmond, Sir John, xlii
Samarra, 82
Samuel, Sir Herbert, xlii
San Remo Conference, xl
San Remo Pact of 1920, 78n
Sardis, 44
Sargent, John Singer, xlii, 241
Sauds, 72
Schreckhorn traverse, 26, 28, 32
"Self-Determination in Mesopotamia" (Bell), 196–97
self-determination of Arab people
  and Arab Intelligence Bureau, 166
  Bell's advocacy for, xiv, 159, 208, 215, 232, 255
  and conflict common to region, xv
  and France, 162
  interpretations of, among Arab groups, 180
  Lawrence's advocacy for, 159
  and Lloyd George, 162
  opponents of, 155, 191, 232
  W. Wilson's advocacy of, 196
self-fulfillment of Bell, 63
Seven Pillars of Wisdom (Lawrence), xlii, 206

Shakespeare, William, 14, 122
Shammar tribesmen, xli
Sharia law, 180
Shatt al Arab, xxxv
sheikhs, 98–99
  Bell's influence on, 22
  and British mandate in Mesopotamia, 180
  dining with, 79–80
  and etiquette of the desert, 65–66, 67–68
  and Lawrence, 152
  tents of, 79–80
  warnings about, 98
Shetateh, 99–100
Shia, 180, 184, 196, 209–10
Simon, Saint, 59
skins, inflated, 83
South Africa, xxviii
steel industry, xliii
Stevenson, Robert Louis, ix
St. Lawrence's Church, East Rounton, xliv
Storrs, Sir Ronald, 152
Strutt, E. L., 30
Strzygowski, Josef, xxxiii
suffrage rights for women, xxxiii, xxxviii, 18–20, 22
Sufis and Sufism, 11–12, 13
Sunnis, 180, 184, 196, 209–10
surveying of Bell, xxxiii
Swiss Alps, 28–29
Sydney Harbour Bridge, xliii
Sykes, Sir Mark, 78, 78n, 196
Sykes-Picot Agreement, 78n
Syria, 58
  and *Amurath to Amurath*, xii, xxxiii, xxxiv, 99–100
  bazaars of, 81
  Bell's fame in, 76
  Bell's identification with, 21
  and *The Desert and the Sown*, xi, xxxii, xxxiii, 63, 94, 98–99
  and desert expeditions, xxxiii, 63
  exploration to be performed in, 96